My Dearest Cecelia

❧

ALSO BY DIANE HAEGER

❦

The Secret Wife of King George IV

My Dearest Cecelia

A NOVEL OF THE SOUTHERN BELLE WHO STOLE GENERAL SHERMAN'S HEART

Diane Haeger

ST. MARTIN'S PRESS
NEW YORK

www.stmartins.com

Design by Kathryn Parise

LIBRARY OF CONGRESS CATALOGING-IN-PUBLICATION DATA

Haeger, Diane.
  My dearest Cecelia : a novel of the southern belle who stole General Sherman's heart / Diane
Haeger.—1st ed.
    p. cm.
  ISBN 0-312-28200-1
    1. Stovall, Cecelia—Fiction. 2. Sherman, William T. (William Tecumseh), 1820–1891—
Fiction. 3. Georgia—History—Civil War, 1861–1865—Fiction. 4. Women—Georgia—Fiction.
5. Augusta (Ga.)—Fiction. 6. Generals—Fiction. I. Title.

PS3558.A32125 M9 2003
813'.54—dc21

                                                                              2002033284

First Edition: March 2003

10   9   8   7   6   5   4   3   2   1

For Ken, Elizabeth, and Alex,

now and always

Author's Note

❧

This book was inspired by actual events. Various subplots and some of the secondary characters, where necessary, are fictionally constructed.

Acknowledgments

I am especially indebted to several people who helped make this book a reality. First and foremost, to C. L. Bragg, M.D., author of Distinction in Every Service, *for so graciously sharing his knowledge of the Civil War, as well as that of the Stovall family; to Dr. Steve Grove, West Point Military Academy Historian; to the staff at the Augusta Library; to the staff of the Historic Charleston Foundation's Aiken-Rhett House; always to my "merciless editor," Marlene Fried, for so carefully reading every word; to Diana Moody, a special thank you for first putting the notion of a story about General Sherman into my head; and to Kelly Costello, for continuing to support me and for having read all of my books so enthusiastically. Finally and most especially, to the memory of my grandmother Eva Corbett Hanke, whose own father, Partrick Corbett, fought with General Sherman's Wisconsin Militia. Across the years, they tied me to this particular story in a special way which I could not have imagined back when my research began.*

My Dearest Cecelia

Prologue

❦

JULY 1891, SHELMAN HEIGHTS PLANTATION, GEORGIA

He left his carriage at the filigreed iron gates and bounded up the shadowy avenue of magnolias and dense, low-lying oaks dripping in soft gray moss. He passed the carpet of lawn, with its vine-draped pergola, and tramped across the neat brick drive. Then he took the painted front porch steps of the temple-style veranda house, with its Greek Doric columns, two at a time. His ebony Stovall hair was slick and shimmering in the blazing Georgia sun. So much youthful energy and optimism were things sorely missed in a life so long lived, Cecelia thought as she squinted and he came into full focus before her. She rocked steadily in the white wicker rocker, giving nothing of herself away.

Pleasant Stovall, her brother Bolling's boy—and their father's namesake—rarely came to visit his old Aunt Cecelia these days. An ache of nostalgia filled her as he kissed her snowy crown of hair and the little knot piled neatly at the top of her head.

"Aft'noon, Aunt Cecelia," he drawled, gazing lovingly down at the elderly, brittle-boned woman in the plain black dress and black button shoes, who was unwilling to step too far from the era and times that had defined her life. The tall, smoothly handsome man in the beige linen suit then stood back properly and tipped his planter's hat to her as he knew she would appreciate. A moment later, he sank into the white wicker chair facing hers, surrendering his hat to his hands.

In the silent shadow of a bristling crape myrtle tree, he looked appraisingly at her for a moment. "Now, I know what you're thinkin', I do," he said with his careful, honeyed Georgia drawl. "But I didn't come 'bout money."

"Is that a fact?" She smiled, and her eyes—the sparkle behind them— made him smile, too. She may have lost everything else—youth, beauty, and the enthusiasm that comes with both—but that sparkle was, and always would be, uniquely her own.

"Yes, ma'am. Not this time. It's a story. I'm writin' a story fo' the paper."

The *Augusta Chronicle*, the paper of which her brother's son was editor, was struggling. He leaned forward, elbows on his knees. "I sho'ly would appreciate yo' help, Aunt Cecelia."

"*My* help?" she warily repeated, lifting a pale white eyebrow.

"Aunt Cecelia, this story—if you'll tell it to me directly, this story could put the *Chronicle* on the map all across this fine country!"

"Now, we both know old folks like me haven't anythin' but an old whale of a tale to tell," she gently responded, looking out across the expanse of her property, the lovely sheltering moss-draped oaks, azaleas, dogwoods, and camellias. "Isn't that what young folks are likely to say?"

That stopped him again, his match met fully in the kindly, generous, and yet mysterious old woman who sat now before him. "I would *never* say that. Not about you, Aunt Cecelia. Besides, I'd wager you ain't never told nothin' but the truth in yo' whole life."

She reached across and, for a moment, covered his hand with her own. "You're a good boy," she said. "I know that."

He smiled at her. "And do I still remind you of my father?"

Cecelia lifted her tea glass and took a shallow sip. "Still and always."

He drew in a breath. Exhaled. "Then, fo' his sake, fo' the love you bear that brother, I beg you to tell me 'bout you and that murderous fiend, General Sherman, Aunt Cecelia. The *real* story 'bout the two of you—"

As she moved to respond, he lifted a firm hand to stop her. "Now I know what you've always said, that you don't talk about the war, or about anythin' or anyone havin' to do with it, but—"

"Those hard and horrible war years are dead and gone. And they're best left that way."

He countered with his best endearing and slightly rakish smile. "This really could mean everythin' to me. A personal account from you—a grand Southern belle of yo' day—a kind of Civil War–time spy—and yo' secret relationship with the most despised Northern general in all of the South— would sho'ly sell papers! And I so desperately need somethin' that'll do that. I'm hopin' fo' me—fo' yo' brother's boy, that you're gon' make an exception, just this once."

Her tired eyes narrowed. "I don't make exceptions, boy. I *can't.*"

"My daughters—yo' own nieces, said you showed them a private note to you from the butcher himself!"

My answer is the same now as then, Cecelia—I would ever love and protect you. . . .

She felt the old defenses rear up as echoed words from so long ago played at the edges of her mind, and she struggled to press all of it back. The girls had found the old card and questioned her in a nostalgic moment. He was a good boy, but she simply could not—would not—say anything more.

"Now, is that a fact? I can't say as I recall any letter."

"You playin' games with me, Aunt Cecelia?"

"I don't like games."

"Well, you sho' the devil are better at them than I am!" He stood, and she could see that little crease in his brow that had been so much his father's, just the moment before his temper flared. "If I don't come up with some sort of story, I'll be ruined!"

Pleasant Stovall ran a hand behind his neck and gazed out at the land that was Shelman Heights Plantation, Cecelia's home for nearly fifty years. It was a grand white-pillared antebellum mansion on a knoll overlooking the shimmering Etowah River, beyond rich oak and magnolia trees, that had all survived the Civil War, the end of slavery, and the election of thirteen presidents, including Abraham Lincoln, Ulysses S. Grant, and Grover Cleveland.

"Very well. You've made me say it. I'm in trouble. Deep trouble. The paper is losin' mo' subscriptions every day, and if it don't turn around soon, I will be plum out of business!"

"Can't you use some of yo' inheritance to tide you over?"

"Hell, that was gone two years ago!" He looked out at the valley again and drew in a deep breath. "Look, Aunt Cecelia. If there *is* a personal wartime note to you from the most famous Northern Civil War general—"

Her face bore a network of fine lines, full of the richness of the years. Some days she felt young again—like the Cecelia her nephew had first mentioned, the young Southern beauty who had lived so naïvely before the war. One he would not recognize or understand if she had come marching up those carefully painted steps now behind him. What would he think of that girl? The choices she had made—promises broken—lies told? To this young, untested man, she was only a favored old aunt. A means to an end.

"I'm sorry, Pleasant, I truly am. But there's just no story."

"I don't believe you."

Her smile was there again, gentle but firm. "I expect one might call that *yo'* problem."

"So you refuse to help me—yo' own flesh and blood?"

"I can't help you because there isn't any story to tell. There never was."

He was desperate now, and he lurched forward in his chair. "But you knew him, didn't you? General Sherman loved you . . . and wanted to marry you, didn't he? You met at West Point! My father, yo' own brother, told me that much 'fo' he died!"

Her dark eyes narrowed and filled with a wild fire they had not held for a very long time. "Boy, I warn you, don't go searchin' fo' somethin' you will *never* find!"

His eyes fixed on hers. The stare was harsh. "Would it change yo' mind, Aunt Cecelia, to know that I recently took it upon myself to send the hated old general himself an open letter through the editorial page of the newspaper . . . and that, after all these years, he actually took the bait, all the way from Ohio . . . and he responded?"

Her lined face paled. "That's a lie! It's got to be!"

"Come, now, Aunt Cecelia, aren't you even the tiniest bit curious 'bout what yo' old Northern lover had to say?"

She reached for the arms of her chair to steady herself, but her fingers hit the side table and tea glass instead. The glass shattered, spraying amber liquid all across the white plank porch. Her fragility clouded her eyes, blocking the sparkle that was so distinctly hers. "You have no idea what you are playin' with! I beg you to let it—and the general—be!"

He stood and looked down at her. "I'll be back in a few days, after you've had time to think about it."

"My answer'll be the same then as it is now."

He pivoted back toward her on the steps, replacing his hat with a smooth movement. "We both know, Aunt Cecelia, that General William Tecumseh Sherman responded to me—a Southern newspaper man, a million miles from his life up in Ohio, fo' no other reason than because my name is Stovall. *He* hasn't put the past entirely away. Why should you? Especially when it would help yo' own nephew? Think about that. *Please.*"

Her weak heart slammed against her thin chest as she collapsed in the wicker rocker and watched him stalk back down the steps not waiting for her response. *Thank you,* she thought, knowing how little more she could have taken. As he went on down the carriageway without turning back, Cecelia's stoop-shouldered elderly maid, Cretia, padded heavily out onto the veranda in her cotton dress and crisply pressed apron.

"Lawd! You all right? You're white as a sheet!"

Cecelia smiled, the deep lines of age fanning out from her eyes. "I'm fine, old friend. Just a bit tired. Perhaps I'll doze here awhile."

"That Mr. Pleasant, he came here to stir things up, did he?" she said, shaking her springy steel-gray hair, hands on hips.

"Mo' than he knows, Cretia."

The color of the afternoon sky deepened to violet. Ice in the new tea glass, replaced, filled again, and then left beside her, had long since melted and made a ring on the glass-top table as Cecelia slid into and out of sleep in her white wicker chair. The hands that curled around the arms were withered, veined, and thin. Her hands had once been one of her loveliest features, everyone had said. But that was a lifetime ago. . . . How much had changed since those early days of gracious innocence, flattery, flirtation, and promise? She longed for those days now from time to time. But those occasions came less and less often with age. And with reality. *Reality* . . . How overrated that particular commodity could be!

Now, as she spent most of her days in the old brass bed upstairs, the one in which she'd borne her children, and watched her husband die, or in this old rocker that once had belonged to her mother, Cecelia preferred the rose-colored tint of a youth lived long ago. The bright side . . . and the way it almost was . . . with William. The despised William Tecumseh Sherman . . . the South's greatest enemy . . . and the secret love of her life. *They would never understand how it was, and I will never tell them. My secret is my greatest jewel, and I will guard it until my final breath!*

Slowly, she climbed the stairs inside the house, holding tightly to the mahogany bannister, her legs aching with each step, but Cecelia was desperate to find the private sanctuary of her bedroom. There, the windows were open wide, and the gauzy curtains blew a gentle rhythm against a highly polished bureau. On top lay a silver music box she had not opened for a very long time.

A thousand fantasies begin to throng into my memory . . . , John Milton once wrote. *And so they do! But with too much shame . . . and the color of too many years . . . What would the world, and the South, think if they knew the truth? That I betrayed my Confederate land, my husband and my honor? . . . May God help me,* she thought, slipping gently toward sleep as the music box played its tune softly beside her, *I would do it all again in a heartbeat; face the danger . . . the deceit . . . the treason. Who in the South—who in the world?—would ever be able to understand that?*

Cecelia took the music box, emblazoned with an English crest, to the top of her bed and, covering herself over with a pale ivory quilt, twisted the mechanism at the bottom and then opened it. Inside were only two small remembrances: a small gold cross and chain, and a calling card. Seemingly insignificant, yet one represented the beginning of something very dear; the other had signified its end. Cecelia was old now, useful to no one. But as she gazed inside the music box, in her memories she was that girl, that beautiful Southern belle, before the awful war, who once had met a dashing West Point cadet from the North . . .

Part 1

❧

But there's nothing half so sweet
In life as love's young dream.

—THOMAS MOORE

Chapter One

~§~

MAY 1837, WEST POINT, NEW YORK

Cecelia Stovall sighed. She was distracted and yet dazzling in a new shell pink gown trimmed with flounces, white silk roses, and ropes of pearls. The wide bell skirt, in the Southern style, with layers of petticoats beneath, rustled and swayed, making a grand impression as she strolled with her three brothers along the brick pathway from the West Point barracks toward the Commencement Ball. But her mind was elsewhere. The words that had been shouted so angrily at her brother Bolling back home in Augusta, only a few days before, still played across her mind. They were pressing her to acknowledge them *and* their meaning: "How could you do it to Anne, Father?" Bolling had asked. "Much less with a slave?" "Stay out of this!" their father's voice had boomed. "You're just a boy who hasn't a clue what I have with yo' stepmother, or what it is to have the needs and pressures of a man!"

Her mind and heart were made so unbearably heavy by those words, and by the questions the scene had aroused. So, too, her father's response to her eavesdropping: *"Very well, young lady! You want to involve yourself in my affairs as well, then so you shall! You'll go to West Point along with them and be out of my sight until you learn to mind your place!"*

Cecelia and her other two brothers had spoken little about it on the rough, noisy train as it clattered and clacked its way out of Atlanta or on the dusty, rattling carriage ride from Albany. Clearly it was something bad. But she feared knowing precisely what. Old Joe and his daughter Cretia had been a part of their lives for as long as she could remember. Though slaves, to Cecelia, they were a part of her family.

And now her family had a dark secret.

"What is there between Father and Cretia?" she had asked her younger brother, Bolling, as the train swayed along a length of track through a seemingly endless field spotted with cotton. Bolling was sixteen but very tall, serious, and, she thought, worldly for a boy his age. Of all Pleasant's first family of children, it was he who most resembled their dead mother. His skin was smooth, his hair, ebony black and very straight. Like her own, his eyes were dark as coal and largely indecipherable.

"You know perfectly well she's one of his slaves," he had said, opening a book and refusing to say more. But there was something more. Of course there was. Her stomach had churned ever since as the unthinkable conclusion had settled heavily upon her.

Cretia was her dearest friend. They had grown through childhood and adolescence together. Shared their lives. All their secrets. Or so she had long believed until a few days ago. Certainly Cretia would have confided something so horrible. Then had come the trip to West Point, along with two of her brothers, and one long, hot train ride after another to spirit them away from the truth. All of that had brought them very far from the South. As it was a long and strenuous journey from Georgia, and plebes were required to remain over summer, her trip was meant to last at least a few weeks.

Now she was going to the Commencement Ball at the military academy where her brother had just completed his first year. And for the first few hours since her arrival, Cecelia had managed to feel a bit of joy at the unexpected adventure. Here, she would be with Marcellus, the eldest Stovall brother, and the one person in all the world who could make sense of things. She had longed to ask him about it from the first moment of their arrival this morning. Thus far, there had been no time. But he would tell her the truth.

Reunited, she was surrounded now by the three of them. Marcellus was tall and dashing in his cadet's gray coat, gleaming brass buttons, and starched white trousers trimmed with black silk braid. Bolling and Thomas were dressed in dark coats and shiny gray-striped cravats. They all moved together into the crowded cadet's Mess, a room already full of handsome, uniformed young men. For this evening, the Mess had been admirably transformed into a representation of a ballroom. Tall, ivory tapers flickered in wall sconces and on tabletops, bathing the open room in a soft, golden glow as the band played the popular tune, "There's Nothing True But Heaven." Already she could see that it was a world away from a Southern summer evening.

"It's lovely." She softly smiled, gazing around at the uniformed men and elegant women.

"Not so lovely as you, dear sister." Marcellus squeezed her arm. "You've grown up while I've been away."

"So it happens with us all." She smiled up at him, her face shining in the profusion of candlelight.

"Glad as I am to see you, Father didn't write to me that you'd be joinin' the boys."

She exchanged a glance with Bolling then, her dark ringlets bobbing, but he looked quickly away. "It seems he decided it at the last minute."

"Well, however you got here, I'm thrilled. Now, do let's enjoy ourselves! And judgin' by the number of eyes upon you just now, the evenin' is young!"

For the first time, Cecelia, too, saw the way the men regarded her. In this place far from home, she became aware of how the eyes of several cadets found her and then cut away amid soft, suggestive laughter. As children, her sisters had been cruel. Her glossy, raven-dark hair was too black to go with her dark eyes, they had said, especially against her white, white skin. She resembled a crow sitting in cream, they had taunted. Taunted, until she began to grow steadily and gracefully into features that became striking rather than hawkish as they once had been, bold rather than unremarkable, as both her sisters now were. In an oddly victorious moment she wished her two married, and heavily pregnant, sisters could see her now—a free spirit in a new party dress, unencumbered by their father's rules, smiling—and admired.

As they moved more deeply into the already warm and crowded hall, with Marcellus holding tightly to her elbow, Cecelia was introduced to a blinding collection of her brother's classmates. The motions and manners she found tedious, especially with things at home still tugging at the corners of her mind. But it was worth anything in the world to her to be back with the one person she loved best in the world, her Marcellus. The one who would *always* tell her the truth.

"Might I have the pleasure of this dance, Miss Stovall?" The voice was deep and unexpected—full of reassuringly familiar Southern charm. Still clutching her brother's arm, Cecelia looked back before her. The cadet was older than Marcellus and admirably handsome in his uniform. He had thick, dark hair, heavy dark brows, and discerning, steely eyes. He extended his hand as if the request had been rhetorical.

"Thank you, suh, but I believe I shall wait until my brother is ready to dance."

"Cecelia!" Marcellus's startled tone stopped her. "Pardon her, suh. My sister has only just arrived after a long journey from Augusta. I'm certain that explains her rudeness. Cecelia, this is my friend, and senior classmate, Mr. Braxton Bragg. You may feel quite free to accept his invitation."

Bragg smiled at her and bowed. The music was beginning again. "Shall we, then?"

Reluctantly, she took his arm as he led her toward the crowded dance floor.

Bragg danced smoothly. Too smoothly, she thought. And the smile that only briefly left his face was marked by a smug self-confidence. Her mind quickly wandered. Words, inferences—and Cretia's last tormented expression as they left home played across what was already heavily on her mind. Anne, their stepmother, had been defensive over the way Bolling had pressed her before they had left. "I know," Anne had told him. "I've always known. . . ."

Cecelia's stomach turned sharply as the unthinkable conclusion settled yet again into the pit of her already nauseated stomach. But Father would never . . . something so unspeakably vulgar as . . . And with a slave! He had a wife, children . . . Of course she had misunderstood. She was too young, too spoiled, and, as he so often said, impossibly romantic about life. Her sister Marie was married and living in Rome, Georgia. Caroline, as well. The reason Cecelia had no suitors, Thomas always teased her, was because her head was filled with too much fantasy. And who the devil, he said, was man enough to unburden her of that?

She had never met a boy who she thought came close to understanding her. And if there ever were to be someone, he would not be like those perfectly proper, dull boys in Augusta. How in the world could she consider spending her life with a man like Caroline had married? Even Marie's husband, handsome though he was, wore his dullness upon his gentility like a proud badge of honor.

When she married, it would be someone wildly industrious, brimming with confidence, and ambitious beyond measure. A self-made boy, not someone living off the family largesse and in their shadow like the man Marie had married.

Men like that reminded her of warm milk-toast that Setty Mae, their cook, had given her as a child. It had been bland but predictable, sure to settle one's stomach. Kind and gentle, Setty Mae had always had a lovely way of coming up with relevant snatches of Scripture when they seemed to be needed the most. "De Lawd, He say Ask and He answer," she had told her one day when she was mixing up a fresh batch of corn bread. Yes, one day Cecelia would meet the right man, and take Cretia to live with them in a grand, lovely house by a river. She had it all planned. Cecelia's dress rustled again as she curtsied to thank the dull, steel-eyed cadet for the dance.

Late and uninterested in dancing, William Sherman pushed himself in among the swell of cadets and guests hoping for little more than a cup of iced punch. There was a last topography paper he had been intent on finishing, in spite of the mass exodus from the drafty, three-story stone North Barracks. Everyone else, it seemed, was here tonight, needing little prodding to enjoy a bit of socializing after a rigorous and deadly serious academic year. He rocked back on his heels, surveying the crowded room where the laughter and chatter had crescendoed. So this was a West Point ball, he mused to himself, largely unimpressed by the trappings of social grace.

Two of his roommates were dancing, but the third, Marcellus Stovall, stood a few feet away, beside a graceful, dark-haired girl in a pink dress with a wide bell skirt. The girl, who was just then accepting a dance, suddenly and very strongly took William's breath away. The sensation was intensely sharp and all encompassing. So *that* was Stovall's sister from Augusta, he thought as his heart slammed against his ribs—the girl about whom Stovall had told his roommates just this morning. Her arrival here with their two younger brothers had been quite unexpected.

As she moved toward the dance floor, William eased himself over to a corner to watch her, trying to make sense of what drew him so powerfully. She was attractive, certainly, but not in that pale, vapid way by which he had come to define Southern women. Miss Stovall had an inner strength that showed past her pretty Southern party dress and the oddly strained expression on her face as the dance began. Seeing it, William changed his focus to her tall and burly dance partner. It was Braxton Bragg, one of the graduates being feted.

William felt a smile tug at the corners of his mouth. He had heard plenty of the infamous Bragg, and his standard procedure with the out-of-town girls. They were the first to be danced with, he had often boasted, and the last to be left at dawn. Bragg, his name, William thought, from the tales he had heard, was a fitting one. William Sherman could not have been more different from Bragg, and from most of the other cadets at West Point. His short, wild hair was the color of fire-lit copper, and looked as if it had been cut by gardening shears. But his eyes, with their long dark lashes, were a dramatic cinnamon brown flecked with gold. The combination, along with a tight, hard body, made him uniquely attractive among the light-haired, smooth-skinned, or more swarthy gentry, with whom he had begun at West Point.

He continued to watch them dance, and he watched the dark-eyed girl's expression grow more strained. When the music stopped, William saw Bragg's meaty hand grip her arm below the elbow, keeping her there with him. It was a subtle move no one else would have noticed, other than someone watching them closely. Something curiously defensive in him churned, and he felt his legs move decisively toward the dance floor before he had made a conscious decision to do so.

"Pardon me, sir," William said formally, trying to keep the clipped anger from his tone, "but I believe this to be my dance with the lady."

"I don't expect Miss Stovall would agree to that," Bragg said icily.

"Then shall we say that I am making the decision *for* her," William countered, feeling a muscle twitch in his jaw as an odd sense of knowing took him over. Her face became all that he saw. He must do this. He must dance with this dark-haired, ebony-eyed girl, now, here, so that she would not walk out of his life.

The music rose up again, and everyone else began awkwardly to dance around the three of them, a swirl of shoes, skirts, lace, and laughter. "Miss Stovall?" Bragg said with an overly solicitous tone. "Shall we continue?"

William's eyes blazed with a fury. "I *said* unhand her."

Bragg let go of her, and Cecelia took a small step back, her eyes never leaving William's. He took her hand then, feeling as if he were taking possession of her soul. There was a strange unexpected shudder of excitement that coursed through him at their strangely immediate connection.

"*We* will dance now, Miss Stovall and I. When we are finished, sir, I expect not to look at your face again this evening. Is that perfectly clear?"

"And just who the devil do you think *you* are, besides a first-year, no-account plebe?"

"I am William Tecumseh Sherman, sir. And you would do well to pay heed to that."

William could see his rival growing angry and the veneer of affability beginning, once again, to shatter. "I shall speak with yo' brother 'bout this presently!" He glared at Cecelia, his heavy black brows merging over his eyes.

"I am quite capable of decidin' with whom I dance, suh, and just now I believe my choice to be Mr. Sherman," she shot back with a defiant flair that surprised both young men.

"I have been good to yo' brother this year—" Bragg stammered at Cecelia, disarmed by her self-possession. "I've helped him along what has been, fo' him, a difficult academic road!"

"And I'm certain he's grateful, suh. But I'm equally certain he never intended payment fo' it to include me."

"I see that I've misjudged you." Bragg's steely eyes narrowed. "A sharp tongue in the place of manners holds no interest fo' me." Without waiting for her response, he looked at William. "And *you* should consider yo'self lucky, Sherman, that I'm on my way out of this place, or you would live to regret this. I won't forget tonight."

"Nor shall I."

William led her more deeply into the other dancers before it could get any uglier, as Bragg stalked off, muttering to himself. It was an instant before he realized he had not let go of her hand. They turned to one another, and only then did her hand fall away. She lifted her face to his, and he felt it was a face he had looked upon all his life.

"I suppose I owe you my thanks," she said uneasily as they began to dance, William taking in the heady fragrance of soft lilac perfume. For an instant, he was controlled by it. "But I confess, I feel at a loss fo' words just now."

William managed a smile. "Now, why do I find that difficult to believe?" They turned, nodded, and turned again in time with the music. "I have a strong suspicion, Miss Stovall, that you could have taken care of yourself."

Her eyes widened. He saw the intelligence there. "Ah, but circumstances, like appearances, Mr. Sherman, can so often deceive."

He nodded, giving her the point as a small, sly smile turned up the corner of her slim lips. The fire in her eyes, he thought, was powerful. She was as sharp as she was lovely. He had never known a girl like her, and a Southern girl with a smooth, honeyed drawl that made him feel dispossessed of himself, as if he were another person looking down at their exchange, seeing her as she saw him. He was convinced suddenly, in spite of all that, that she found him foolish, unimportant. It was how her brother Marcellus openly referred to Northerners. Unimportant.

"I do thank you kindly fo' intervenin' in my behalf, truly I do, Mr.—"

"Sherman," he said deeply. "William Tecumseh Sherman."

"But my father always warned me not to trust Northern men."

"My heritage alone changes your impression of me?"

"My father says it must. Whether or not young men can come together at a place like this, the North and the South are two entirely different worlds."

"Respectfully, Miss Stovall, that remark disappoints me." With his retort like a punctuation mark, the song was at an end. William nodded and returned her to her brother's side. Although he did not realize it then as he moved toward the garden doors, that very moment marked the beginning of his obsession. It was a sensation with which he would do battle for the rest of his life.

"Damn it to hell!" William snarled, not at all certain then why her opinion mattered. He meant to say that she had surprised him. But instead self-preservation and fear had caused him to walk away.

Outside, the warm summer breeze cooled him even as he tossed down his gloves, and the sweet music of the crickets distracted him from the surprising power of his encounter with Cecelia. William wondered, as he touched the stone balustrade, what exactly had happened in there with a fellow cadet, but moreover, why had a Southern girl who should not have touched his defenses been able to do so?

"Well, now. You're not going to just leave things like that, are you?"

William turned with a start. He had believed himself alone on the terrace. But behind him, beside a twisted vine of wisteria, full of flowers, stood a compact, dignified man. He had a shock of umber-colored hair, arched brows, and gray-green eyes flecked with gold that were directed on him as he stood holding a full cup of punch. The man was alone, a total stranger to William.

"I beg your pardon, sir?"

"The girl. You don't plan to end up in the same position with her as that insufferable looking lout with the heavy eyebrows, do you?"

William glanced back inside for a moment before he replied. "I don't expect either of us has particulary impressed her this evening."

The other man chuckled and extended his hand. "Name's Lee."

"Sherman. My friends call me Cump," he responded, shaking his hand in return. "You a cadet?"

"I was. Graduated in '29. Second in my class. I've a commission now as first lieutenant of engineers supervising the work in Saint Louis Harbor."

"That *is* impressive. But what on earth brings you back here now?"

"I'm the commencement speaker tomorrow. Never having won a demerit here seems to be a lightning rod for the other cadets."

William shook his head. "I had two demerits my first month."

"I'll wager you haven't had a great many more since."

"True."

"You learn quickly."

"Not quickly enough, apparently, to win a second dance with the illustrious Miss Stovall."

"And that matters to you?" Lee asked as they both watched her dancing now with a different upperclassman William did not recognize.

"I don't exactly know if it does or not."

"Then it seems to me, you owe it to yourself—and Miss Stovall—to find out for certain."

William looked back at the dance floor for another moment and watched her dance. Lee was right. Something very odd inside him told William it was absolutely essential that he find out. Still he faltered. Lee saw it.

"Not that I don't appreciate the advice but—"

"She's a Southern girl, and you're from the North. Is that it?"

"She seems to think so."

"I met Miss Stovall myself this morning at the church social. She reminds me of my own wife—proud, fiery, yet delicate as glass—and in need of a man who can handle all three."

"And you think I'm that man?"

"Well, son. I wouldn't make a guess on that." Lee gazed out over the river, a sweeping black space behind a frame of tall pine trees, as he took a swallow of punch. "But you sure as hell aren't gonna find out standing here with the likes of me!"

William smiled. A heartbeat later, he extended his hand. "Thank you, Lieutenant—"

"Lee, son. The name is Robert E. Lee."

"I would be honored if we might try that one more time."

Surrounded by a collection of other young ladies and cadets, Cecelia turned to the voice behind her. William's eyes met hers again. They were such an odd color, his eyes that blazed with mysterious fury. She had not expected him to return after her nervous foolishness, and she had pinched her wrist repeatedly with anger. Now she felt her face warm as he looked into her eyes.

"Very well, suh," Cecelia said, struggling to find her voice. "Perhaps we did get off on the wrong foot the last time." *Lord, what is it about him? He makes me absolutely weak in the knees!*

"We shall see," he cooly replied as he wound her arm in his.

There was a power between them that had risen up like a huge wave the very moment William Sherman returned to her side, and it startled Cecelia. Inexperienced though she was in these matters, she was absolutely certain that this was far more than attraction. *It cannot be! This sort of thing—this sort of connection with a stranger does not happen! Still, here it is, this feelin' that I have known him all my life.* When the dance was over, they walked together to the side of the room where there was too much activity around them for anyone to notice the intensity between them. William got them each a glass of punch, then stood facing her.

"Your eyes are so dark, they are difficult to fathom."

In his very quiet tone there was no pretension, only honesty. She realized he had not expected a response. He did not condescend to her, or flatter her overly. He spoke to her as if she were an adult. A woman. It was the first time in her life anyone had ever done so.

"And *yo'* eyes earlier toward Mr. Bragg, suh, startled me. I found them as cold as they were cruel. Truly," she said with an unexpected tremor to her soft drawl, "I would pity anyone who might ever become *yo'* enemy."

"You need never worry about me, Miss Stovall. Perhaps this is a wild, impetuous thing to say, but no matter what, you may trust that I would ever love and protect you."

Soon, the next dance ended, and couples pushed in around them, but William's eyes never left Cecelia's as they remained beside a white Ionic column that shielded them from the open glances of anyone who might be passing by. Remaining like this with him, the world—*her* world—tilted, then changed. *This feelin' is not possible!* she was thinking. *I know nothin' of him beyond those eyes, and yet they tell me everythin'!*

"Sho'ly you don't mean *love*, suh." The word passed across her lips in a strained, shocked way reflecting the loss of control she felt inside.

"I never say anything I don't mean."

"But, Mr. Sherman—"

"I am as direct as I am level-headed. You shall never find cause to dispute me on that."

Cecelia tipped up her chin, taking her eyes from his, unable to bear a moment longer the open admiration she saw there. Yes, she would be all right so long as she did not look directly into their gaze. His eyes mirrored the future—and she very clearly saw herself there.

"You're quite certain of yo'self."

"Early disappointments made me a realist and have left me no time at all to perfect the art of flattery, I'm afraid."

"I suspect that shall endear you to the young lady you will one day come to court."

He lifted two fresh glasses from the refreshment table beside them and handed one to her, drawing his eyes away from hers for only an instant. "The young lady I one day mean to court will desire purity of heart over flattery, or I won't court her at all. Nor would there be any purpose in our being together unless we intend to spend the rest of our lives in open devotion. For me, that's the only way the story can end."

"You see yo' life as a story, Mr. Sherman?"

"Everyone's life is a story, Miss Stovall. I'm just determined to give mine a happy ending."

She was warm—warmer suddenly than she had ever felt in her life. Cecelia opened her fan, a small ivory thing with lace, and edges painted with salmon pink roses. She wanted more than anything in the world suddenly for them to touch—for him to take her hand again, or to feel his fingers brush hers even absently. *His name is William . . .* , she was thinking. *Like the great warriors . . . Like William the Conquerer.*

"Let's not dance again. But will you walk with me to the terrace for some air?"

Her mind spun even as he asked her—even as she wound her arm once more with his and let him lead her outside. The moon was full as they stood at the stone terrace edge and gazed down at the silvery Hudson River with two other couples who had come out before them.

"How did so curious a man ever find his way to West Point?"

"The same way that I came to meet you, I expect—with the light of the good Lord shining down on me."

She shivered, cold suddenly in the warm summer night air. She was so powerfully drawn to this mysterious Yankee that she could not catch her breath, but she did not even mean to try. "You know, you really shouldn't say things like that—speak about courtin' or love."

"Why not speak the truth? There's so much to do in this life and so little time for all of it."

She saw a new excitement light his eyes as he said that. It made her smile, and the thrill inside her flared. "And what is it you wish to do in this world, William Sherman?"

He gazed heavenward, as if the dark sky were his canvas. "I think I will command an army one day . . . travel the world . . . and, of course, lead and inspire my men while I'm at it."

She was smiling up at him, watching the secrets behind his eyes slowly yet powerfully revealed to her as a flower unfurls itself to the sun. "You sound like Marcellus," she tried to say, tried to make what he said seem unimportant. "I do believe, as a child, a soldier was all my brother ever wanted to be. But mostly, I expect, now it is fo' him to measure highly in our father's eyes."

"Was your father's expectation what brought *you* to West Point, as well? Perhaps to find a husband among the cadets?"

"Oh, gracious, no." Her laughter was honey soft, barely audible. "My father has far mo' grand ideas than *that* fo' his daughters. We are Southern royalty, he always says. And he'll never settle. I don't suppose yo' own father is anythin' like that."

William looked away from her and out toward the shimmering river, silver now and glittering beneath the quarter moon. "My father died when I was a boy. I have no idea what sort of match he would have wanted for me. But he always saw West Point as a path to greatness. All I knew was he was intent that I somehow find a way into it."

"And so you have," she said with special gentleness. And yet her heart battled her mind. Her father and Marcellus would tell her this was nowhere near right, this unbelievably charged power and the sense of a future for the two of them. It frightened her to think of going against her family. But it was more inconceivable to consider never seeing William Sherman again. Cecelia wondered as he spoke and smiled—was it actually possible to meet a man like this, a virtual stranger, and yet know within moments that your future would be inextricably wound with his?

Cecelia wrapped her arms around herself against a sudden chill. "You're so certain of yo'self."

"Only of the direction ahead of me. Not where I have been in this world so far."

"Has it been so bad?" she asked. "Where it is you've been?"

"I wouldn't fancy living it over, I can tell you that."

"You seem a gentleman possessed of fortune, as any other cadet here."

"As I believe you suggested earlier, Miss Stovall, appearances can be deceiving."

"Are they with you, suh? Have I misjudged you?"

"Only your favorable opinion of my heritage. The rest, I plan fully to rise above, given half the chance."

"Yo'self-assurance is inspirin'."

"I am flattered that you think so."

She smiled at that, finding it impossible to keep any sort of logical defense against him. He made her heart race, and heat flushed into her cheeks as though she were on fire. "For some reason, I feel quite certain you will accomplish everythin' in life you hope to."

Suddenly, he was shaking his head and washing a hand across his face. "I really can't believe I just told you all of that."

"Are you sorry that you did?"

He met her gaze again squarely. Again the charge between them flared. "Not sorry at all."

"Ah! There you are!" Marcellus's rich drawl broke between them like glass, and Cecelia took a defensive step away from William before she pivoted back. Thomas and Bolling were beside their older brother. "Sherman? Well, suh, I trust you have been a gentleman with our sister."

"Your sister had grown warm with all the dancing. I simply escorted her out here for a breath of air with all of the others who felt the same. She was perfectly safe, I assure you."

"Yes, well, by her tremblin' she appears to have gotten quite enough cool air," Marcellus surmised, glancing suspiciously from one of them to the other.

"Indeed." William nodded to Marcellus before he turned back to Cecelia. "Miss Stovall, I've enjoyed our dance and our conversation. A pleasant evening to you all."

"And to you, suh," Cecelia said, summoning up everything within herself to speak lightheartedly, dampening the power she had felt between them, which she could not dare reveal to her brothers. What exactly would come of it remained the only question. What she did know, down to the very core of her soul, was that this would not be their last encounter. It had only been the beginning.

Chapter Two

Late the next afternoon, Marcellus Stovall sat cross-legged on the bare wood floor, just beneath the small window of the dark barracks room that he shared with three other plebes. The room was unbearably hot due to lack of ventilation. Stiflingly so. Life here was a gruelingly monotonous schedule of drill and study, whether hot or frigid. Scrambling off their mattresses at dawn to the bugle's harsh blare, with sleep-filled eyes, the cadets studied until breakfast at seven, then drilling and classes. Afterward came more drilling, marching, and handling muskets as the day wore on, until sundown. After supper, they were expected to study again until taps were sounded at ten. The only articles issued by the school were an arithmetic book, lamp, broom, bucket, and two blankets. As there were no beds at West Point, each cadet slept on a mattress on the hard and sometimes very cold floor.

Aching for fresh air now, and for old freedoms, Marcellus turned his critical gaze on one of his roommates, then on the two others, all deeply engaged in open books. Committed and bright, all of them were bound for success here, Marcellus thought spitefully, and all when he despised West Point and the year he had struggled, trying to match them.

The tight race to excel here had never been his own idea.

He glanced again at his three roommates, especially the taut, copper-haired Yankee with eyes that were shockingly intense—even a little frightening, particularly if they were cast in anger directly upon him. Marcellus looked away ruefully and fanned himself with the back of a term paper. William Tecumseh Sherman had been sponsored here by an impressively wealthy neighbor—one who just happened to be a United States senator. Payment for that had been veiled yet clear: Do well, graduate with honors, enough to return to Lancaster with the stature sufficient to marry Ellen, their plain-faced daughter.

Sherman was a sort who appreciated this chance and was driven to succeed.

Stewart Van Vliet and Edward Ord were more tolerable as companions, only in that they were not poor Yankees, and thus, did not chafe quite so much at his own sense of social insecurity. Together, the four of them were a cross section of the country with nothing in common in their lives or the worlds from which they had come. Ambition alone united them, and it created an odd brotherhood.

Still, Marcellus disliked Sherman, and he disliked West Point even more. Where he wanted to be was out on the edge of town at the deliciously welcoming Benny Haven's Tavern, putting back a few too many whiskeys. Reckless? Of course. Foolhardy? Without a doubt. But this life was his to live—to find triumph in, or ruin, as he saw fit. In spite of what old Pleasant Stovall divined for him. That, however, was not the plan for this evening. Marcellus had something more important to attend to.

As he moved toward the door, one of the other roommates, a ruddy-faced, sandy-haired boy from Maryland, called out to him. "You aren't planning on going out after curfew, are you?"

"Mind yo' own business, Ord," Marcellus snarled, tossing a civilian button-down jacket over his uniform in a defiant swirl.

"We've got final exams first thing," Sherman plainly added, not taking his eyes from the pages of his open book.

"Look, Yankee boy, when I want yo' advice I'll ask fo' it! I've got an appointment over at the hotel, and I'm gon'—curfews be damned!"

Instantly sorry, but unwilling to concede a burst of temper, he turned and headed out the door. Alone a moment later, the two other roommates exchanged glances with William, who was certain Marcellus was on his way to see Cecelia. He sat back against the wall of the small, cell-like room that had been home to them these past grueling months.

"He's a fool." Stewart Van Vliet shook his head as he looked back down into a volume of Machiavelli's *The Art of War*, a book that was required reading for the exam tomorrow.

"Not a fool," William observed in a sandy tenor as a shaft of light from the oil lamp between them played across the square line of his jaw. "Stovall's just in over his head here, and he knows it."

There was a brief silence before the slim, pale-faced boy from Vermont looked back up. His eyes were wide and discerning. "Not so different from me, actually, or a lot of the rest of us. My father wanted me here. Truthfully, I don't expect Marcellus or I will last till next winter." He shook his head. "You know—you're different. What's the story, Sherman? You sure as hell don't talk much."

William looked at the boy in the clotted summer silence, considering how he could or should respond to that. He was a world apart from any of the other first-year students whose family wealth and prominence had bought them a place here.

"I don't suppose I've got anything much interesting to say to boys like you and Stovall, that's all."

He looked back into his book without reading it. That had been a lie. William had plenty to say. He felt like a volcano most days, brimming with ideas and ambition that he was not free to acknowledge here among the boys and instructors who found him curious in the first place.

He thought of Ellen with a small grimace of resignation. As a friend, he cared for her deeply. She had just always been there, a tag-along at first, later a friend he trusted completely. And he did owe her for her faith in him. He owed all the Ewings a great deal. He simply felt nothing more for her than that. But right now, Ellen was on his mind in no more than a fleeting way, like a leaf that rests on a tree branch before it is cast off with the wind.

Marcellus had been gone for an hour when they heard the expected sound of boot heels outside in the corridor. The sharp click of the door handle was followed by the appearance of a stone-faced cadet, a grade above them, as he strode into their small room.

"Bed check," he flatly announced, glancing down at his roster. "There's to be four of you. Where's the fourth?"

William lifted his head a fraction as Van Vliet shot him a worried glance that did not go undetected by the young guard. The very serious cadet checked his chart again. "It's Stovall who's missing?"

The air in the small room was thick and warm tonight. It felt like a coffin. For a moment, the silence was deafening. "Sherman, sir," William calmly said. He stood and set his book onto the mattress, preparing, for some unknown reason, to lie for a plebe who not only kept his distance, but disliked him, as well. "Tell him the rest of it, then," William urged as he looked over at Van Vliet.

Stewart shot William a look of panic, his lips tightly sealed against the recriminations for what had clearly been a breach of academy law. "Poor Sherman had a nasty case of, shall we call it, *the revenge?* Whatever he ate at noontime has been tormenting the rest of us since—if you get my drift. We booted him out of here a few minutes ago to deal with it."

"Nevertheless, I've got to report him. You all know leaving the barracks after curfew without permission is strictly forbidden. *This* is a serious matter."

"So was Sherman's gut!" William easily volleyed with the slightest irreverent smile. "I'm sure he'll be back any minute if you wait."

"I can't wait," the cadet angrily returned. "I've got the rest of this floor to check before I can get to my own books. No matter what his reason, Cadet Sherman *will* see a demerit on his record for this."

After the senior class man had gone, Van Vliet and Ord gazed at William in wide-eyed disbelief. "Why in hell did you do that for a cadet who seems to despise you?" Edward Ord asked.

William opened his book again and sank back easily against the wall, thinking of Cecelia and wishing it were he who was seeing her at the hotel just now instead of Marcellus. "Come on, boys. Stovall has far more demerits than I do. It was a gesture. Nothing more than that."

Only Marcellus remained in Cecelia's large room with a view of the Hudson River, a silvery snake in the last of evening's light. The other brothers, he said, had her for an entire year. Now it was his turn to get caught up, and so he sent Thomas and Bolling down to eat in the hotel restaurant. Moments later, Marcellus propped himself against the headboard of the ornate dark oak bed, then crossed his legs at the ankles. He was too thin, Cecelia thought, and his lovely pale skin had been replaced by a pasty gray pallor. It surprised her when she became aware of it. He was not happy here. But then she had known he would not be. Coming here for Marcellus, in spite of the romance of battle, had been all about living up to their father's will. It had been that way for all of them.

"Are you sure you should be here?" Cecelia asked him. "Don't you have a curfew or somethin' at night?"

"You let me worry about that, will you? Now give me news from Augusta," he playfully bade her.

Cecelia had set out a worn daguerreotype image of their mother in a small frame onto the dressing table with the rest of her things. She glanced at it for a moment, then at him. "It's still lovely. Hot now, of course. The flies are as thick as molasses on one of Setty Mae's sweet potato pies." She turned around to face him, the name bringing up all the feelings and confusion she had been trying to suppress. Her own smile fell. ". . . And speakin' of home—I believe Father is beddin' Cretia."

She waited for his eyes to register indignation. Shock. Something. But it never came. Marcellus carefully drew a silver flask from the inside of his jacket and took a long swallow of the contents. She could smell liquor as he exhaled a heavy sigh.

"You didn't know?" he said blandly. There was no question in his words. Grainy shadows played across his face as a cloud outside the window moved across the sun.

She sank onto the corner of the bed, the springs letting a faint squeal. "*You* did?"

He took another swallow. "It is . . . let us just say, not a revelation."

Cecelia's mind spun. "It certainly was to me."

"And so *that's* why he sent you here with Bolling and Thomas," Marcellus calmly declared, perfunctorily. "To give you time to adjust to one of life's realities. Can't have his firebrand daughter stirrin' up the pot of *that* particular stew."

She sprang to her feet again, tilting up her chin. Her voice was full of anger. "Is it a reality that a man with a wife should bed his slaves?"

"Mo' often, I suspect, than either of us would imagine."

She spun away from him, wounded by things she longed now not to know. "That is vile!"

"Yes. Much of life is not the pretty picture painted for young girls," he responded. "I expect now is the appointed time for you to begin learnin' that."

"But father has Anne, who has been a proper wife to him! She has given him more sons!"

The deep blue-black Stovall eyes—eyes she had always loved for their calm honesty—grew cold and stony. He was not going to share her indignation in this. He was not going to grieve with her over the innocence of which she felt herself so firmly being robbed. And in that, she longed for the Marcellus she had always known. Playful. Loving. Happy. He was none of those things here at West Point. He was not the brother she knew. In the face of that, her openness to him closed itself off, protectively. She felt like a stranger now, a shell rising up around her, as her arms went tightly around her waist.

Marcellus saw the change. "If you're gon' grow up, you might as well do it all the way, Cecelia. This has been a devastatin' year fo' father's business."

"Father's the richest cotton merchant in Augusta!"

"He certainly was. But times have been tough lately. Between you and me, he's lost money. A lot of it. Now, don't get me wrong, Anne is a good woman, but she has a way of remindin' him a bit too often 'bout that failure, and the lack of cash she has available now. A man's pride suffers. Things happen."

"I just always expected mo' of father," she murmured brokenly.

"Ah, take care with that, my dear sister. We men are fallible creatures, all of us. Put any of us on a pedestal, as we do you, only at yo' own peril."

I will not cry, she thought. *I cannot. The things I grieve for are already lost.*

Her dark eyes narrowed, her determination returned. She was angry now. And, she felt, betrayed. Not only by her father and Marcellus—but also by the fatal ghost of expectation. Shreds of her childhood innocence were peeling away from her like autumn leaves from a tree.

"Are you willin' to tell me there is no such thing as a man who will not disappoint me?"

"What I am tellin' you is to beware. The man to whom you eventually give yo' heart may break it without even knowin' he has done it."

"And what if I break his first?"

"Knowin' you, sweet, dear sister, I'd expect *you* to hold on to the love of a good man with the determination of a lioness—quite likely to the great peril of everyone else around you!"

William was fastening the last of the brass buttons on his gray dress coat the next morning when Marcellus came back into their airless barracks room. The door closed. Marcellus remained beside it, arms crossed over his chest, studying William. "Ord told me what you did fo' me last evenin'."

William did not respond. He faced the mirror, combing his thick waves of copper hair, doing his best to tame one of the many parts of him that resisted. Yes, that wildness was ever there as a warning. In his blood, which burned for excitement, and in his hair, the way it betrayed the comb, his true nature showed.

"I haven't been civil enough to you to warrant yo' savin' my hide."

"True enough," William replied.

"Then why'd you do it?"

William continued with his hair, adding a small amount of taming oil from a slim brown bottle. "Seemed like the right thing to do at the time."

Marcellus studied him warily. "Pity, is it, Yankee? Because you're smarter than me in every subject here . . . except maybe women and drinkin'?"

"Can't say I'm the pitying sort."

"Nor am I."

They both participated in the silence until, without turning around, William said, "So tell me, Stovall, is sneaking out worth the risk of getting caught?"

"Most nights, hell yes!" he chuckled dryly, sinking exhaustedly onto his mattress. "A good woman—and especially a bad one—is always worth *that*."

"So, which did you find last night?"

"Honestly, she was a bit of both." His cavalier smile fell just a bit. "Truth is, I went to spend a bit of time with my little sister."

William's slim face, handsome but hardened by a childhood of disappointment and an adolescence of obligation, was softened by an unexpected rusty laugh. It moved up from his solar plexus and erupted. The laugh was so spontaneous that Marcellus responded with his own deep-bellied chuckle, quite in spite of his accustomed reserve.

"Looks like I owe you one, Sherman."

"You owe me nothing."

"A gentleman, suh—especially a *Southern* gentleman—always pays his debts."

William nodded. "All right, then. Three years more here is a long time, and I'd sure as hell rather have you as a friend than an enemy in this rat hole of a room when the lamps are out at night."

Cecelia strolled the ground around The West Point Hotel with Bolling later that morning, down a mossy brick path. They conversed about home; about the littlest Stovall, their half brother Georgie; how much he would be missing them all; and about how thick and sultry it would be getting soon back in Augusta. All the while, she was thinking of William, and this place—how both had somehow changed her already.

Late yesterday, she had stood on the academy grounds and looked out across a sea of uniformed cadets, all standing at attention. A young Southern woman, sheltered for her entire life, Cecelia had never seen so many young, vital men all with a purpose far greater than sitting on the veranda, sipping a julep.

They were a gray-and-white wave before her, their polished brass buttons glistening in the sun, cut grass on the tips of their shiny black boots. Back home, her father always said that Yankee boys were nothing like Southern gentlemen. A world apart, he blustered. But here at West Point, their palpable dreams and their dignity bonded North and South. It struck her as she had watched the mixed collection, tin soldiers in the crimson setting sun, that they were all so young yet so full of commitment and ambition. It poured from each of them. Each with families, with his own goals—each from some place entirely unlike any other. And yet, undeniably here, on the brink of so many lives not yet fully lived, they were the same.

And in the center of this elite corp of young men whom her father would never understand was William Tecumseh Sherman. William was intense, confounding—and unforgettable. He certainly did not possess the genteel smoothness of a Southern man. Nor, Cecelia thought, was he possessed of the more distasteful affectations which her father never mentioned.

She knew nothing of war or conflict—the world that these vital young cadets might one day come to find—and she had been humbled and disturbed by realizing that, since yesterday.

"Marcellus told me 'bout father and Cretia," she suddenly blurted, wanting to press away thoughts that were still difficult to reconcile.

Bolling glanced at her and, for a moment, stopped walking. The warm breeze tossed his dark hair. "Then you know it's none of our affair."

"But she is—"

"She's not like us, Cecelia," he firmly drawled, refusing to speak what they both knew because he was too genteel, too refined. What he *meant* was that she was a slave. A Negro. ". . . and father is married. You mean that, as well. *You* still believe in the dream of fidelity."

"I thought I did."

He began to walk again, and she followed, sunlight cutting in and out above them as they passed through a lacy cover of thick evergreen trees. "Did Marcellus also tell you that if you were old enough to know about such things, Cecelia, you must come to terms with the notion that men are very different from women? They are ruled far mo' by their desires than by sentiment."

"Does that include you?" she asked, an angry incredulity seeping slowly across her soft tone.

"I expect one day it shall."

"Am I to believe that no man is what he seems? That no man is capable of fidelity, commitment, or the greater concept of real love?"

"It hasn't a thing to do with love, Cecelia!" her brother chuckled. "Not with Father, not with any man."

"I won't accept that!"

"You will, I'm afraid, have little choice once you are married, once you have children to bind the two of you."

"That sounds like a miserable sort of blackmail, not an existence or life at all." She wrapped her silk shawl around herself and gazed out at the river, which lay beyond a stand of broad, leafy trees and down a sweeping slope. "And not at all a life fo' *me!*"

"I don't know that Anne looks all that unhappy. She has her child by Father, and she is wife to one of the most prosperous men in Augusta."

"And her husband regularly beds with one of the slaves who is forced to serve *her* afterward!"

"Oh, do grow up, Cecelia! Life is not all pretty party dresses and juleps on the veranda! Not by a long stretch! You wanted the truth; now you have it!"

She was so angry with her brother's "truth" that she nearly decided to miss the Sunday church service on the West Point grounds, which she had agreed to attend this morning with her three brothers. It seemed so wholly inconceivable. Everything was harsh and tawdry in the warm, revealing light of day, and nothing, not even a sobering church service, seemed capable of washing away the stain on her innocent perceptions.

She came reluctantly into the church, with its powerful scent of incense and the heavy strains of organ music. And only then, as she glanced around, anxious to leave, did she notice William already sitting in the back of the church behind her. Seeing him here was a surprise, as nearly everything about him was. Her brothers were all so cavalier, so tolerant of the ugliness their father had wrought. That they condoned and even anticipated it for themselves was more than she could bear. Where was love, honor—commitment of the heart?

The sermon at the little stone chapel on the grounds of West Point was long, and her mind kept winding back to that, as a sanctimonious baritone priest droned on about duty as related in Ecclesiastes. She was not prepared to do a duty to any man the way her brothers had laid it out. To acquiesce. To trap herself by their conventions. She glanced around the little chapel as colored light filtered through the stained glass, shading the faces of the young men who had gathered there to worship. Suddenly, she could not breathe, could not think of anything but this betrayal, and the shreds in which she saw lying all her most dearly held illusions.

"I need some air," she whispered to her youngest brother, Thomas, who was on the end of the pew beside her.

"I'll go with you."

"No, stay. I'll be back directly."

Outside, the bright sunlight bore down like a great weight. Heavy, unbearable. Cecelia found it difficult to think or to breathe for the tangle of memories that was choking her as they flooded back—poor, poor Cretia.

Cecelia's relationship with the young house slave, of her same age, was a complex one. They had become close friends as children, and early on, circumstance had trumped society's constraints. A privileged Southern girl whose mother had died and whose two older sisters were more concerned with their marriage prospects had needed a friend. Cretia was not going away like everyone else in her life. Pleasant Stovall owned her, as he owned the girl's father, Josiah, who the family called Old Joe. Cretia's mother had been sold shortly after Cretia's birth, to a business associate of Pleasant's visiting from Atlanta. The story was that a man had taken a liking to the woman when he'd seen her, and so he had offered an exorbitant amount to take her with him. It was all quite in spite of the husband and the small child she had been forced to leave behind. So a kinship between two motherless girls had been cemented. It flourished even in the face of their one greatest obstacle: the color of each girl's skin.

When they were both seven, Cecelia had given Cretia one of her own dolls because Cretia had only ever had rags tied with rope to hold and comfort her in night's darkness when she missed the safety of a mother's arms. Even now, she remembered every moment of that first poignant encounter that had made them friends.

"Miss Cecelia, I can't take it!"

She thrust forward a pretty cloth sewn doll with glass button eyes and a dress sewn of blue-and-white gingham with Irish lace at the hem. "Of course you can!"

"My daddy'll say I made you feel sorry fo' me! And he say even Negroes have they pride!"

"Oh, pooh, Cretia! No one *makes* me do anythin'! Don't you know that by now?"

Cretia bit back a cautious smile. "That much sho'ly is true. But I still ain't got no right to take it, Miss Cecelia."

"I *want* you to have it. It's a gift. And it would be terribly rude of you to refuse a gift, now, wouldn't it? You would hurt my feelin's, after all." Cecelia was smiling, trying openly to give Cretia something dear for the friendship Cretia had given her. The memory of that instant was bound by images and feelings, one week later, when Pleasant Stovall found out what had occurred, and personally took the doll away from his houseman's daughter.

"Give it back to her, Daddy!" she said more stubbornly than his other daughters had ever dared. "The doll was mine to give, and I wanted Cretia to have it!"

"Oh, nonsense," he had cruelly laughed, as though his own daughter was as brainless as a bird. "You'll be givin' the girl ideas. Before you know it, she'll be wantin' a party frock like yours, and to sit out on the veranda with the rest of us, too!"

Cecelia put her hands on her hips defiantly. "And what would be so awful if she did?"

"That ain't her life, chil'! She's here with us for dressin' you and Anne. Not dressin' up herself!"

The chasm between the two girls, who had played beneath the house, in the shade of the lush and shady moss-draped oaks, who told one another their secrets and dreams, grew suddenly to something thick and overwhelming. Cretia looked dumbly at the ground.

"I know what yo' tryin' to do, chil'," Cecelia's father said more softly. "You have a good heart in you. But yo' intentions, they ain't never gon' change what she is!"

Seeing Cretia as she really was, in that shattering moment, not as an equal friend, but separate, her future condemned by her blackness, filled Cecelia's eyes with tears. "I can *try* to make it a little nicer."

"Fool girl!" Pleasant had said in his fury, ripping the cloth doll in two with a horrid tearing sound. "There's no earthly point! Don't you hear what I'm tellin' the both of you? There ain't no friendship that can ever go beyond the bounds of this house! The more *you* try to create one, Cecelia, the more any Negro is gon' resent the hell out of you one day!"

Cecelia slowly reached down, grasped the shredded doll, and drew up the pieces. Through her own tears, she saw that Cretia's eyes were wide and dry. None of it had mattered to her. Or had it? It was the first moment Cecelia would recall with absolute clarity of the world's unfairness. Sadly, that moment was only the first of many more.

And yet their friendship had gone on, in spite of Pleasant Stovall, or Cretia's father, Josiah, who seemed to know what Father called his "place," and never dared cross the line. Determined stubbornly to make a difference, over the years, Cecelia secretly had helped Cretia learn to read, and had given her other dolls, dresses, and shoes. As they grew, Cecelia spent countless private hours helping Cretia learn to speak properly, in spite of the risk if they were found out. The only way for her friend to fulfill her potential, she believed, and to break the bonds society had put upon her was for Cretia to have the weapon of education. These lessons seemed to cement their already deep and rich childhood bond, and to make this newest revelation all the more devastating.

Suddenly, without even realizing it at first, Cecelia was weeping. She had come to a tree in the churchyard and rested her arms against its great trunk. She was sobbing for Cretia—and for the man she had always believed her father to be—the man he could never be for her again. And she was weeping for the loss of her own innocence. When she felt a hand on her shoulder, Cecelia turned with a start to see the concerned face of William Sherman behind her, and his handkerchief proffered. It was another moment before she could speak.

"Come," he said, taking her hand and leading her to a bench wrought of a great log split in half and shaded by the heavy, low-hanging branch of an old evergreen.

"I do so hate that I'm cryin'." She sniffled, trying to control herself. "I hate that it matters so much. I hate the vulnerability in that!"

"It's more difficult to be vulnerable than almost anything else," William said knowingly. "It's too open. Too exposed."

Cecelia wiped her eyes with the handkerchief again and held it on her lap. "That's it, precisely."

"But the good can come in then."

"If there is any good left."

"There is always some bit of good in everything."

"I hate optimism just now."

"For most of my life, that's all I've had."

"I'm sorry," Cecelia said, meaning it.

"Don't be. It's what I needed to survive, and survive I did."

"It's my family. My father particularly." It was still difficult to comprehend, but Cecelia felt entirely safe and natural with William—safe enough to share her burden. "He's like a rock, a great icon in Augusta, where we're from. Everyone adores him, and I've always looked up to him."

"But no longer?"

"My father remarried befo' my mother was barely in her grave. Lawd, that was hard to bear. Now he and one of our servants—" She paused, remembering only soft flashes now of Louisa Stovall. Occasionally her mind could conjure the hint of her mother's smile, or she might recall the air, thick with perfume, the fragrance of musk roses, that had clung to her dresses. But that was all that was left. The rest of their mother, her essence, had vanished into time—dust to dust, replaced so easily by Anne, who had borne their father a child almost immediately after their hasty marriage, pressing Louisa into the past, along with the four children she had borne and loved and left when she died.

Suddenly the words were difficult to speak. Not because of William but because of the dark truth they carried. "It's not Cretia's fault. She can't stop him, after all. Can't tell him no. He owns her."

William shook his head and was silent for a moment. "Now it is *I* who am sorry," he finally said. "I can only imagine how you feel. I don't understand slavery myself. It just never seemed right, one person owning another, like a pet or a piece of furniture."

That stopped her. She had never thought of it quite in those terms. Cecelia handed him back the handkerchief. "We've just always had them. They were always there, and it seemed fairer than turnin' them out to uncertainty. I mean, my father always said, what sort of life would they have without us?"

"A free one. Freedom to make their own choices, their own mistakes. The way it is for you, Cecelia . . . here in New York."

Her fingers were gently at her lips. She was quiet as the reality settled upon her.

"They're property for your families, no better than the horses or the cattle . . . the family dog. In the North, where I come from, they have a chance at the same sort of fortunes and failures—family life and joys like the rest of us."

"You treat them like anyone else up in the North?"

"I can't say life is as easy as it is for the rest of us, no." He tipped his head, considering the blacks he had known and seen growing up. "It's still hard, for sure. There's still prejudice. But what I'm trying to say is at least they have a chance. No one separates men from their wives . . . babies from their mamas . . . the old from the young . . . To my way of thinking, all of that, no matter how long you've been doing it, or what reasons you give yourselves, it's just plain wrong."

"You make us sound heartless in the South."

"I believe slavery *is* heartless, and I wouldn't be a bit surprised if this country went to war over the whole issue some day."

Looking at him, she stiffened. "That's crazy! It's the right of the state to decide!"

"Owning people is what's crazy, and there are people whose consciences won't allow it to go on forever."

"They've just always been there. . . . It's the way it has always been. No one's ever made me think of any of it like you have befo'."

"I suspect you've never met anyone like *me* before."

She laughed before she could help herself. "That much is certainly true."

"I'm still sorry about your father. I'm sorry he disappointed you. And I'm *very* sorry for the girl—for Cretia."

"I am, too." Cecelia lowered her eyes. When she looked up at him again, she said, "You make me think, William. But not in the way my brothers do. You don't patronize or talk down to me, like I'm a child meant to be molded. Meant to have only half-truths, only the ones they *believe* I can handle."

"Well, I don't see you that way. Maybe that's it."

"How *do* you see me?"

He leaned back, looked up at the sky, and took his time. "Back home, Mrs. Ewing had a bird in a cage when I was growing up, a little yellow finch. It used to sing and keep her company. But it stopped singing after a while. I figured it just lost the will."

"How terribly sad. Did she ever end up settin' it free?"

"Not exactly. But Mrs. Ewing's not a bad woman. She cares about things. Some time after, she had the wings clipped and let it out to hop around the yard, in the sunshine so it could wander for a time every day. That little taste of freedom pretty much changed everything."

Cecelia looked at him in a startled way. "You think that's what comin' here has done fo' me?"

"I don't know. I suspect that'll be for you to say, how you're different, or the same."

"I feel like *everythin'* is changin'. Nothin' feels the way it used to."

"Most of life is like that. Just when you think you've got a handle on it, everything changes."

"And yet that doesn't seem to bother you."

"I'd never have survived this long if it did. The life I've had so far has taught me to accept things as they come, and not to question them too much. Accept the good and deal with the bad. I seize life, like a big, shiny apple. I take a bite when it's offered, and always want more."

It was so simple, so plain-spoken, that it startled her in the complexity of emotion she felt sitting here with him. Boys back home talked with her about dancing, her dresses, and perhaps the state of the weather. But not William. He spoke to her as if her thoughts mattered. They sat together like that, beneath the shady canopy of trees, talking of ordinary things and meaningful things. From this single encounter, Cecelia knew she would never look at Cretia or Josiah in the same way again. Never *think* of them in the same way again. On so many levels, it was a conversation like she had never had with anyone. Deep, thought provoking, emotional—and she liked it. She liked how it made her think, question, and consider. She liked it, and William Sherman, quite a lot.

"You certainly make me feel foolish about some of the things I've been taught to believe," she said later, after she had lost all track of time.

He covered her hand with his own, and after her first impulse to pull away, she remained, drawn powerfully by the warmth and command of his touch.

"And do I make you feel brave, too?"

She looked at him. There was a little silence as the intensity between them grew to something that felt very powerful. His eyes, the ones she had feared last night, bore truth now, and safety. "Brave?"

"Do you have enough courage to see me again? With or without your brother's approval?"

She shrank from him, surprised. "Are you askin' me to lie to Marcellus?"

"Think of it as taking things as they come, Cecelia. Take what the two of us are feeling for one another, and don't question it. I won't, and you can do the same. *If* you want it badly enough."

Suddenly, with the offer there between them, making what she had felt from the first now hard and concrete, Cecelia gave in to a rush of panic. She had always obeyed rules. Her father's rules. Southern rules. She had always, *always* done what was right. Even if now that veneer of *politesse* had begun to peel away like old wallpaper exposing something sordid and ugly beneath.

"I couldn't! I mean, how could I? I will always be a Southern lady. And you are a man who—"

William drew up her hand and kissed the palm, stopping her words. "And I would ever treat you as the precious jewel you are. I told you that."

"I can't sneak around behind him! And anyway, Marcellus would know!"

"Did you know about your father?"

Her stomach squeezed, and her own eyes filled with tears before she could will them away. When he saw them, Cecelia turned from him. In response, William took her shoulder and gently brought her back around.

"Look, I'm sorry. That was unthinking of me. But you know we've got to see one another again."

She did know it. But she exclaimed, "This is madness!"

"Yes," he said, mirroring her own word as he leaned in very closely, still clutching tightly to the handkerchief with which she had dried her tears. "Yet it's powerful madness. And for my own part in it, there's nothing I want to escape."

She hadn't realized how long they had been sitting there until the church doors were opened and Marcellus, Thomas, Bolling, and the rest of the congregation came out and down the stone steps into the sunlight, all squinting and shading their eyes from the light as Cecelia had done. Marcellus approached them first, and William stood then, as she did. A slight warm breeze came up off the river; she watched the two greet one another and observed the uneasy alliance between them.

"You all right?" Marcellus asked her.

"I think it has just been too much with the trip and all. Mr. Sherman kindly lent me his handkerchief and was keepin' me company until the service was over."

"Now, apparently," Marcellus said with a nod, "I am indebted to you twice."

"You make too much of small gestures."

"There was nothin' small 'bout sufferin' a demerit that rightly belonged to me. I owed you fo' that, and now fo' kindness toward my sister."

"And I thank you fo' *both* of us, Mr. Sherman," Cecelia said.

William nodded carefully. "Miss Stovall."

As he turned to take his leave, Cecelia felt something rise up within her— desperation. It was strange and disconcerting in its power, but she could not overcome it. "Mr. Sherman, wait . . . please!"

Marcellus looked at her as William stopped, then turned back. The moment crackled with an odd tension between the three of them. "Next Saturday," she said cautiously. "Yo' free day. Sho'ly you are given time enough to join us at the hotel fo' lunch."

"Please do, Sherman," Marcellus agreed. His gaze shot from his sister to William and back again, sensing the power between them. "You could enlighten us all to life growin' up as a Yank. Somethin' so foreign to us all is bound to be entertainin'."

Her brother's smile was good-natured. William smiled back. It was a straight, white smile, full of no pretension at all. It was, Cecelia thought, one of his most powerful qualities.

Chapter Three

❧

They met at one o'clock the next Saturday after graduation, in the dining room of the West Point Hotel. Crowded with summer guests, it was a bright airy room, bearing a high ceiling and with a large crystal chandelier overhead, and a wall of tall windows facing the river. The sun brought streams of buttery yellow light in across the crisp ivory-colored damask table linen and brightly polished silver.

Cecelia sat beside Thomas but across from William, whose face was in the shaft of sunlight, half in the shadow that the heavy blue velvet curtains cast. She looked at William, his tight, hard body, his head topped with mussed coppery hair, all of it coming together in a wildly sensual way. He was the same man of honor enough to come to her aid, and her brother's, as well.

Calm yourself, she thought as she watched his deep, penetrating eyes, which from time to time settled on her with open admiration. A rush of attraction shook her, when she realized that. Her heart beat wildly as he leaned back in the tall, blue, velvet-covered chair, looking at her again. Thomas was telling him about Georgia, the dogwoods, and the lush camellias, all the things he must see if he ever made it to the South. He would come to Georgia. Cecelia knew it with an odd kind of premonition that shook her almost as much as it thrilled her.

"So, is it true that you're an orphan?" Thomas crassly asked, taking a large forkful of buttered trout as a smile ever so slightly turned up the corners of his mouth.

William's own fork hung in midair for only an instant, settling into the challenge before he set it back on his plate. "My father died when I was a boy, and my mother was not left with sufficient means to care for us all. I was fortunate to have been offered accommodations with a family friend," he charmingly replied, refusing to take the bait.

"I was given to understand from Marcellus," Bolling interjected, "that you are the ward of Senator Ewing."

"The senator's generosity did not require the premature death of my mother."

"How fortunate fo' a boy with ambition."

Cecelia's eyes darted to each of her brothers, seeing suddenly that the younger two meant to have a bit of cruel fun with him. "Mr. Sherman has set out to make a great deal of his life from his adversity," she defended, "which will be far mo', I suspect, than I will be able to say 'bout either of you."

All of them were stunned into silence by her flash of spirit on behalf of a virtual stranger. "Now, sister—" Bolling smiled. "—Thomas only meant that it is always a marvel when one triumphs over humble beginnin's."

"And all the mo' remarkable if he goes to put it to good use," Marcellus countered as he drew a glass of dark burgundy wine to his lips.

Amid the clinking of glass and silver against china, a new tension sprang up at the table. Sherman was not good enough for any of them, least of all her. That was what this was all about: an understated, purely proper Southern way of cutting someone down to size, and all the while maintaining a dignified smile. Her stomach turned. In that instant—and for the first time in her life—she despised her brothers and, by extension, what it meant to be a Southern family of means. She loathed what it had made of them all.

"Sho'ly you know I meant no offense," Thomas said politely.

William folded his napkin and laid it across his plate, the polite luncheon and Cecelia's hopes at an end. He stood stiffly and then bowed to Cecelia. "Miss Stovall, it has been a pleasure."

Cecelia leaned toward Thomas, murmuring between gritted teeth as William walked out of the room. "I could kill you with my bare hands!"

"I was merely makin' conversation. Can I help it if he's not well suited to hold his own against Southern boys?"

"That's quite enough," Marcellus intervened. "I owe Sherman. We've got to remember that."

"So you were polite out of duty alone?" Cecelia tightly asked.

"Well, we don't have a great deal in common with boys like that."

"Oh!" she exclaimed, shoving her hair back in a blaze of anger. "I am ashamed of you all!"

"Precisely where do you think you're gon'?"

"Fo' a breath of air! The environment here is as foul as death!"

"You certainly can't go out alone!"

"Watch me!"

"It wouldn't be proper!"

"I've had my fill with what should *seem* proper! Now get out of my way! And don't you *dare* to chase after me!" she warned, moving swiftly out of the dining room.

Cecelia held up her wide bell skirts and broke into a run as she moved through the hotel front door, realizing only after she had gone out into the warm summer sunlight that she was not so much running away from her brothers as toward William.

She doubted he would have had a horse or carriage and, knowing only one path back toward West Point, she charged toward it with all the purpose she had ever felt in her life. It was the first time she had ever set out anywhere entirely alone, and her heart raced with that knowledge—and with the hope that she could catch up with him.

The trees were thick and lush, shading the archway like a tunnel as birds sang from the branches above and the dirt path wound along the edge of the Hudson River.

"William!" she called out as she went farther and farther from the hotel and she saw the silhouette of one man rather too far ahead to know for certain if it was him.

Running after him, she watched him move, the fluid yet powerful grace of him. Unaware of her presence, he was magnificent in his stride, possessed of such great dignity.

"William, please wait!" she called again.

The figure stopped as Cecelia held up her skirts again and continued on toward him. When she reached him, she was out of breath, her pale cheeks flushed. He stood staring at her in the rich lacy shadows that the trees made.

"I'm so sorry! Please! My brothers were horrid!"

William reached up to brush back a strand of her dark hair, which had come free with her running. His hand stilled there against her cheek. Her chest rose and fell heavily, and she could feel her heart slamming against her rib cage. His hand did not leave her face in that moment when she had no idea at all what to do next—or what he would do. When William looked at her, Cecelia thought he was looking through her, right through to her heart, and that he knew exactly what she felt. Her cheeks burned.

It was certainly not proper to be alone out here like this with him. She shivered, realizing it, but beyond that she did not care. The air between them eddied. As he moved, an object slipped out of his jacket pocket. Cecelia bent down to pick it up.

"A sketchbook?" she asked in a voice that came barely above a whisper.

He seemed embarrassed and held out a hand to take it from her. "It's nothing important."

"I'd like to see it."

William did not protest as she pushed back the worn leather cover, but his tone was apologetic. "They're not at all good. I just sketch things sometimes, to pass the time . . . to record things here, places, people, so I don't forget them."

She looked up at him. "These are brilliant, William."

He laughed. "Edward Ord, one of my roommates, calls them chicken scratch."

"Yo' roommate, suh, is a fool, and certainly no judge of talent!" She looked back at each of the sketches, richly detailed and true to life. The detailed image of a barn surrounded by trees. A rigidly standing cadet bearing a bugle for taps. And a riverside setting, lush and inviting, framed by leafy trees that dipped down to the water's edge.

"This place?" she asked. "It looks near here."

"It is. Just down that path. I go there sometimes when I need to be alone, to think. I don't believe another human being even knows it exists."

She moved a fraction closer. Bending on a sudden impulse, Cecelia reached up and touched his face, as he had touched her. William took a sharp breath, made a small gasp, and her fingertips came alive at the uneven, slightly craggy warmth of his skin. She had never touched something so purely male before, and her entire body reacted to it.

"Would you draw me?" she asked, her voice shaking.

"You are the *only* girl I have ever wanted to draw."

In a moment that was as charged with excitement as it was frightening,

William pulled her to him with an arm at the small of her back in a gentle, tentative way, and kissed her. As he drew away, Cecelia extended her hand to him, her whole body trembling. He took her hand and held it tightly. The *knowing* that had possessed her reason—and certainly her better judgment—took over all else.

Cecelia knew not a single member of her family would easily approve a Northern boy with no family of note, no distinctive heritage. But that made her no less determined to insist.

His hand was firm and sure, as he drew her back against himself. "You're the first girl I've ever kissed," he confessed with a charmingly timid smile.

"And you're the first boy *I've* ever kissed."

"Would you think me forward if we did it just like that, one more time?"

"Absolutely."

Attraction shimmered in the air between them. William tipped his head. "And if I didn't?"

"Then I do believe, suh, *I* would have to kiss *you*."

"Cecelia Stovall, you are the most incredible girl!"

His simple words rang like the sweet, sultry music of a wind chime in her mind. It blotted out anything her brothers could have said. No matter what happened in her life from here on, she would never forget this moment of pure, rare truth with a man. And she would revel in it for as long as she could.

"It's curious, don't you think, how people come together?" she said as they drew apart a second time, her lips slightly bruised from the power of their deepening connection.

"Only thing more curious are the things that keep them apart," William replied, pulling her close yet again and beginning a slow, hypnotic touch of her face, neck, and arms, as if he were trying to memorize the contours of her.

Cecelia could feel the warmth of his body through his summer uniform, the power of his desire, so close against her. A red-hot heat was snaking its way up her chest and into her face at the very same time. And suddenly, she thought she might actually understand about the physicality between men and women. She could see how they came together and why, wanting William so blindly as she did at that moment. It was the first time in many days, she felt even the slightest understanding for her father. It made her wonder if this was the power that overtook him, too, the same sensation that ruled him when he went to Cretia, despite promises made to Anne. Despite honor and all else. For that same power, she was willing to risk anything now—and forever—to be with William Tecumseh Sherman.

"Show me yo' special place?"

"I've never gone there with anyone. And it's pretty well secluded."

"It'd mean a great deal to me if we could share that." She smiled. "Like a grand secret between us that no one else would be a part of."

He hesitated, glancing back at the path in the direction of the West Point Hotel. "I really should get you back to your brothers."

"I don't give a *fig* about my brothers, after the way they treated you! As far as I'm concerned, they can worry about me awhile longer!" She ran a finger along the brass buttons of his gray uniform coat. "Show me? Please?"

He took her hand then and led her down a narrow path edged with shrubbery that moved them that much farther away from the imposingly grand hotel. They walked silently down a gentle rise of earth until they came to a clearing strewn with coppery pine needles and dotted with lushly wild ferns. The air was cooler down here so near the water's edge. A robin trilled somewhere in the lacy tree branches above them, and Cecelia knew she never wanted to leave this special secret place, and the peace it brought her, so long as she could remain here with William.

"It's as lovely here as you drew it," she said with an open smile.

"I'm glad you think so, too."

In the silence, as he lay his coat onto the ground, Cecelia realized he was creating a clean place for her to sit. She couldn't help but see that William's bare arms were well muscled, his chest tight. She cleared her throat, feeling another hot rush into her face and she purposely looked away, out across the river that now was as clear and still as glass. A moment later, he held out his hand to her, and she sank down beside him.

She smiled. "This isn't the least bit proper."

"Your brothers wouldn't think so."

"Still, I'd like to come here, too, sometimes." She drew her knees to her chest and felt the cool breeze reviving the senses he had stirred. "Just to have a little while alone to think."

"It will await you gladly," he said with a chivalrous air.

Cecelia broke a small piece of fern from one of the branches beside them, knowing this was a place she would want to remember. "Thank you, William, fo' sharin' this."

"Only with you."

A few minutes later, he took her hand as they began to walk back toward the hotel and the three brothers they both knew only too well would be waiting and angry.

"How will I see you again?"

She thought for a moment, then looked over at him as they walked, her arm wrapped in his. "The Fourth of July festivities are later this week. Will you be able to attend them?"

"All the cadets that stayed here for the summer will go. Could I meet you there?"

"I shall look fo' you."

"I'll be looking for no one *but* you."

She came alone out of the arch of trees after that, the slip of fern tucked safely in the pocket of her skirts, and William at a pace behind her. But the distance was not great enough to dissuade her already suspicious brothers. "What in God's name have you done with our sister!" Bolling angrily demanded, stalking forward, away from his brothers, the first to confront them.

"Nothin' worse, by far, than what you did to *him* at lunch!" Cecelia haughtily shot in response, then walked away from William without looking back.

She could not afford to stay; she knew the truth was plain in her eyes. And it was not yet time for anyone to know what Cecelia Stovall felt for William Tecumseh Sherman.

Chapter Four

✧

Done for the visiting families of the first-year cadets required to remain over the summer, West Point celebrated the Fourth of July in grand style.

There was a band, long tables lined with food, candles beneath hurricane glass, and American flags strung up like banners between shade trees, all at the little clearing on the river near the North Barracks. As William waited for a glimpse of Cecelia, he saw Robert Lee instead, standing near the bandstand with a group of West Point instructors. He waited a moment, uncertain whether he should speak, but Lee had been so kind to him a week earlier, so interested, that he felt compelled to pay his respects before the impressive graduate returned to his post in Saint Louis.

"Your commencement address was splendid," he said, coming up behind the group of men. "I managed to hear a bit of it with a few other cadets last week."

"Why, thank you," Lee said, turning around and recognizing William immediately with a large, welcoming smile. After the instructors had disbanded, Lee drew away from the bandstand together with William. "So tell me. How did you fare with the young lady?"

William could not help smiling. "She now feels as I do, I am happy to say."

"Splendid news." Lee's smile was genuine. "It didn't take any sort of particular genius to see that the two of you had quite a visible connection."

"There's a good deal against us. Especially her family."

"Everything worthwhile in this world comes with a price, son. Perhaps now you must decide if it is a price you are willing to pay."

Then William caught a glimpse of her, in the company of two of her brothers, strolling beside the tables laden with cakes, pies, and cookies. "Cecelia would be worth any price I had to pay, Lieutenant Lee. Any price at all."

"Knowing one's future is a rare gift, Sherman. See you take care with that."

"Oh, she *is* my future, sir. Strangely enough, there is not a doubt in my mind about that."

After they had said their good-byes and William wished the lieutenant the best of luck back in Saint Louis, he concentrated on moving close enough to be seen by Cecelia but not by Bolling or Thomas. William moved stealthily around trees and the other family members who had come to keep the first-year cadets company over the long months of the summer break when they were not allowed to leave the academy. There was laughter and music, and enough distraction, William thought, to find a bit of time alone with Cecelia. He had but to wait for the right moment to steal her away. She saw him soon after that, beckoning her. But the moment for her to join him did not come until well after supper when a concert of favorites began.

As the band played a rousing rendition of "My Heart's Desire" for the patriotic audience, William crept up near Cecelia on the vast green lawn and motioned for her to join him over behind the cookhouse. She did so a moment later, and William embraced her.

"I've missed you!" he murmured, and kissed her tenderly.

Cecelia smiled at him as she touched the line of his jaw. "I do believe this has been the longest week of my life."

"Do we have a moment alone?"

"Most likely only just that." Cecelia looked back as the crowd gathered to listen to music. The sun set swiftly around them all, and the late evening wore a heavy cloak of haze behind which they could hide. "I told the brothers I'd gone to find somethin' to drink."

William smiled at her, then drew her arm through his just as the fireworks display out over the Hudson River began to explode in shimmering waterfalls of red, green, blue, and silver. Given the cover of darkness and bright lights, they walked down to the river's edge together to watch. In silhouette that protected them from discovery, William put his arm around her waist, and Cecelia settled her head on his shoulder as they watched the night sky. In spite of the colors overhead and the deafening boom in her ears, she was aware of little else other than his sheer solidness beside her, the warmth of him pressed against her.

"Do you believe in fate?" he asked into her hair, caring not a whit for the dazzling show before them.

"I didn't. Until I met you."

As the current of emotion crackled between them like the powerfully brilliant fireworks overhead, William turned her toward him. He cupped his hands on her small face and bent his lips to hers. A moment later, he took a small lit lamp from one of the tables and led her away from the crowd, all the rest of them gazing in rapt attention at the bursting colors still lighting the night sky.

The evening was warm, but a breeze off the water cooled the air and scented it with a mossy fragrance as they neared the hidden clearing. That scent mingled with the fragrance of pine from the protective grove of trees around her. Crisp fallen needles crunched beneath her feet as she moved from the path and carefully between the trees and around silvery shafts of moonlight tangling there. *He will not hurt me*, she argued with her heart. *The truth is still there in his eyes, and I believe him.*

He drew her to him and kissed her more passionately than he ever had before. Cecelia was aware, as he drew his lips away from hers, of his arms across her back and the sensation of her breasts against his chest. She felt as if she were actually melting into him—into his chest, his soul, and into his heart.

When William pulled himself away from her, Cecelia saw that he was flushed and his breathing was heavy. "I had no right to kiss you that way. But I'm still not sorry," he said huskily, touching her cheek with infinite tenderness. "I can't be."

She looked at him, allowing his sentence to trail away. "Do you . . . *love* me?" she asked tentatively, flushed with emotion, her body alive with a host of new sensations.

"I know how sudden it seems, how wild and unexplainable. But yes, I do, entirely and hopelessly."

"Then *I* shall never be sorry either."

He traced a finger along her cheek, down her neck, and then held out his hand. "Come on," he said, his voice breaking.

He took her hand, and they walked down the steep sandy slope to the bank of the river where the water lapped softly at the shore. A cloud slipped across the moon and what bit of light there had been was suddenly eclipsed by shadows and cool, sweet breeze.

Her voice was no more than a whisper as she lay her head on his shoulder again and he slipped his arm around her waist. "My brother says all men break their lovers' hearts, sooner or later. Tell me, William Sherman, do you intend to break *my* heart one day too?"

He drew away from her again, as if fighting some great internal war, and ran a hand through his unruly thatch of copper hair. He was too unaccustomed to the sort of raging arousal that coursed through him when he was with her. All his life, William had needed people. His mother, the Ewings, the superiors here at West Point. Cecelia was the first person who he believed ever truly needed him. Mixed with his attraction to her, that was a powerful draw.

"What I told you that first night, I mean every bit as much today. I shall *ever* love and protect you, Cecelia Stovall. That is plain fact, no matter where life takes us. As to your question, I'd like to believe I'm the one man who will never disappoint you."

Cecelia drew him back to the place he had sketched and pulled him down beside her. She was smiling. "Do you have a pen with which you might draw me?"

He laughed, surprised by how capable she was of quickly changing his mood and his desires. "I always carry it. Just in case I see something I don't want to forget."

"And have you seen that now?"

"Drawing or not, Cecelia, I could *never* forget you."

She chuckled, lightening the moment, and then tipped her head. "Is there enough light left?"

"Just enough and I've the lamp." William settled himself before her and opened his sketchbook; then he found the chalk. Cecelia watched him—the intensity in his eyes, the furrow of his brow. She felt the lift of her heart as she studied the nuances of him. Yes, she knew inexplicably that this was a man she could love forever, and with her whole heart. He was a man she could marry, and to whom she could give herself completely. Whatever he desired. She flushed at the realization of that. William saw the sudden rise of color in her cheeks, and his chalk stilled on the paper.

"Are you all right?"

"Mo' than all right. Now come on, silly. Start drawin'!"

His hand moved feverishly across the small white surface, and his gaze moved from her to the pad and back again in rapid volley. He was so intense, so surprising. So full of contradictions and dreams. William Tecumseh Sherman was wonderful, and even knowing him as briefly as she had, Cecelia could not imagine his not being a part of her life.

"May I see it?"

"Not until it's finished."

"When will you do that?"

"Tonight in the barracks, I'll do a bit more shading, after I've studied for my last exam."

She gave a slight pout. "But how'll you remember the proper angles?"

"There isn't a thing about you I could *ever* forget."

When he was finished, William closed the flap over the book, stood, and helped her back to her feet. "Thank you," he said in that deep, rich Northern voice that captivated her.

"Fo' what?"

Facing her, William put his hands on her shoulders and drew her near. His kiss swiftly became passionate, and it was more difficult this time to part himself from her. "For giving me an image of you that I will keep forever, to light my way in this world."

"You're gon' make yo' own brilliant way in this world, William. I just know it."

"Well, very little about it has been easy, so far. Nor will changing my future be. Senator Ewing took me in and obtained this appointment for me, but at a great cost. He was planning to make me respectable enough to marry Ellen, his daughter."

Cecelia had not seen it coming, nor could she have guessed how painfully the words would descend upon her. "Then you're already—promised?"

"I have promised nothing to anyone—before this moment, that is."

He kissed her again and, a moment later, said, "I've got to come to Augusta, meet your father. But I don't get my first leave from West Point until next summer."

"That doesn't matter." She smiled. "I've known almost from the first that I love you too. I will wait fo' you to come."

In the lamplight, she saw an unmistakable foreshadowing in his eyes. Somehow, William would make a mark in this world, and she already felt herself a part of it.

"And I *will* be there. You can depend on it," he said, his voice a low rasp, his body taut and raging with desire for her. He moved hungrily to kiss her again beneath the trees, tall sentinels dutifully protecting them from the rest of the world.

It was different this time, the promise between them sealing his desire. William pressed her back into a soft bed of pine needles, and she did not object to his hands as they moved down the length of her body, molding the skirts of her dress to her thighs. The power of her own desire shook her, and the world around them began to spin like a carousel, a play of light, color, sound, and feeling, all of it converging on her now as he tasted her lips, touched her body, held her as closely as if they were one.

William now trailed a finger from her chin down to between the cotton-covered rise of her breasts. She felt him shiver, and yet still did not stop him. Again he kissed her, wanting more this time, his mouth moist and warm, his strong hands tracing a path along the smooth planes of her body. His own rock-hard form was firm against her. The reality shocked her—especially that part of him she would one day know fully. The thought of that knowledge filled her with wild desire rather than the fear she had always expected.

As he touched her in a rhythm to his own rasping breathing, she moaned, knowing the awakening of a fierce kind of hunger that was more powerful than breathing.

She ached for him to draw up her dress, to do everything in this quiet, private beautiful place that was a haven for them. Where they were simply William and Cecelia. Not young, not separated by North and South, or by family ideal. And even though they were not married, she knew one day they would be. And she trusted him with her life and her heart. Giving him the rest of herself now would seal that promise forever.

Cecelia knew enough of her father's prejudices to fear his reaction to a man like William, and so this act, this moment of pleasure she had not anticipated, she now wanted. To secure what had begun between them. As he kissed her passionately, his body covering hers, and her heart beating madly, like a bird's wings, her skin beneath her dress was bathed in perspiration. *Lord help me . . .* , she was thinking. *But I want this with him!*

Then, without warning, on the very edge of her surrender, William pressed himself away. He rolled onto his back on the bed of dry pine needles, let out a rasping breath, and closed his eyes. "It's not time for us yet. Not for the full pleasure a wife gives to her husband. That I must wait for," he managed to whisper as his chest rose and fell.

Cecelia watched him in the heavy silence that had fallen so suddenly between them, struggling to catch his breath, his face strained with the unmet passion, and her heart swelled even more grandly with the love she felt for him. But she knew he was resolute. She trusted him, and he would not take advantage of her honor beyond what they already had shared.

A moment later, as they lay side by side, William opened his eyes to the heavens, then took up her palm and kissed it gently. Still holding her hand he said, "I'm not a frivolous sort, Cecelia."

As he made his declaration, William reached up and unfastened a small gold cross and chain from around his neck. She gasped softly as he linked it around her neck.

"This is the only thing I have of any value at all in the world. It has been in my family for generations. My father gave it to me before he died. It had been given to *him* by his mother."

"I couldn't possibly take it! It's far too special!"

"It's all I have to give you as my promise that I *will* come to Augusta the first moment I can."

William looked at her lying there beside him, knowing he had never wanted anything so much as this woman who believed in him. She was special. They were special, together. As he helped her brush some of the needles from the length of her skirt, he could feel her legs trembling beneath it. As his own were. He had never been with a woman before—not fully, nor even this close, and the depth of his desire for Cecelia had nearly overwhelmed his sense of honor. Taking both her hands, he entwined his fingers with hers and then brought them to his lips. His smile bore such confidence, she thought.

"Wear this until the day the future is absolutely sure between us."

She glanced down at it, holding the cross out between two fingers. Tears were shining in her eyes. "You know I will."

Marcellus had seen them come up from the river together again. He had seen them pause. He had seen Sherman touch his sister's face in a manner that was far from casual. Marcellus had not intended to upend his life in this way. Not with his own future at West Point in such tumult. But knowing that Cecelia had gone off alone like a common strumpet with a penniless Yank of all people, one she scarcely knew, tainted her in a way that was repugnant to him.

It had become a Pandora's box for them both.

Marcellus burned with anger. Cecelia, his own baby sister—who depended upon him, looked up to him—had never lied to him. Worse almost, he had let his guard down with Sherman, actually begun to like the bloody Northerner.

The devil take William Tecumseh Sherman!

He had planned to confront them there, then thought better of it. From his fascinating study of the art of war, he knew well that the element of surprise was a winning strategy. He understood that, even as a lowly West Point plebe whose own current standing was bleak.

Marcellus waited inside the tiny cubicle of their barracks room, trying hard to bide his time. William would pay for defiling his innocent sister. Oh, yes, pay dearly he would! So what if Sherman had done him a favor a few days ago? His sister's virtue was far beyond the realm of payment. It was an hour before William returned.

Before Sherman was fully inside, and with the element of surprise, Marcellus threw a fist wildy, powerfully, and exactly, slamming William back against the wall. Edward looked up in openmouthed surprise.

"What the devil—?"

"Stay out of this, Ord!" Marcellus grunted. "Did you think I wouldn't find out?" he raged, grabbing William by the collar and pressing him tight against the wall. "You've ruined her!"

"I *love* her!"

Edward Ord sprang to his feet and hurriedly closed the door. This sort of thing could land all three of them in the brig for the rest of the summer.

"*Love?* You barely *know* my sister!"

Then, without warning, William cast Marcellus off him boldly and threw a punch with such force that Cecelia's brother went careering against the opposite wall with a great thud, landing like a rag doll on his mattress in a wilted pile.

"I love her, nevertheless!"

Marcellus laughed bitterly, rubbing his jaw. "Stupid, fool Yankee! *That* will never come to anythin'!"

"Keep it down, boys!" urged their roommate, his hands up in warning.

"Because I am not from that select, private club called the South?"

"My father is a man of means, Sherman! The most prominent cotton merchant in Augusta, and arguably in all of Georgia!"

William arched a brow. "And I haven't pedigree enough to satisfy him, is that it?"

"You haven't any pedigree at all! Yo' father is dead, and yo' mother sold you over to the highest bidder! You're dependant upon the kindness of the family who took you in! Do you really believe Pleasant Stovall would turn over one of his daughters to a future with the likes of *you* simply because a tumble in the grass one July evenin' suited yo' fancy?"

"She's *not* a tumble, you idiot!"

"Well that's the most you'll ever get from her, so I hope you enjoyed destroyin' her honor!"

William reached down swinging at him hard, pressing him back into the bedding with the force of another sharp blow to his jaw. "You really are a vile bastard!" William growled.

A bright red ribbon of blood streamed from the corner of Marcellus's mouth. "And you, my Northern hayseed, are *well* out of yo' league!"

"Cecelia loves me!"

"Give it up, Sherman! Trust me, you stand *no* chance with my father! None at all!"

For a moment, the airless, white-washed room was filled with silence, and sour with the unspoken rancor. "What do you have so against me, Marcellus?" William's pride forced him to ask as he sank onto his haunches beside Cecelia's brother, who was dotting the blood from his lip with a handkerchief. "Your sister could do a lot worse than a man with ambition and an absolute determination to make a name for himself. One who adores her."

"And back in Augusta, she could do a whole lot better!"

Having made his cruel point in spades, Marcellus struggled to his feet, smoothed out his shirt and pants, ran his hands through his dark, straight hair, and moved in long strides toward the door. The small, hot room smelled of their sweat and acrimony long after Marcellus had gone out of it. William went to the window and watched, knowing Cecelia's brother was going to her, and that he would try his best now to put an end to things.

"Quite the sanctimonious prig," Edward Ord calmly observed, cutting into the silence that remained. William did not respond. "My mother married a man of means because her family willed it. She hasn't had a day of happiness since."

William spun around, helpless anger blazed in his steel-gray eyes. "Why tell me that, exactly?"

"Because if you love her, you've got to fight for her!"

"And just how do you suggest I do that? You heard him yourself."

"Fortunately for you, he is *not* the final arbiter of your life. Steal her away, and marry Cecelia tomorrow, Sherman, before anyone can stop you!"

Outside the window, they could hear the echo of taps being sounded in the courtyard. He raked back the hair from his forehead in frustration. "Ord, I haven't a *clue* how to accomplish that. I don't even have the money to pay a preacher, much less to keep her somewhere safe until they come to their senses!"

Ord's long face sparkled with mischief. "Then it's lucky for you that *I* do."

William came away from the window and sank onto his mattress, feeling the weight of defeat. "I can't take your money. I won't have a way to pay you back for years."

Edward Ord was still smiling. His was a pale, pleasant face, long and regal in an English manner. Back home in Maryland, his nanny used to tell him when he was a boy that he was descended from English royalty. The son of King George IV and his secret wife, Maria Fitzherbert. It was a subject his own father refused to confirm or deny.

"Then you'll owe me—with interest. And, believe-you-me, I *will* collect!"

"Why would you gamble like that?"

"I've never met anyone like you, Cump. Ambition burns in you like a damn beacon! You've got great things in store. That's no gamble."

"I *will* pay you back," William declared, a new spark of hope lighting eyes that seemed gray now in the dim lamplight.

"Oh, I know you will. After all, what else is there in store for a man named Tecumseh but sheer greatness?" He was laughing good-naturedly. "The way I see it, you've got some sort of life ahead of you. I just hope I'm around long enough to know what the hell that is!"

Early the next morning, Cecelia sat inside the already sweltering carriage, next to Marcellus, with Bolling and Thomas facing her on the opposite leather seat. Shadows from the tall trees along the road played across her oldest brother's face as they made a sharp turn away from West Point, toward the town of Albany. Still it was Thomas's expression, even more than the change in direction, that betrayed what was really about to happen. He turned away from her startled gaze, but it was too late. Cecelia looked at Thomas, then at Marcellus.

"We're not gon' sight-seein', are we?"

The odd silence was broken after a moment by Marcellus. "No."

Her heart began to race as she shot a glance at each of her other two brothers. No one would look at her as the carriage swayed and the horse's harness jangled in the silence. "We're not gon' back to West Point either."

"No."

Marcellus's face was hard. He wore no expression at all. In that moment, as a heavy, dark panic set in, they were not her brothers, not men she trusted and loved, with whom she had shared a carefree childhood. They were now her enemies. They were men to be feared for the ability to betray her heart with a casual ease.

A lump rose swiftly in her throat, forcing tears into the blackness of her eyes. *I will not cry . . .* , she thought again as she so often did. *I cannot. That would only give Marcellus too much satisfaction that he has won, that he is the one in control of my destiny.*

"Where are you takin' me?" she finally forced herself to ask as the tears she struggled against pooled in her dark eyes.

"I've been given my release from the academy, by mutual agreement," Marcellus told her flatly. "Father is sendin' me abroad to make the grand tour until he can decide what to do with me."

"But Father was so bent on you bein' here!" She lurched forward. "He pulled so many strings, went through so much to see you admitted!"

"We've both known in these past days that I am not cut out fo' this place. Better I leave now before any real damage is done to his precious pride or reputation."

"So you've written to Father?"

"Several days ago, yes."

"About me?"

"Yes."

Knowingly, she said then, "And I'll wager he is sendin' you as far away as he possibly can—with an errant sister as companion."

Marcellus's face remained impassive. "Yes."

Hot rage began to choke her. "All this to keep me from William Sherman?"

"All this and mo', Cecelia. Whatever it takes to bring you to yo' senses."

"I'll never stop lovin' him!" She shouted in wild warning. "You cannot stop me from *that!*"

"It'd be a pity if that were true." His voice was strangely calm. "After all, you *will* meet the right sort of man one day, and you *will* marry, then, with *all* of our blessin's."

"If it's not William, I won't! I love him, Marcellus! How can you be a party to this? . . . How can any of you do this to me?"

"We love you," Thomas said flatly.

"And *I* surely do despise *you*! And I will *never* forgive any of you! I will love William Tecumseh Sherman until the day I die, and there is not a wretched thing you can do about that, no matter how you betray me, or how far away you spirit me—you can't have my heart!"

Cecelia turned her face toward the window of the carriage and closed her eyes. The tears that had lingered, shining in her eyes, fell now, wetting the high lace of her collar. For a little while, she had allowed herself to hope. She had believed his infectious optimism, his open passion for her. But now something very different was true. There would be no dream. No hope. No William. Not for her. And right now that loss felt like a small death inside her. It certainly had been the death of a short and very wonderful dream.

Chapter Five

Cecelia despised everything about London. The pervasive gloom along the Thames, even on August mornings. Pretentious accents on ordinary people. But she hated it most of all because it was the place designed to come between her and William. No matter the history, the sights, or the grandeur, London was her prison.

Cecelia held back the long, ivory-colored lace curtain and stood stiffly at the window of her hotel room that looked down onto Grosvenor Square. Light played on the black carriages as they passed back and forth below, and she heard the jangle of a harness, then a horse whinny. Here, she was a hostage, her every move watched closely by Marcellus, under the sickening guise of his concern. At first, the tension had been thick between them. But as the weeks passed, and her eldest brother had settled comfortably into the knowledge that he had averted a potential family disaster, his mood with her had lightened.

He had tried his best at coaxing her from her sadness by buying her expensive English gowns, shoes, hats, taking her to the theater, and most astoundingly, seeing them to the front of the line as the new young Queen Victoria stood on the balcony of Buckingham Palace greeting her subjects.

"I want to see you smile again," he had said by way of explanation. "I'm doin' all that I can to bring that 'bout."

"There's nothin' to smile about," she had answered mechanically.

They had quarreled again. He followed it with contrition. And so it had gone for the long summer days they had spent as far from West Point as the Stovall money could send them. But what she had declared in her anger remained true. No matter how far away they led her, they could not tear her from her feelings for William. Those, she could and would protect as her most precious possession.

"Are you ready? We're gon' be late if you're not."

Marcellus's voice drew Cecelia from her thoughts with a jolt. He stood behind her in the doorway, dressed in gray trousers and a black coat, white shirt, and gray neck scarf, hands shoved casually into his pockets. He was smiling, as if he hadn't a care in the world. It instantly made her angry.

"Late for what?"

"Why, for tea, of course," he blithely chuckled. "Have you forgotten? We're meetin' a new friend of mine. I told you about Charles last evenin' at supper, remember? He's a Southern boy, too, here in London seein' a bit of the world befo' he settles into life back home in Savannah."

She gave her brother a steady, contemptuous stare before she responded. "You're tryin' to match me up to make me forget William."

"Guilty as charged, dear sister." He bit back a smile, intending to look sheepish and charming.

All she felt was a shiver of distaste for him. "No."

"No?"

"No, I won't go, Marcellus. I have no intention of helpin' you get over yo' guilt about what you've done to me."

He advanced, hands outstretched as she pivoted around from the window, facing him fully. His heavy boot heels clicked over the parquet floor.

"You're bein' quite pigheaded."

"I know my mind, brother." Cecelia straightened her back. "And you are sho'ly losin' yours if you believe trottin' out some proper Southern boy will make me betray my heart!"

"Well, it sho'ly won't if you won't try!"

"Try to love someone else to ease *yo'* guilt? Hell itself will freeze over befo' I will *ever* give you that!"

"Cecelia," said, coddling her. "You've really got to try."

There was silence as she drew forward, looking up at him. "Let me send a letter to William, and I will meet yo' friend. Mind you, meet him. No mo' than that."

"Out of the question. Father'd have my hide if he found out!"

"That's my offer," she bargained. "Take it or leave it."

"Cecelia, there's no point in it! You've made a start of it. It's been two months! Do the right thing; let him go!"

"Father knows only what you tell him."

His dark brow furrowed. "You cannot give Sherman hope, Cecelia, because there isn't any."

"I don't believe that. I *won't* believe it!"

"Not yet, perhaps. But you will. You'll have to. William Sherman may not have been my favorite cadet, but he deserves better. He deserves a life, Cecelia, and a marriage he is not fo' the rest of his life tryin' vainly to live up to. Think of it like that if you have the courage. It would be selfish of you to give him the slightest bit of hope that there is a future fo' the two of you that would not involve resentment and failure."

She was silenced by the cold truth in her brother's words. There were tears standing in her eyes that she fought furiously to control. "You're just sayin' that because he's from the North. Because he doesn't approve of some of our Southern ways! If I married William Tecumseh Sherman, he would always be there to make *you* defend that, defend things like what father does with Cretia! What we do with all our slaves!"

Marcellus was calm now, coldly so. "I said it, sister, because it's true. And I think you know it. Write yo' letter. I'll require a look at it first, but it shall be sent to yo' Yankee. *If* you do this one thing in return fo' me."

"Don't tell me you're actually gon' to try now to make yo' actions sound kind."

He took her hand, moving toward her as though he smelled success. "I love you. You know that. Write yo' letter," he urged. "I will send it. Then let's go to tea."

It amazed him how gullible she was for a girl of eighteen. And for a Stovall, it was downright remarkable. Of course, he had no intention of mailing her girlish love letter to that no-account Yankee. Life, after all, was about strategy and winning. Thank God he had learned at least that much in his one disastrous year at West Point.

Marcellus smoothed back his raven-black hair and waited at the bottom of the mahogany staircase at the Hotel Winchester Hill on Grosvenor Square. After all, he reminded himself, Charles was far better suited to his sister: Dignified. Refined. Wealthy. From a solid Southern family. And bright enough to want a good match, wherever that found him. Sherman was like a mixed breed mutt. Marcellus found himself smiling at his own comparison. All right if Charles Shelman lacked . . . fire. At least he was still a purebred.

Marcellus straightened his tie and glanced at his pocket watch. This was a day none of them would soon forget. He was not at all certain how Charles Shelman had pulled it off, but tea today would be at Buckingham Palace, the Queen's new residence, and not at a hotel, as he had told Cecelia. Granted, they would be among a collection of two hundred other guests, but an introduction to the young sovereign would surely be the highlight of their trip, and probably of their lives. He only hoped Cecelia would see it that way.

Sherman. Shelman. The irony of a single letter was not lost on Marcellus. Nor was the sheer perfection of matching Cecelia with the latter.

"Are you about finished? he asked anxiously.

She came toward him, wearing a serious expression as she handed him the letter. "Do you promise you'll mail this?"

He glanced at her words, which began, "My darling William."

His stomach twisted. "A promise is a promise," he dryly replied. *But the ends do justify the means,* was what he was thinking as they finally went together out the door.

The crowded Garden Room at Buckingham Palace was full of potted palms, lattice, and white linen, and it was also very hot, but Cecelia's fascination with her surprise made any discomfort inconsequential. The young woman at the head table, in the blue-beaded gown, was an honest-to-goodness queen, like Anne Boleyn and Elizabeth I. Cecelia felt, sitting here amid starched table linen, gleaming silver tea services, and great crystal vases filled with flowers, as if she had stepped into a fairy tale. Tea for Her Majesty's garden club and their guests was a rather more grand affair than any garden club back home, Cecelia thought. She looked over at the stately line of liveried servants wearing crisp white gloves, flanking one whole wall of the vast room papered in a green-and-white bamboo design. Unable to avoid being impressed, she turned back to her host.

Charles Shelman was a man of average height, with thinning, sandy blond hair, a shiny, high forehead, and small, closely set hazel eyes. He had a well-groomed mustache and neat triangle of a beard, all tamed meticulously by barber's oil. He was not so much handsome, she saw, as sophisticated, with an easy confidence and a smoothly schooled tenor, rich with a familiar Southern drawl.

"Mr. Shelman," she said primly, leaning only slightly toward him at her left. They were seated at a large, round table of quietly dignified English guests who chatted among themselves, leaving Marcellus, Charles, and Cecelia on their own. "You must tell me how a man from our little state of Georgia managed to arrange somethin' like this."

Shelman sank back into his chair and dotted his lips with a white linen napkin. He glanced at Marcellus, then smiled widely at Cecelia. "Now, Miss Stovall, is there a desirable gentleman in all the world without at least a bit of mystery?"

"Sho'ly, suh, you know this event will be spoken of fo' years to come in the Stovall family. I only desire to get the facts correct."

"I simply sought a means of makin' an impression."

"Before we'd even met?"

"Yo' brother described you exceedingly well. I chose to trust that I would be well served to make a bold impression with you, from the first."

Cecelia felt her cheeks burn beneath his admiring gaze. "This *is* rather forward, Mr. Shelman."

He took a swallow of tea and then calmly replaced the cup into its saucer. "Alas, you can plainly see, Miss Stovall, I am not an overly young man given any longer to the wild fantasies of youth. I know what I want, and how to get it."

"Such as this invitation?"

"That"—he smiled easily—"and a good deal more."

Cecelia looked away, discomforted by his confidence, which bordered on arrogance. His presence beside her, and the implied expectation, made her miss William all the more. Her heart surged as she thought of him preparing now for his second year as a West Point cadet. Still unable to get leave. Unable to come after her. Told only that she had been dragged to the other side of the world, that she was lost to him forever. A hostage herself, Cecelia had no money of her own—quite intentionally—to alter that.

At the very moment when she would have excused herself from the table and from the expectation in Charles Shelman's hazel eyes, a royal page presented himself very formally between them.

"Her Majesty would receive you and your guests for a private introduction now."

Cecelia felt her heart jolt hard in her chest; then it began to beat so swiftly at the thought that she could scarcely catch her breath. Not only was she here but, by some odd twist of fate—or the workings of a determined Southern man—she was also about to stand before real royalty! She was light-headed and full of panic at the same time. She shot Shelman a stricken glance. Her eyes then moved to her brother. Marcellus's expression, however, only showed pleasure. Shelman was the first to stand.

"We mustn't keep a monarch waitin'!" He smiled, then extended his hand to her.

Across the room, bathed in light from an intricate stained glass, at the head of a very large table, the eighteen-year-old queen was dwarfed by the size and shape of the very grand upholstered chair in which she presided over the gathering, hands curled over the claw-shaped chair arms. In the years to come, Cecelia would remember little of the moments leading up to the encounter that followed. But the actual meeting, the words exchanged, the very dignified and gracious young woman who would rule England for sixty-four magnificent years, stayed with her forever.

Seeing Charles approach brought a sedate smile, followed by a nod of acknowledgment from Queen Victoria. "Mr. Shelman. How pleasing to see you again."

"Your Majesty." He bowed deeply.

She was pretty, Cecelia thought, shining dark hair parted in the middle and pulled tightly from a round, kind face. Feeling a new burst of panic rise within her, Cecelia curtsied beside him and felt her knee creak as she clumsily rose again.

"You are enjoying tea here at the palace?"

"It is certain to remain one of the highlights of my life."

"I see that famous Southern charm is alive and well." The young queen was smiling as she looked at Charles. "And is this the young woman about whom you were telling me?"

"Miss Cecelia Stovall, yes, ma'am."

Cecelia felt herself pale, her heart still fluttering against her chest. It was all so unbelievable. The queen of England knew of her?

"Come forward," Queen Victoria commanded in her soft, cultured voice.

Cecelia wondered suddenly then how William's friend Ord might wish to be in her place. The irony of that was not lost on her. Supposed secret child of a king in one country, Cecelia standing here meeting his unacknowledged cousin, a million miles, and a world away, in another.

"Is it true, Miss Stovall, what they say about Southerners? That you will hold on to the unspeakable practice of slavery with all that you possess?"

Cecelia was startled into silence by the question. It was the last thing in the world she had expected to be asked, and she had no idea how to defend herself without offending a queen. The image of all those headless victims at the Tower of London darted across her mind, and her heart raced ever more wildly.

When she finally tried to speak, her mouth had gone so dry that the words came out in a cracking squeak. "It is a part of our way of life which I have personally begun to question, Yo' Majesty."

"Would that there were more in the South like you, Miss Stovall. Perhaps there could be real change before something truly dreadful occurs. I am advised that the practice of keeping slaves may one day lead to all-out war in your country."

Cecelia shot Marcellus, beside her, a helpless glance. The young queen looked at Cecelia with utter fascination, as if she were an oddity.

"I hope that will not need to be the case."

"Yes, well, one fights for one's beliefs." She took an absent swallow of her tea before she set the cup back in its saucer to be filled again by a waiting page. "In case of war over slavery, tell me, Miss Stovall, upon which side are you likely to find yourself?"

Cecelia felt tightly trapped by this inquisition that had seemingly begun as idle tea chatter, and she longed now for the protective anonymity of the crowd around her. It occurred to her then that the queen of England was attempting to educate herself on American policy by examining a specimen of the country rather than hearing only what advisors thought perhaps she would wish to hear.

"I am a Southern woman, Yo' Majesty," she replied, struggling hard to find a firm voice. "I would have no choice but to stand beside my family. But my best friend in the world is a Negro slave in our house, and the very moment I am able, I fully intend to buy her freedom, and her father's, as well."

The queen shook her head. Even so, Cecelia could feel the assuring warmth of Charles Shelman's smile upon her. She had not done so badly, she realized then, considering the firing line into which she had just been unwittingly led. The liveried guard beside the queen moved toward them, signaling the end of the discussion.

"If your country's problems do continue, Miss Stovall," Queen Victoria said as an apparent afterthought. "I hope, for your sake, that your heart and your allegiances are reconciled."

Cecelia left Buckingham Palace, got into the waiting carriage with Marcellus and Charles, and was halfway down the Mall before she could utter a single word.

"Fo' the rest of my life," she acknowledged, "I shall never quite believe that actually happened." She was speaking indirectly to Charles, who sat across from her and Marcellus, hands in gray silk gloves, and resting properly atop a very English burled wood walking stick.

"Her Majesty is an engagin' enough sort, don't you think?" he asked casually as they crossed Piccadilly in their swaying carriage. Although they had met only that afternoon, Charles spoke as if he had known the two of them all his life.

"Outstandin'." Marcellus smiled. "Do tell us how you actually managed an extraordinary invitation like *that*."

He glanced out the carriage window again nonchalantly as they moved into ever more heavy traffic in the steady clop and sway that moved them along.

"The man rumored to be her most likely candidate for husband, Albert of Saxe-Coburg-Gotha, is not particularly outgon'."

"You've met him, *too*?" Marcellus chuckled with incredulous admiration.

"A bit of a dreadful stutterer, actually. But he is fascinated, so they say, by America, and by Americans. Ingenuity, pluck, all that sort of thing. We met briefly at the races last month, through an earl, out in Dover. Knowin' England's dependence upon cotton, and my ties to the sale of large quantities of it, he invited me to her private box the next day. The queen is actually quite openly smitten with him, and I think Her Majesty hopes surroundin' him with people who are confident, some of it will rub off on him. Of course"—his eyes twinkled mischievously—"I was only too happy to oblige. I've been in their presence on two other occasions. But she was never quite so hospitable as she was today." His gaze descended on Cecelia as the carriage ground to a halt in heavy afternoon traffic, near Green Park.

"You'll pardon me if this all seems a bit too convenient to be believed."

Charles shot Marcellus a quick glance. "Very well. I confess, yo' brother here has shared his concern over some *confusion*, shall we call it, concernin' a passin' acquaintance you'd made at West Point."

"Passin' acquaintance?" The words sputtered across her lips, and she was dumbfounded. "Euphemisms, Mr. Shelman? I despise that sort of prevarication and distortions of the truth! The *truth*, suh, is that William Tecumseh Sherman is the love of my life, and a further truth is that the queen of England just asked me to defend the entire practice of slavery in front of two hundred well-heeled English guests!"

"You make too much of it, Cecelia—may I call you Cecelia?" Before she replied, he continued undaunted by the strained expression that had taken over her delicate features. "They are interested, here in England, in the sort of lives we lead so far from their shores. I had hoped meetin' Her Majesty would impress you—as I was quite certain, from yo' brother's description, that *you* would impress *me*."

"And I'm certain that it did, Charles." Marcellus intervened, having heard the contentiousness rising in Cecelia's voice. "My sister sometimes forgets herself." He glared across the seat as the carriage turned onto Grosvenor Place, freeing itself from the tangle of traffic and moving onto cobbled stones of the smaller lane. "It was a most gracious surprise to have brought both of us with you. We shall forever be the talk of Augusta, thanks to you."

"Miss Stovall? . . . *Cecelia?*"

She looked at him, the sensation of longing for home now ardent within her.

"Did it impress you?" he pushed. "Bein' presented to the queen?"

"How could it not?" she replied in a tone that was cool with formality. "It *has* been a most interestin' day."

"May I assume by that you do not mean altogether displeasin'?"

"You may assume it."

"Then, with yo' brother's kind permission, may I call upon you again? Perhaps fo' supper on an evenin' next week?"

It was all crystal clear to her suddenly. The eldest son, keeper of the Stovall legacy, had failed at West Point. Producing Shelman, like the golden goose—a wealthy cotton merchant—was a way to save face and save their father's business from ruin. She was to be the sacrifice to preserve Marcellus and their father. She was being played for a fool. Her dear brother and Charles Shelman had orchestrated every bit of this in order to woo her and move her heart from William Sherman to a more suitable and Southern alternative.

No matter what, she would not let that happen to herself.

"My sister would be free next Saturday evenin', Charles," Marcellus affably interceded. "I've a business call to make out in Kent, on behalf of my father, and I'd be grateful for yo' attentions that evenin' on my sister."

There was no point in objecting. Marcellus meant for this dinner to take place. For now, this *was* home. Until Cecelia somehow demonstrated that she had returned to her senses, they would not be leaving England. And so it was settled. With hardly a word spoken by her, Cecelia would be forced to indulge this arrogant Southerner. Either that, she quickly reasoned, or face more endless days than she could imagine here in England with a spiteful brother whose sole job, it appeared, was to see her forget about William. The sooner she indulged them both, the sooner she would be allowed to return to Augusta. One supper with Charles Shelman, she decided, no matter how unattractive he seemed, would certainly be worth that.

Over the days that followed their dinner, Charles Shelman seemed to turn up, like a bad penny, wherever Cecelia and Marcellus happened to be. In the lobby of the King's Opera House, he was standing alone in an impressive black cutaway evening suit and white tie. And he just happened to be sitting in the same row as the Stovalls for the performance. Afterwards, also conveniently, Cecelia thought, he insisted they join him for a quiet supper at his hotel. Then, two days after that, at the races in Brighton, he was sitting in an open carriage, waving them over with a grand smile.

None of the blatant coincidences were lost on Cecelia, who saw, very clearly, all the things that Charles Shelman could afford for her, and which William could not. His family business in cotton merchandising was the largest anywhere around Savannah—larger than Father's company in Augusta. An infusion of cash for Father's vulnerable business was a clear motivation for the Stovall family—and it was to be achieved at her expense. Such calculation steeled her resistance against him all the more.

Charles would never achieve his desire. He would never win her as a wife, no matter what he tried next.

Chapter Six

Two months in London slowly became three. The days, now that it was October, were long and tedious, and as much as she wanted to return home to Georgia, Cecelia found herself looking forward to moving on to Paris, and especially away from the constant presence of Charles Shelman.

There was nothing greatly wrong with him, she had decided. She had begun to see him more as a smart and very clever self-made man than her first wary impression had allowed. But his open interest in her kept her defenses up. She loved William, and she always would.

They gathered in the courtyard of their hotel to tell Charles good-bye on a late October day that was crisp and clear. The dark green ivy that had grown up and along the brick walls enclosing the courtyard cooled the air to a crispness as much as the single low-hanging elm tree that was a centerpiece to the space. Marcellus stood beside Cecelia, she in a rich green traveling dress with puffed, flounced sleeves, he in a dust-brown overcoat, trousers, and a slouched hat with two guinea-hen feathers tucked into the band.

Charles's face was calm, his expression stoic as he stood very formally, embraced Marcellus, and then drew up Cecelia's gloved hand. He permitted himself only a slight smile. "I wish I were gon' on to Paris with you instead of back to Georgia."

"Rest assured, Mr. Shelman, I would happily trade places with you."

"Ah, but Paris would lose all allure fo' me if *you* were not there."

She did not blush at that, or make any response to his flattery. Cecelia had grown accustomed to his forward manner these past long weeks, and now had less of an urge to run from them than she had at first.

"Have a safe journey," she said with intentional formality.

"You do the same." He nodded. "And rest assured, we *will* meet again."

He paused for a moment, allowing the declaration to settle upon Cecelia before he reached out to shake Marcellus's hand. "Take good care of her," he said, as if he had some sort of claim on her already. "I shall call on you both in Augusta as soon as my schedule permits."

Marcellus glared at her. "We will await you anxiously, won't we, sister?"

"Indeed," she replied, mindful once again that the fastest route home was through compliance. They walked him through the darkly paneled hotel lobby and out to a bustling Grosvenor Square, where a horse coach stood, ready and packed with his things. Charles climbed inside and leaned out the open window.

"You haven't told her yet, have you?" he asked Marcellus as the coachman climbed up onto his seat and drew up the reins.

"No, but I will."

"See that you do it soon. I fear yo' sister shall need Paris to grow accustomed to the idea."

As the coach lumbered off with Charles waving, Cecelia turned to her brother. "I'm almost afraid to ask."

"There's nothin' to fear," he said with a smug smile. "Charles is on his way to ask Father for yo' hand in marriage. Thanks to the letter of support I've sent along with him, I'm quite certain there'll be no objection."

He turned then and looked at her appraisingly, waiting, she knew, for the slightest protestation of her love for William. One word like that and she might never see Augusta again. It made her see clearly how she had been changed here. In her mind, Cecelia saw an image of herself, her face swollen from crying, her heart broken. How many nights since she had come away from West Point had she passed that way? Wanting to run. Having no money with which to do so.

She looked now with clear-eyed resolve at her brother. She drew in a deep breath, feeling the pressing weight of disappointment once again. Marcellus had always been her favorite. She his. Now her brother was her captor. Her enemy. She may not have attended West Point herself, or had the education of a man, but Cecelia Stovall was learning very quickly just how to play the game of one who had—and she did not intend to lose.

After one beat, then two, she turned from him and went back up the brick steps to the hotel. "It'll be interestin' indeed," she said wistfully, "to see how it all turns out in the end."

Part 2

❧

So I awoke, and behold it was a dream.

—JOHN BUNYAN

Chapter Seven

AUTUMN 1837

"Kill him, Sherman! Kill him *now*!"

William lunged forward, dagger drawn, as was the order, while other teams of cadets hollered, jostled, and sparred around him on the open field. But, unlike the others, Edward Ord, his partner in this exercise, froze entirely. Even as William hunched down and flashed the dagger, Ord did not move. Although they had trained in the same group on many occasions, this was the first time they had been teamed up in any way.

"Come on, man!" William urged through gritted teeth. "They're watching!"

But Ord was stymied, unable to get the rhythm of his own defense with the battlefield sensations around him. William knew only too well that weakness would earn Ord a dreadful turn at all-night guard duty, with incredibly harsh assaults from drill instructors and upperclassmen, which was something to be avoided at any cost.

"Clip him, *sir*! Do it with the butt of your weapon if he won't fight you! Go in for the kill! Kill him *now*!" the drill instructor goaded William in a screeching howl very near his ear.

Complying, William leaned forward in a showy lunge. "Give him a show, Ord!" William urged in a low voice. "Fight me!"

At last, Ord made an attempt with a mild lunge forward, but it was enough of a movement for William to play upon, and he responded by arching back, arms up submissively. Enough of a movement, perhaps, but not for the instructor, who bolted off his platform toward them in a swift, combative burst. The drill instructor was in his final year at West Point, a young man with a hard body and a face full of sharp angles. He was suddenly down on the field between them, shouting at Ord, his expression close and confrontational.

"This is *not* a Southern garden party, *sir*! You will either kill your opponent or be killed by him!" he shouted. "Is—that—clear?"

"Yes, sir!"

"Louder, Ord! So I believe it!"

"Yes, *sir*!"

"Useless lily!" he murmured, shaking his head as he walked away.

Seizing the moment, William once again lunged at him, dagger poised, and as Ord moved, William slipped a booted foot around his ankle and flipped him onto his back. Ord turned over, shock lighting his blue eyes.

"Come on!" William went on goading. "Let's give 'em what they want!"

"I'm not like you! I can't!"

"You can! You've *got* to!"

Finally, William could see just a spark of fire ignited in Ord's eyes in the instant before he lunged and thrust an unexpected fist at William's jaw.

"Hey!" William shouted, feeling a trickle of blood ooze down his chin, far more surprised at Ord's sudden show of strength than at his own unexpected injury.

"Not half bad for a lily boy, hmm?" Ord smirked just before William clipped his shoulder with the butt of his rifle.

Later, in their barracks room, Edward Ord sat smiling as he balanced a book open on his lap. "Whatever you thought you owed me before today—" He sheepishly smiled. "—you have paid back. You saved my hide out there."

"I guess from now on, it's one for all and all for one," Van Vliet surmised.

William rolled his eyes and gave a crooked smile. "Original, Van."

Ord ran a hand through his hair. "I guess I haven't gotten the mentality of a warrior yet. It just wasn't like that for me in Maryland. I always fancied myself a gentleman, not a soldier."

"The drill instructor sure the devil knows *that*!" Van Vliet ruefully observed.

William looked at him squarely. "Why are you here if the military isn't the life you want?"

"My father's idea, of course. He wanted to impress his friends with how far he could take his son."

"A lot of us have stories like that," said Van Vliet.

"One thing's for sure. No matter what we came from, at West Point we're all in it together just helping one another survive," William observed as he lay down on his mattress, then crossed his legs and his arms underneath his head. "If we all *do* make it through these next three years in this place, Northerner or Southerner, it won't matter a lick. We'll be bonded as friends for life."

William stood in uniform beside Edward on the parade field. Beneath a warm wreath of sunlight, they and the other cadets surveyed the raw group of new plebes, trunks and suitcases in hand, from which each second-year cadet was now entitled, like the other senior cadets, to select one to do personal tasks and errands until the school day began. More serious hazing was rare.

William did not much care for the practice of having a glorified personal servant, one who was so designated against the man's will. To his mind, it felt far too much like slavery. He had not enjoyed being an aide to an upperclassman the year before. But it was part of the West Point tradition. The order of things—plebes serving the upperclassmen. Besides, he silently reasoned, any plebe he chose now was far better off under his tutelage than beneath several recent graduates, such as Pierre Beauregard, and the Southern malcontent, John Pemberton, whose familiarity with slave holding made their freewheeling and relentless orders almost intolerable to fulfill.

William and Edward studied the group of tentative young men still in their civilian clothes glancing around, wide-eyed, as they were assessed by the upperclassmen. He had not realized until that moment how far he had already come, and how the challenges of this place had changed him.

"That one resembles you," Ord observed of a young man with cropped chestnut-colored hair, intense blue eyes, and a square jaw. He stood alone, beside a leather-covered traveling trunk, dressed in a plain brown suit. They moved toward him. He was taller than William, but there was a similar facial shape and similar Midwestern demeanor that knitted them visually.

"What is your name, sir?" Edward Ord asked, hands linked behind the back of his crisp uniform as he and William stood facing the new, uncertain, cadet.

"Grant, sir," the boy replied in an affable tone. "Hiram Ulysses Grant. But my friends call me Sam."

Grant had a lot to learn, they both thought, remembering their own first year. "I am your superior, sir. For the time being, we shall *choose* to call you Grant," said Ord.

"Yes, *sir*." Grant was formal again, his stance firm, eyes directed straight ahead, as if he knew the routine already. He was not given to shock for being laid low by an upperclassman.

"Good." A quick study. He would do well here, William thought. Ord's smile grew. "At ease, plebe."

Ord and William chuckled as Grant went to join the other new cadets, wandering uncertainly toward barracks assignments, just as they once had done. "If you don't want him," William said casually. "I believe I'll take him on."

"Be my guest. After all, Tecumseh—Ulysses. Now, there's something peculiarly grand in the sound of *that* particular combination that may well play itself out for me to see."

.

It was four o'clock when mail call sounded with the familiar taps played on a single bugle, held by a statue-like uniformed cadet. It was something oddly childlike in William that kept him hoping, even after all this time, that he might yet receive a letter from Cecelia in spite of the abrupt way she had been spirited out of New York by her brothers.

As he walked with Ord and Van Vliet from the rifle range, William's heart quickened, only to slow, as it always did, with a crashing thud, when his name was not called. She loved him. He had believed that. He had believed *her*. It was Marcellus who was keeping them apart. But he wondered now about the power he possessed over her, an absolute ability to keep her even from finding the means to post a letter. Was that possible? Knowing Marcellus's warlike determination when he chose to execute it, of course it was. He shook his head as cadet after cadet was called to retrieve his letters and packages from home.

"She still hasn't managed to get a letter through?" Ord gently asked.

"Damn him to hell!" William softly raged, both of them knowing he meant Marcellus Stovall.

"Do you suppose they've returned from England by now?"

"Only if the bastard has managed to sufficiently turn Cecelia against me."

"Next summer, when we get our leave, you can go to Augusta."

"Damn it, Edward, do you honestly believe for a moment that the Stovalls will let her wait for me? I'll be lucky if they haven't managed to marry her off to the first rich British lord they find!"

Edward Ord looked back to the man calling mail, hoping more for William than he did for himself. William Sherman had quickly become his best friend in this place—and his friend was suffering.

"If Cecelia isn't writing to you," he cautiously suggested, "it's only because she can't. Stovall has obviously found a way to keep her from posting anything. You've got to know that."

"Sherman . . . William T."

The sound of his name, called aloud by the mail clerk, almost did not register with him after so many weeks of hearing nothing. Then very suddenly, William's heart jolted hard.

"That's you!" Ord smiled widely. "Get up there, man!"

There were two letters for him today, but the one envelope he took and slipped to the top was worn and soiled, as though it had suffered greatly in its transport. The queen's post marking from England told why. For an instant, William forgot to breathe. He ran his fingers across the slim, sloping writing, certain Cecelia herself had addressed it. But as much as he wanted to tear it open and read it here and now, beneath the dry blazing afternoon sun, with cadets swarming around him, he could not. He must savor it, no matter what it said. And he must be alone.

Because it was late Friday, the cadets now had a bit of personal time as the new crop of plebes settled in, preparing for classes Monday. William took the letter and went to the only place that felt right reading it. He took the long walk down the path along the river to the shady spot where he had taken Cecelia. Where he had sketched her and talked with her, the place where they had kissed and spoken words of love. Words to which he held tightly as he broke the seal and opened the envelope. Only to find that it was empty.

Marcellus!

William squeezed his eyes for a moment, feeling it impossible to catch his breath. Then, in a fit of helpless anger, he tore the envelope to bits and cast it to the wind. He had thought himself prepared for a great fall, and yet there was no way to make himself ready for this! What had she meant to tell him? What had she said that he would never hear? He could just imagine that smug

face smiling down at his sister, mailing the envelope in order to satisfy her. All
the while, Marcellus had already removed the contents.

William looked out across the cool green surface of the lake, calm now as
glass, and silvery in the reflection of the setting sun. Then he glanced down at
the sketch he had done of her, his most dear possession. In it she was smiling,
happy. He had drawn her that way because he had wanted to think of her that
way always. Her onyx hair, the deep coal black eyes, and skin no watercolor
shade could ever recreate. His heart lurched as he thought of how Cecelia had
been obviously duped into believing, when her brother had mailed her letter,
that he had actually left the contents inside!

He closed his eyes again, feeling that he had been hit very hard in the solar
plexus and could not catch his breath. Marcellus Stovall was still in control of
her letters and her life. She would be kept from William. Until he gave up.
Until he forgot her.

"By God, *that* will never happen!" he murmured as a soft breeze moved up
from the river and through his hair, pushing it back from his forehead. "I will
never do it!"

How many times he had thought about risking everything to go after her.
If he had even a penny to try it. If he did not owe the Ewings everything for
this appointment. And what would they live on if they made a stand, if
Cecelia went against her family and they eloped? Cecelia Stovall was accustomed to the finest things, and he was a young man with nothing. Only the
promise of a future. A low-paying military commission, *if* he survived and
succeeded here.

William lost either way he played it. But one thing was clear. If he gave up
West Point to go after her, he would not even have a military future to offer her.
William touched the image of her face that his hand had created from a fleeting moment in time. How would he ever see her again? What had Cecelia
needed to promise for Marcellus to have mailed her letter? Considering it all,
gloom descended upon him, dark and thick as dusk came steadily to settle
around him, and a bullfrog loudly croaked in the marshy reeds along the
river's edge.

They *would* see one another again. Somehow, no matter what became of
each of them, that much he promised himself unfailingly. How odd it was that
these two particular letters should have arrived, and together, after weeks of
receiving nothing at all. Two young women: one he loved desperately, and one
who held the importance of a sister to him. He opened the second letter now,

the one from Ellen, more casually, taking no particular care with the envelope as he, at first, had done with Cecelia's. Ellen, he thought. A senator's daughter. His childhood playmate. Like part of his own family.

Ohio
September 12, 1837

Dearest Cump,

It has been a beautiful summer here at home. Warm and breezy, without the mosquitoes we usually get this time of year, and that, Mama says, is a blessing. We've all missed hearing from you as often as we did when you first arrived at West Point. Hearing the stories about your roommates, all the things they have you doing. Mama says to tell you she hopes you aren't ill.

I remember that time, a couple of years ago, when you had the influenza, and Mama was so worried she called the priest to see to Last Rites for you. Phil had to be nice to you for months. None of his silly games. I never saw him look so bereft. Until that Tuesday when you left us for West Point, of course. You know he's not much for letter writing. (Some days he isn't much for speaking full sentences!) But still, you are his best friend in the world, and he misses you. We all do. Me especially, I suppose. You were always my champion against the brothers, Cump, and now I'm pretty well on my own with their teasing and their low humor. Are you planning to come home when you get your first leave next summer? Phil sure would like it, I know. Mama would, too. She says a special prayer for you with grace every evening at supper, as I suspect she will until you return home.

Come home next summer if you can, Cump. And write again soon. We miss you.

With the greatest fondness,

Ellen

"Well?" Edward asked expectantly as William came back into the small barracks they shared. He and Van Vliet were each on their own cots, reading. William sank onto his cot and combed his hands back through his hair, letting out a great sigh. He had read Ellen's letter in a cursory way. His mind and heart were still too taken up by Cecelia—the arrival of her letter and the longing it brought.

"She was as duped by Marcellus Stovall as I have been."

"Was there an address? Did she write it on hotel stationery perhaps?"

"Do you imagine a man like Stovall would have been that foolish?" he fumed.

Edward scratched the back of his neck; then he shook his head in pity for his friend. William truly loved that Southern girl whom he had seen only at a distance. Personally, he could not quite fathom the attachment, or the speed with which it had formed. But why did anyone love another person? What was that powerful bond that could rise up so swiftly between them? It made him consider the strange story of his own heritage. The man, a king of England, who was supposedly his secret grandfather. George IV fell madly in love with a woman who was entirely ill-suited for a match with English royalty. A widow, a Catholic, with everyone, every law, against them. Whether or not he actually believed his own connection to their story, it was still a tragic, sweeping, and romantic tale.

Edward glanced again at William, suffering in silence and teetered on the verge of his own sad, destructive love. Ord hoped his friend would have the strength to move on. He was young. Life was long. And Cecelia Stovall seemed well beyond his reach.

"Is there anything I can do?" Edward asked, still not disturbing the silent study of their roommates.

"They want me to give her up," he managed to rasp, head still in his hands. "Arrogant bastards . . . And they actually believe, because of their money, that I will."

But they didn't know him, Edward Ord was thinking. No one really did. Nor did they fathom the obstacles he had already faced—everything that had led him to this place. But Ord did not say it. William was a good friend to him here, and he had shown Ord great kindness. But like many others, he had seen his roommate angry, and his icy stare, most of all, was unforgettable. The last thing in the world Edward wanted was to be on the wrong side of William Tecumseh Sherman.

Chapter Eight

✎

Ellen Ewing put down the newspaper, her green eyes wide with surprise. Outside, a cool September wind tossed more amber leaves to the ground. Mama was right. Papa's good friend William Henry Harrison was considering running again for president of the United States! And, after all he had done for the campaign last year in 1836, if Harrison defeated that evil President Van Buren in three years, Papa would surely be named to some high post in Washington as payment! Mama was preparing for her husband's departure for Washington this very morning, to help with a new early campaign strategy. As Papa drank his coffee, Mama was upstairs taking stock of which of the senator's proper suits were fashionable enough to bring to the capital, and what she would yet need to buy and have made.

She was scuttling back and forth on the floor above them, in busy little clicks, followed as she went by a covey of her servants. When Mama was in one of her moods, the whole house suffered for it.

Turning away from the commotion her mother had brought with the morning's announcement, Ellen glanced out the large-pane window, draped in swags of yellow silk, and sighed. She was a pretty girl in a soft, pale, and delicate sort of way, every bit her mother's daughter. Like Maria Ewing, Ellen had small green eyes that bore a splash of blue above a slim nose and a perfect milk-white complexion.

Ellen's full face still sparkled with the glow of extreme youth, lost long ago to Maria, who had borne her children in rapid succession. Still, the comparison between the two was rarely lost on people, and her sweetness, combined with the pale beauty, had brought a number of neighbor boys more steadily to the fore. But Ellen had always wanted only one suitor: the copper-haired boy who had long been her champion. The one boy she had loved for as long as she could remember.

Cump was such a silly nickname, she thought now, but it was what everyone here had always called him. A family name. A name that tied her more closely to him than any other girl would likely be. Cump would have been here with her, she knew, cheering up Mama in spite of her mood. Her brothers, even the older ones, were all less brave than she. Immediately after breakfast, they had all gone outside and collected around the craggy, gnarled oak tree like they were waiting out a storm. And in a way, they were.

Mama truly could be insufferable with her obsessions. But she was greatly loving, too. After all, hadn't she been first to think of taking Cump in, after his father had so tragically died? Then she had put that same notion into Papa's head, convincing him that Cump, a Ewing family favorite—who had lived with his family just down the street—was as smart as their own son Phil, and would reflect well on the senator's great sense of charity. She had woven that theme into him until he believed it was his own. But victory in her obsessions had served only to strengthen the occurrence of them. She was brilliant that way. Knowing precisely how to get what she desired. The brothers feared her. Ellen, however, knew that their mother was someone from whom to learn.

But so many things were changing. Cump had gone off to West Point. Her own brother, Phil, Cump's best friend, was working as a young lawyer in their father's office. And now Papa would be going off to Washington, leaving the rest of them behind for the better part of the next year, getting Mr. Harrison elected, at last, to the presidency.

Her thoughts were stopped suddenly by her father's late entrance into the breakfast room. A great white-haired bear of a man, Thomas Ewing nonetheless exuded quiet kindness, and Ellen felt herself smile as he stalked purposefully toward her. There was nothing he would not do for his children. His daughter, most especially.

"Morning, Papa." Ellen smiled as he sank into the armchair beside her. In the same fluid moment, Harriet Beasley, their house maid, was at his side with a silver pot of hot coffee which she used to fill his Blue Willow China cup. Then she retreated silently to her place next to the sideboard.

"Morning, kitten." He smiled at her briefly in response, drew a huge swallow of coffee, and then opened his newspaper and disappeared behind it. "Just eggs this morning, Harriet. That's all I've got time for."

Her father did not ask where the others were. Considering the commotion his wife was stirring above the breakfast room, Senator Ewing seemed to revel in the haven that this cozy and brightly wallpapered haven became.

"Mr. Harrison is going to win the presidency next time, isn't he, Papa?"

"We'll do all we can, kitten."

"I'm glad for you. You worked so hard last time to get him elected."

"Be glad for *all* of us if that buffoon Van Buren does not prevail a second time around."

"Mama says you will be going to Washington now to help with the early campaign strategizing."

The paper crunched, and he smiled at her over the top of it. "She has herself in quite a state about it this morning, doesn't she?"

"I wish I could go with you."

He smiled at her. "You know very well that you leave in a week's time for Madame Picot's school in Philadelphia."

She turned her lower lip out in a pout. "You know I don't want to go."

"Nonsense. It's where all the finest young ladies are educated."

"I'd rather go with *you.*"

He screwed up a single snowy eyebrow, then took another swallow of coffee as he studied her. "Let me guess. At least then you would be close enough to take the train to New York to visit Cump, and there would be no headmistress to stop you."

Ellen giggled behind her hand, and her cheeks quickly flushed. "How'd you know that?"

Senator Ewing covered his daughter's small, cold hand with his own large warm one. "You've loved that boy since you were a child, and absence, they say, does make the heart grow fonder."

"Oh, it does, Papa! I miss him so desperately."

"Has he written to you yet?"

"Not since the end of his last term in the spring. You don't suppose he's . . ." She could hardly say it. ". . . that he's met a girl, do you?"

The senator chuckled. "A girl? At West Point? Well, certainly not the sort *you* would ever have to worry yourself over."

"So could I come with you?" she pressed, leaning forward, her green eyes bright and sparkling. "Could I come with you to Washington?"

Thomas Ewing patted his daughter's hand. There was kindness even in his condescension. "Ellen. My darling little Ellen. You are fast becoming a beautiful young woman, but a girl you yet are. You must learn, as the Bible tells us, that to everything in life there is a time and a season. It's not your time with Cump yet."

"But will it ever be?"

He dotted his lips with a white linen napkin, then swiped it across the bushy white mustache above it. "If Cump Sherman is still who you want when he finishes at West Point, then, dear girl, it is Cump you shall have."

"But Papa, that's three years away!"

"And three more years for you to turn into the stunning swan you are sure to become."

"I can't possibly wait that long!"

"My darling girl, Cump is not ready for you yet either. He certainly is not prepared to provide for you in the way I shall insist upon."

"He always said he wanted an army commission when he's through." She sank back into her chair. "That cannot possibly pay well."

"I'm not certain Cump yet knows *what* he wants. Like you, he is young and inexperienced in the ways of the world."

"Will *you* be able to change that?"

He smiled. "I've done everything else in the world for him, haven't I? Who else could have given him the golden opportunity he now has? How will he ever be able to refuse his benefactor when the time comes?"

She smiled back, filled with new confidence. "Or the benefactor's daughter?"

"Precisely. When the time is right, that's it, my darling, precisely."

Chapter Nine

❧

The approach of Christmas had softened Pleasant Stovall's heart and reduced his fury enough so that on the tenth of December, safe in the assumed knowledge that the threat to his daughter had passed, he sent word to Venice, and bade them to return.

Cecelia was overjoyed to leave the damp cold of the Italian water city that had been as much of a prison as Paris. She wanted desperately to return to Augusta and her family. She had missed them so much. Her half brother Georgie, especially, who she was certain would never forgive her for going away in the first place. It had been only six months, and yet Cecelia felt ages older, changed by the experiences in Europe, but most especially by what had happened at West Point.

In spite of her insistence to Marcellus that she could never care for the man, Charles Shelman wrote to her frequently. They were fat, newsy letters in his bold, black script, telling her endlessly about his return to Georgia, his increasing wealth, and his own ever-deepening desire to marry and begin a family. Thank the Lord, she thought, that he lived at too great a distance to call on her with any regularity.

If William wrote to her, she was never allowed to see his letters, a fact that still broke her heart. Worse still was the knowing that her life was not her own, that her family meant to steer her in a direction of their choosing. But they had miscalculated greatly if they believed she would submit to their plan. That much she had worked out even before the coach made the long drive up Greene Street, toward home.

Seeing the house as they turned onto the private brick drive that approached it from behind, seeing the driveway lined with low-lying magnolia trees, Cecelia's heart quickened. Soft gray moss dripped from the branches, brick terraces, and boxwood-bordered paths that lined the yard. There really were so many things she had missed about this place—so many memories.

And, even so, there were many things she had outgrown.

How she would reconcile it all remained unknown.

Marcellus helped her down the coach steps as a gaggle of Stovall offspring, other family, and servants flooded out into the cool, cloudless, and gray December afternoon.

"They're here!" her father's wife shouted, rustling toward them, wrapped in an ermine-and-velvet cape.

As Cecelia moved up the steps, she caught sight of little Georgie, still on the porch clinging to the painted white railing, looking warily out at her through big, black Stovall eyes. Yes, this child of her heart was still angry at his big sister's going away. It would take a bit of doing to mend things between them. But at least she was home now.

Behind Georgie, Cretia, Setty Mae, and Josiah stood bearing great welcoming smiles. Cecelia's heart squeezed a little seeing Cretia now, between the two older slaves—knowing what she had endured because of that father Cecelia once had so loved.

Once, she had believed in the fairy tale of a family's absolute loyalty. Once she had believed in the fairy tale of dignity for *all* women. And, once, she had believed, with her whole heart, in a happily ever after. But, like precious glass, the Stovalls themselves had shattered that all.

As Cretia and Josiah moved away, Cecelia saw her father and Anne. They came toward her, Anne's warm smile was full of kindness. Then, glancing up at Cretia from father's deep embrace, Cecelia felt a jolt of revulsion mix with everything else. How could he do *that* to Cretia, who would have been so helpless against him? To good-natured Anne, who had given him children? Cecelia stiffened, then pulled away.

"Oh, but it's good to have you back home!" Pleasant declared with a wide, easy smile, appraising her at arm's length.

You have aged, she thought. *It's fitting that those manipulations of yours should have changed you, as they have forever changed me.*

"Thank you, Father."

"You must be tired after so long a journey," Anne said kindly in what was a wisp of a voice. "Would you like to rest in yo' room till supper?"

"That'd be lovely."

"I've had Cretia turn the bedcover down, just in case, and start a fresh fire in yo' hearth. She's burned a bit of rosemary, too, to make everythin' fresh and sweet."

Cretia's gaze was proper yet strangely vacant. Had it always been so? she wondered. Had the damage complicity wreaked always been obvious to those mature enough to see it?

"Cretia, go along with Miss Cecelia now, and get her settled in."

"Yes, ma'am," Cretia nodded, turning blandly from the family scene and heading back up the stairs.

As Cecelia climbed the steps, with their familiar pressing squeak, she saw that Georgie had waited, silent and wary, uncertain of how angry he intended to remain. Coming upon him, she stopped and knelt.

"Do I not get at least a hug to welcome me home?"

He tipped his head, considering the question.

"I wrote to you, you know," she reminded him gently. "Did you have yo' mama read you my letters?"

He pouted. "I didn't want to hear them."

Her hands were on her hips. "And why not?"

"They made me too sad, havin' to think 'bout you."

Her eyes filled with tears she had not expected. He was so small and filled with innocence. Cecelia took his small body into her open arms and held him tightly.

"I'm sorry I had to go away," she softly keened. "But I'm home now."

"And will you stay this time?"

An image of William came into her mind and the thought she had so many times, that if he would only come to her, she would run away with him anywhere. But that was a girlish notion. He could not leave West Point. He had his duty to the Ewings. His first commitment was to them. And she admired his sense of honor. So, in spite of how the Stovalls fully intended to organize and steer her life—toward Charles Shelman, particularly—she would wait three more years until William graduated the academy. Then, as now, she would be fully prepared to go with him anywhere. Become a military wife. Because she loved him, and because she could not bear to spend the rest of her life without that. If they thought they could force her into a marriage to someone else before that, they didn't know the woman inside Cecelia Stovall at all.

They were both quiet as Cretia helped her with the stays in her gown, and then with her pantalets, in a bedroom that crackled and brimmed with the mingled fragrance of firewood and rosemary. Hers was a large, south-facing room near the staircase, with a view of the gardens, boxwood hedges, and trees from the long casement windows. The furniture was French, all hand-painted, with delicate garden scenes. And over her bed, framing it, was a sweeping length of fabric. There were large botanical prints on the walls, and the huge rose and celery-colored winter carpets were Aubusson, probably just newly laid back down.

Opulence for the few who lived in this elegant house at the expense of the many slaves kept to maintain it.

In summer every year, the slaves owned by Pleasant Stovall would be subjected to the massive task of switching the heavy carpets throughout the whole house, rolling them up, carting them off, and then replacing them with cooler rush mats. Cecelia had seen the backbreaking process take two days, which was carried out in addition to the regular schedule of duties, only to have it repeated in winter with the carpets.

For the first time in her life, looking down at the carpets, Cecelia felt awkward with the girl who had grown up as her friend—a girl who knew what backbreaking work it was to move them. There was such a chasm dividing them, one she had foolishly never pondered before. How on earth could she possibly set that right?

As if sensing each other's thoughts, the two were tentative with one another. Quiet. Awkward. In spite of her superior station in life, and all the advantages it brought, Cecelia felt helpless. She was nearly as powerless now as her family's black slave to change the horrendous status quo. So many thoughts moved through her mind as Cretia helped her don a thin, cotton nightdress in that silence, and she climbed between the thick, downy bedcovers for an afternoon rest. Cecelia wanted desperately for them to talk as they once had done, with familiarity and ease. She also wanted to ask about the unspeakable thing. But there were no words for something like that. There never would be words to ask how something so wretched had begun.

"I've missed you," she said instead.

"Thank you, miss."

"You been doin' yo' readin' and writin' while I've been away?"

"Oh, Miss Cecelia, you know yo' daddy don't take kindly to Negroes doin' such like that."

"To the devil with my daddy!"

"Miss Cecelia!" Cretia's dark hands splayed across her mouth.

"I mean it, Cretia. You've as much right to read a book as I do!"

"No, miss," she said blandly. "You know I don't."

And she did know it. Of course she did.

"But you've always been good to me," Cretia corrected herself. "I can read some, and speak mo' properly because of you."

"We're friends, Cretia. We always have been."

"No, Miss Cecelia. You're the master's daughter. And I am—"

"*And you* are a jewel—to me most especially."

She slipped between the bedcovers noticing, for the first time, the drab olive-colored dress Cretia wore as she stood before the dress-form, holding Cecelia's brilliant blue silk gown over her arm. Something deep within her stomach twisted with a wrenching ferocity. *God forgive me never seein'. . . .* Cecelia grieved now for the girlhood Cretia had lost at the hands of her father, as if she had lost it herself. A simple trip to West Point had enlightened her more than she could ever have imagined.

Cecelia drew the covers to her chin. She studied her friend in the shaft of sunlight that came through a part in the heavy, closed draperies for a moment, and then, thinking of her brothers, she said, "I need to confide in you. Because you are the only one in the entire world I can trust now."

Cretia was still holding the brightly colored dress over her own drab sleeve. She brought it to her chest as she moved warily toward the bed. "Miss?"

"Cretia, please. Do quit soundin' so formal with me. We've always been friends. We've always shared things. And that is not gon' change now just because I've been away for a while."

"Oh, Miss Cecelia. Everythin' changes. It is bound to."

"Like what?"

Please let her have the courage to tell me, Cecelia was thinking. *I cannot help you if you don't confide in me. . . . And can I really help her, even so?* She pushed that last errant thought stubbornly from her mind, refusing to be undone by it. She would not, could not, accept that things could not be changed. Not if one wanted something badly enough.

"I'm in love with a boy whom Marcellus and my father despise. It's why they made me go abroad. It's why I will be a virtual prisoner here now until they marry me off to someone more *suitable*."

"I'm so sorry." Her voice, deep and husky, and so totally distant, said that her own suffering made true sympathy difficult to conjure.

"The point is, I need you to post a letter to him for me."

"Oh, miss! I couldn't!"

Cecelia lunged forward, the bedding falling down around her as she grabbed Cretia's folded arms. "You're the only one who can! I trust you with this, and there's nothin' in the world that is more important to me! Marcellus let me send only a curt, short note from London, which he altered before puttin' it back in the envelope. I'm certain it only confused William the more. I must explain, in my *own* words, that I love him, and that I will find a way to save myself and wait until he is free from West Point!"

"Miss, you know there's no way slaves are allowed to post letters like that."

"Perhaps not. But a free Negro can. Yo' father can give it to his friend, Thaddeus, over at the Simpson place, can't he? Please, Cretia." Cecelia leaned toward the bedside table and took the silver watch that had belonged to her mother, then handed it to the young girl. She lowered her voice. Her words were cautiously spoken as she intended to help her the only way that she could. "If you sell this, you and yo' daddy would have enough money to make yo' way up North. I hear there is somethin' called the Underground Railroad. I know you could find yo' way to it. You'd be free, Cretia! Free from everythin' and everyone here in Augusta!"

To Cecelia's surprise, she handed it back. "No, thank you, Miss Cecelia. Runaway slaves are hanged from the nearest tree. You know that."

Cecelia pressed the watch back into Cretia's callused palm. "Then don't sell it. But you keep it, you hear me? If you do this one thing for me, you *deserve* a reward, and there may come a day when you just might be able to use the money this will bring. Take yo' good time, my friend. Ask 'round as to a safe way to sell it, then hide the money well."

There were tears shining in her friend's coal-dark eyes. It was the first time Cecelia could ever remember seeing Cretia moved. "Miss Cecelia, this belonged to yo' mama."

"Yes, it did. But there was nothin' so much in the world she would have wanted as to see me happy. If givin' you this can, one day, bring me the happiness I know I will have as William's wife, it will be well given. *Please*. Cretia, tell me you will *try* to do this one thing for me."

"I can't say my daddy'll go 'long with it. His life—'fo' comin' here, it was bad. He doesn't like takin' risks with the master now."

"Show Josiah the watch. Make him see what havin' this could mean fo' the two of you, as well as fo' me, *if* you ever do decide to try to go away. And unless a lot changes fo' you in this world, you may want that. *Please*, Cretia. You have my total trust with the most important thing in the world to me. Will you do it fo' me? Will you at least try?"

Cretia's eyes were wide, two glittering onyx pearls framed by a face full of too much suffering.

"I hope that helps you to realize how serious I am 'bout trust between us. If there is *ever* anythin' you need to share, any secret that becomes too heavy, a burden on yo' heart—I hope you'll come to me in return."

"I'll remember that, Miss Cecelia," she said.

But Cecelia knew, even so, that her friend's brutalization was as locked away inside Cretia now as it had ever been. And this was not the thing to change that. At least not yet.

The house smelled of cinnamon and wood polish as Christmas came, and everyone was put into a tailspin at the announcement that Marcellus had invited Charles Shelman to stay with them until the new year.

"Don't go gettin' any ideas," Cecelia warned her brother as they sat together in the light-filled, wicker-furnished conservatory. Panes of glass, framed in white, painted wood, warmed them and the jungle of plants that Anne maintained to amuse herself. Georgie was playing stick-ball, and they watched him absently, still a short and stout boy with full rosy cheeks, as he ambled up and down the little lanes of plants. It had been a long time since Cecelia had been able to have a civil conversation with Marcellus, let alone remain in the same room for any length of time.

"The ideas have been there since we met Charles." He smiled. "You may not see it yet, but he *is* the perfect husband fo' you."

"*You* say so," she sniped, touching the part of her collar that concealed William's cross as she spun away from Marcellus.

"Indeed I *do* say so. And as much as I hate to point it out, sister, there is not any grand sort of contingent linin' up as competition."

"That doesn't matter a whit to me, since I know the man I want."

"Well, you can't have William Sherman, if he's who you mean. That's fo' *damn* sure!"

"I wouldn't sound so sure of yo'self, if I were you. I usually get my way with Father, sooner or later." She was smiling, but her anger was raw and building again. Because of Marcellus, especially, she felt desperate and capable of something dangerous.

Trying to outrun the sensation, she left the conservatory, but he followed her.

One after the other, they descended the sweeping marble steps, then stopped at the landing that displayed a bust of the Revolutionary War hero, the Marquis de Lafayette, who had once visited Augusta.

"Well, not this time, Cecelia. Father is dead set against it. We Stovalls are Southern royalty, with the bluest blood of the South runnin' through our veins. Queen Victoria could see that. Why can't you?"

She spun toward him in a whirl of raspberry velvet, edged in ivory lace, her face brightened with anger. "Because *you* have slandered William to Father, is that it? Successfully made him out to be a no-account Yankee, with no understandin' of our lives down here, and nothin' to offer me?"

A dark eyebrow arched as he regarded her. His lips turned up at the corners just slightly. "I couldn't have said it better myself."

Cecelia hit his chest with her fist, but it only made his smile widen. "You know better than anyone that William was sponsored by Senator Thomas Ewing of Ohio. How much of a no-account is that?"

"Cecelia, do be reasonable. William Tecumseh Sherman is the senator's charity case, for Lawd's sake! An experiment. A move to better his own political career. Make him seem more charitable, true man of the people, that sort of thing."

"You know," she said in a tone that was suddenly very low as her voice shook with anger. "I don't believe I ever realized just how truly frightenin' you are. As a child, I mistook yo' arrogance for strength, because I wanted desperately to love you. Now my misjudgment of it only makes me feel ill."

"Misjudgment of people, sister dear, appears to be yo' particular specialty. But we Stovalls are here for you, to see that it doesn't become the definin' factor in yo' life."

"And that I don't embarrass you!"

"Now that you mention it"—he smiled cruelly—"that, as well."

Charles Shelman looked different from how he had in London, Cecelia thought as he stood with a broad smile in the foyer of her family's home, handing his walking stick, cloak, and hat to Josiah. The house was decorated for the season with lacy boughs of holly and ivy; the wood tables and cane-bottom side chairs were all polished to glowing. Charles seemed older with a calmer, more dignified air about him than she remembered. In London, he had seemed eager to her, self-absorbed and unattractive.

He was introduced all around by Marcellus. First to Father and Anne, then to Tom and Bolling, and little Georgie. Afterwards, calculatedly, Marcellus drew Cecelia forward by the upper arm as she stood in a new holiday gown of sea green silk with a fitted bodice, bell skirt, and long lace sleeves, flounced at the cuffs. Her hair was pulled away from her face, the back in ringlets, with a string of ivory pearls laced through it.

"And of course, you remember my sister, Cecelia."

Charles took a step toward her. "How could I ever fo'get such loveliness?" he smoothly remarked, taking her hand and lightly pressing a kiss across her ice-cold fingers, in the European manner.

Cecelia could see that Anne was impressed. And Father's smile was broad and genuine. "Welcome indeed to Augusta, Mister Shelman. We're happy to have any friend of Marcellus's. Stay as long as you like," Pleasant remarked.

"You are all too kind." Charles nodded, still wearing his confident smile.

"Only Southern hospitality." Pleasant draped an arm across his wife's shoulder. "Somethin' those Northern sots know nothin' about."

Cecelia was quite certain that had been for her benefit alone. A none too subtle reference to William in the face of his more palatable competition. She still didn't like Charles any better, she thought as he went with Anne and Marcellus into the drawing room. Coffee and Setty Mae's cinnamon cake were being laid out on white linen by a very proper and silent Josiah, dressed up in his formal dark green livery and white gloves, reserved for only the grandest occasions.

"Are you certain you wouldn't like to freshen up a bit first?" Anne asked, linking her arm through his. "See yo' room?"

"If Miss Cecelia would be the one to show me the way, perhaps I would at that." Because he smiled when he said it, a big toothy, attractive smile, Cecelia thought it entirely disarmed her father, who grinned broadly in response. Everyone knew why Charles Shelman had come to Augusta, and they hadn't the least intention of disappointing him.

"Excellent idea, Cecelia. Do show him the way. Josiah, have one of yo' boys bring up the luggage."

"Yassuh." The old black man nodded in a way that revealed none of the contempt he felt.

"You really are awfully certain of yo'self, Mr. Shelman," Cecelia said as they ascended the stairs and she was certain they were out of range of anyone who might criticize her less than hospitable tone.

"There isn't any other way to be, Cecelia, *if* one means to get one's desires in life."

They reached the landing. Cecelia stopped and glanced at him. He was still smiling. Not an overly tall man, what he lacked in stature, Charles more than made up for in the way he carried himself, the way he stood, and especially in the confidence with which he spoke. He wore expensive clothes, as he had in London, and smiled affably enough to melt anyone's reserve. Anyone's except Cecelia's. For her, there was still something that made her recoil just slightly every time their eyes met.

"And do you always get what you want, Mr. Shelman?"

"Sooner or later, absolutely always."

"My brother told me you still mean fo' that to include me."

"I do."

"Respectfully, suh, the two of us are on divergent paths in this life. I don't plan to be among yo' conquests."

He was still smiling, enormously pleased with himself, it seemed, and with her. "Well, I do love life's most difficult challenges the best."

She turned then toward the hall where the guest room overlooking the back garden lay. "At least don't ever say you weren't warned."

"Ah," he laughed, and followed her. "I was just gon' to say the very same thing to you!"

Chapter Ten

❧

As that first West Point summer had turned to autumn, then autumn passed Christmas, turning to a second frigid and biting New York winter, there was never a day when William did not think of Cecelia Stovall. At parade drills, he wondered if she were still in England. During the endless lectures on battlefield strategy and military command, he wondered if that single envelope would be followed by another.

But as New Year's Eve passed them into 1838, the only letters that came were from Ellen Ewing and her older brother, his childhood friend, Phil. William began finally to allow the forbidden thought to move across his mind and to settle there. There had been only that one attempted letter from Cecelia. Perhaps she had been trying to end things properly, without giving him the slightest shred of hope for a future. Could that be why there had been no others?

Perhaps what Cecelia had felt for him, the things she said, had been sweet—and temporary. A moment in a strange place. A young man in a uniform urging her to forget family, loyalty, place, and obligation. But England—and Marcellus—had helped her to remember. Because somehow, quite simply, he knew she would have found a way to write to him again by now if there were any other explanation.

He did not blame her. Nor did he feel anger at her betrayal of a promise. All he felt was a wrenching disappointment that she did not believe, as he did, in something that had felt to him like happily ever after.

By March of 1838, William refused himself the bittersweet pleasure of looking at the drawing he had made of her. His summer romance was over, and he was a second-year West Point cadet, with a promise to fulfill to the Ewings. He would make a success here. For them, and for himself.

"Pardon me, sir."

The deep, straight tenor brought him from the fire in his barracks brick hearth that blazed and crackled. The small fire took only a bit of the wrenching cold from the otherwise spartan unheated, white-washed pine floor room. William turned around, like the others, still wearing his great coat and gloves until lights out. His plebe chum Sam Grant stood formally behind him, cheeks ruddy from the cold.

"Your science notes back from Donovan, sir."

He had been an admirable aide. Firm, unflinching, and passably similar to William in manner for them to be taken for brothers. Both were Ohio boys; both were determined to make a success of West Point, to change what would have been the ordinary course of their lives. Very early on, they had established an understanding. A cautious friendship had followed.

"Thanks, Grant. That'll be all." He took the notes and then tossed them absently onto his mattress. It was too cold to study or read—too damn cold to do anything but let thoughts and memories torture him.

Edward Ord came to stand beside him at the fire. "You're thinking about Cecelia again."

"I'll get over it," he said blithely, not meaning it.

"It's long after curfew. What do you say we make our way over to Benny Haven's to drown a few of your sorrows in an ale or three, with some of the fellas?"

"And what would be the point? It would just all be here waiting for me in the morning."

Ord slapped his shoulder a couple of times, then was silent, thinking better of saying anything more. As they stood, side by side, neither man speaking, William wondered if it would get easier. But he already knew the answer to that. Now he just needed to find a way to live with it until next summer when he could go to Augusta and hear from her directly that she didn't love him anymore.

❧

Cecelia pulled Cretia down beside her on the edge of the bed, making her stop the busy movements around the bedroom, which were designed to avoid Cecelia's concerned gaze.

"Can you not tell me what troubles you?"

"No mo' than I deserve."

No one deserves that, no matter what my father told you!

Cecelia bit back the angry words floating in a mouth full of venom. It was Sunday, and the rest of the family was at church. Cecelia had told them she felt ill, hoping to have a small bit of peace. And with William Sherman at such a safe distance, they chose to leave her.

"Oh, fo' heaven's sake! I wanted you to tell me on yo' own. I wanted you to feel you could trust me. It's why I confided in *you* about William. Why I trusted you with my letter. But I know about my father and what he's been doin' to you."

"Lawd have mercy." The phrase came as a soft gasp, and Cretia seemed to shrink away, but Cecelia held fast, by taking her hand very tightly.

"I want to help you."

"Nothin' you can do."

"How do you know that?"

"Master Stovall made it clear enough. I'm his property to do with as he pleases."

Cecelia's stomach turned. William's words rang back in her mind. *Owning another person, it just isn't right. No matter what the reason.*

Cretia was a flesh-and-blood girl like herself, with hopes and dreams of her own, and yet she had none of it in her future. No happiness, no peace . . . no life . . . and certainly no freedom.

It was vile. A great evil, and Cecelia's awareness was like the opening of a Pandora's box. From what she now knew, there would be no turning back. But for all her convictions, how in the world could she help Cretia, let alone Josiah, when she had no control at all over her own life? But Cecelia knew she had to find a way to make her father stop before all the life and hope went out of Cretia forever.

"Do you trust me?" Cecelia asked.

"I try."

"Then trust me that I will think of somethin' to help you make it stop."

Cecelia knew how unlikely something magical like that would ever be. But she wasn't giving up hope. Certainly not yet.

It was all so simple, really. A little eavesdropping could mete out such a great reward. If one were patient, open—and if one knew how to use information to its greatest advantage. The floorboards outside Cecelia's door gave, and then creaked only slightly as Marcellus moved cautiously away. And really, it was for her own good. She would do well with Charles Shelman.

For the past several years, as the local economy had softened, Father had needed to become something of a Renaissance man. He had become a partner in Stovall & Hamilton, a retail grocer whose company provided ice in the summer to Augusta residents. This was along with his fluctuating cotton concerns, and all just to keep the family well inside their established lifestyle.

Now, the juggling would finally be at an end.

Charles Shelman was wealthy, settled, Southern—and it did not hurt that, by a union between them, the Stovall cotton business would receive a much needed influx of cash. Shelman had agreed to that already, as an early show of faith, with Cecelia as the final reward.

Since leaving West Point, Marcellus had needed to find some means of recouping his image in his father's eyes. Finding Charles had certainly fit the bill. Father was ecstatic. And he was off the proverbial hook. Marcellus smiled as he descended the carpeted stairs leading to the foyer. An added bonus was that now he would be free enough from Father's disappointment to marry Sarah McKinne, the girl he had loved since they were children, and to build a house for them in the small Georgia town of Rome. It would be nearer Sarah's family and blessedly away from the overreaching power of his own.

It had been a short courtship, but Marcellus knew what he wanted. And he was learning ever more quickly how to get it. At first, their desperate father had wanted someone more grand, and certainly more wealthy, for his eldest son. But time and patience changed a good many things. Pleasant had been just happy enough with the wealthy suitor for Cecelia that he had agreed to Marcellus's marriage, as well—and of course there was his deepening hold on the family business now that he had proven his fidelity by finding a backer. Yes, indeed. Things were looking up.

❖

It was after midnight before Cretia climbed the two flights of stairs to her room in the dark and chilled third-floor attic. There had been dinner dishes to take out to the kitchen house, clean towels and underclothes to bring back in for morning, and the last of the chamber pots to empty before she could think of sleep, or any small bit of peace for herself. The family, however, had retired hours ago.

Feeling old and used up, decades older than she was, Cretia thought about the games she played in her mind when things were at their worst. When the master came to her. She closed her eyes, hoping he would not come up those stairs tonight. She was too tired for games. For him. For the hopelessness his taking her brought.

With hands that felt numb and heavy, she drew her dress off over her head. It was the same one of two dresses she wore every day. One for most days and one for when she might be seen by guests. The fabric of both had come from one of Anne's old winter dresses. The fabric of one of them used to have delicate rose-colored flowers.

A single candle lamp glowed on the plain wooden table beside her bed. It flickered and made shadows dance on the wall. But it did not warm the small, garret room that held no fireplace, and no other means of heat but the drab blanket on her bed.

She could see her breath in small, white plumes as she exhaled and sank exhausted, beneath the blanket, too tired to be cold. The bedsprings squealed and, at that moment, the door clicked open. *Damn him*, she thought. *Please, not tonight . . .* But wishes, she knew, were for white folks. Cretia closed her eyes, not looking at him, for she knew who it was. Who it always would be.

Pleasant Stovall had moved her room, along with Josiah's, from out over the laundry and kitchens with the other slaves, and into the main house, and he had done it for a reason. He hadn't wanted to go to her out there with all the other Negro men around him. So he had made it seem like an increase of status. But there was no privilege in the price she paid.

Pleasant came toward her now, wearing a heavy velvet, forest green robe with a corded tie girding his stout middle. "Good Lawd, but it's cold in here!" he said, rubbing his hands together, careful not to raise his tone so that her father, next door, wouldn't hear them.

Of course Josiah heard, and knew what had long gone on between his daughter and the master. But Stovall had provided well for them, by slave standards. They lived in the main house, not out in the drafty carriage house or above the laundry, and they worked in the house, not in the stables, the wash house, the sweltering kitchens, or on one of the vast cotton fields on the plantations outside of town. Nor did he beat them. And yet a part of her had long wished for it. She knew it would have been better than the sexual demands made of her by the master and, one day likely, by one of his sons.

This was city work, with white folks, she was taught to believe. Here, father and daughter had a modicum of respectability. And so, they owed Stovall the fulfillment of his desires.

"Ain't got no fire fo' warmin', suh. You'd be better downstairs on a night like dis." Her tone was bland, unafraid, full of the weariness she felt from running up and down stairs, fetching and carrying, and serving all the Stovalls since before dawn. And all words came in the uneducated dialect he expected.

"Oh, nonsense, girl. I know just how to warm us both."

She hated his body, all white and fleshy, and hairless. The way he smelled was not like a man at all, but perfumed, like a white woman, from bottled scent. He pulled the blanket back, then slipped in beside her.

Beneath his velvet robe with the braided cord, he was naked. He did not waste time up here. That much was a small blessing. The best she could do was to try to keep from getting a baby by him, and to remember how much worse her life, and Josiah's, might be if she fought him.

After the first time, five years ago, when she was still such a child, Cretia had realized the value in silent acquiescence, no matter how her heart and her innocence bled away. Now, even some bit of the disgust had faded behind the duty. As Cecelia had her hair curled, went to music classes and garden parties, Cretia had emptied the chamber pots, lit the fires, pressed clothes, brought in water, carried dishes, filled the wood boxes—and serviced Master Stovall.

Thanks to Setty Mae's ancient African recipe—part of which she drank down just after he had been with her, the other part, she put inside herself and lay very still until morning—there were no babies. So far. She was to do this religiously, until the day when he would tire of her and find someone else. But that was not going to happen tonight.

As he unfastened the velvet cord at his waist, Cretia saw a sudden image of naïve Cecelia, always believing they were friends. Always believing that there was even the slightest thing in common that could bond them into something real and enduring.

The thoughts vanished as Pleasant turned her roughly onto her belly and mounted her. But the more compliant she was, the sooner it would be over. And tonight, that was all she cared about. Cretia knew what he wanted. What he *always* wanted. At least, thank God, he never kissed her. That, she mused ironically, he saved for his poor wife.

She closed her eyes as he pushed into her to gain his own satisfaction. She knew of course that her daddy heard them as the master groaned. The walls up here were thin and cold. But they never spoke of it. In the light of day, it did not exist. Josiah's earliest memory had been of a life picking cotton fourteen hours a day, every day of the week. He had been whipped, and scarred, and he had seen his love torn from his side. It had been a devastating existence for the man who had been given his name by a God-fearing, Bible-reading former owner, a man who had scarred his flesh, and his heart, forever.

Life with the Stovalls at least was a calm, predictable existence—better, he often said, than a Negro should expect. Josiah would not rock the boat with the Stovalls, no matter what befell his only child. He just no longer had the fight in him.

Pleasant collapsed onto the bed beside her with a satisfied groan, and Cretia pulled up the single drab blanket over her bare body. She must remember the tonic. The moment he left, she must mix it. There would be time. He would not stay long now that he was finished with her. He never did. Now he would be anxious to get back to the comfort of his own grand poster bed with the intricately painted headboard and the thick down mattress, the warmth of his bedroom's oversize fireplace, directly one floor beneath her own.

Cretia felt no tears anymore, and very little shame. She may have to endure this, but she would not be undone by it. It was an act. He took what he wanted, then left. It kept her father from the fields, and it made the beatings that had defined his youth only a horrid memory. But Cretia was not like her father. When the time was right, she would rise above this, somehow. It was that hope alone onto which she hung the last of her very fragile girlhood dreams. Dreams that were a world away from those of Cecelia Stovall.

Over the next days, as the snow lay in white patches on the brown front lawn and the bleached landscape of winter covered the horizon, Cecelia told Cretia everything about William. In their moments alone, as Augusta moved into spring, she described every detail, from his face and hair to the flecks of gold in his eyes, to the rich sincerity of his Northern accent. Both his laughter, and the times he spoke with great commitment. And she loved it when her most trusted friend asked her questions, as it helped to keep the image of him alive for herself.

These months were filled with uncertainty, but Cecelia refused to be uncertain. They *would* be together. She would make it happen. She certainly would *not* marry Charles Shelman, no matter how much money he gave her family in anticipation of a union. Too much had happened. Too much had changed her.

"I do wonder if William has tried to write to me in return," Cecelia said on an early spring evening in April as the two girls sat alone in Cecelia's bedroom. They were preparing her for Marcellus's engagement party. Cretia was curling Cecelia's dark, shiny hair into precise onyx ringlets with tongs she pulled from the fire. It was to be a grand affair down in the second-floor ballroom. The wine had been brought from France, the rich and elegant menu had been planned for days, and the orchestra from the theater in town had been hired to play. The guests were to number one hundred.

"If he *did* try to write, yo' daddy'd sho'ly burn the letters as soon as they came into this house."

"And he would probably be angry with me. But he has said nothin'."

Cecelia glanced at Cretia behind her in the reflection of the mirror at her dressing table. She caught the disparity, harshly, once again in the satiny yellow firelight. Her own rich gown, sewn of violet-colored silk and embroidered with delicate pink roses, came up to smooth, milk-white shoulders. Cretia's drab cotton dress, without the benefit of petticoats, clung to her small body. It was the same dress she had worn yesterday, and the day before that. The skin of her arms and neck were black, the color a flat parched black, dry and untended. So different from her own skin made soft and smooth by a variety of oil and milk baths, lotions and creams. Behind her, Cretia was a shadow. Her conscience. She grimaced. The image was difficult to bear.

Cecelia wanted to give her friend something new to wear. She thought about it almost continually. But she knew Cretia would never take it. It would draw further attention to herself, attention she was trying very hard to avoid, from Pleasant Stovall.

"I don't know why he still hasn't written, or at least sent someone else with a message fo' me." For a moment, Cecelia was silent. She bit her lower lip. "You did manage to see that letter to him mailed, as I asked you?"

Cretia turned from the mirror and bent beside the fire to heat the hair tongs again. "You asked me, Miss Cecelia, and I have to do as you wants."

Downstairs, the sound of laughter and voices deepened. The guests were arriving. They could hear the heavy front door open and close, then the clink of cordial glasses, brought, on a silver tray, to each guest in welcome.

"It is as I *want*, Cretia." Cecelia gently corrected her, something she had been doing since they were children, hoping to help her friend better herself if the opportunity should arise. It was also why she had secretly taught her to read and to add her numbers even before she had fully understood the implications of the differences between them. "And I hope you believe that helpin' me marry William will help you, too."

"Yo daddy'd never let me go."

Her voice went lower. "We can't just give up! Maybe there will be *somethin'* we can do."

"Nothin' anybody can do. That's just the way things are."

"Well, I am *not* givin' up on you. Just like I'm not givin' up on William and me, until every last little bit of hope runs out."

A knock sounded at her door. They both glanced over at it. It was time for Cecelia to go downstairs. Into the other world. Her one blessing was that Shelman had needed to return to Savannah on business, and he would be unable to join them this evening. *Good*, she thought. At least she would not need to look quite so happy to suit her father. Cretia clasped a gold-and-pearl necklace at Cecelia's throat, then handed her the matching earrings as she went to open the door. It was a black footman named Theo, who answered to Josiah.

"It's time," he said in a crackling baritone drawl.

Cretia glanced back at Cecelia, her violet silk gown shimmering like fire in the lamplight. Cecelia came toward her and took Cretia's hands. Leaning in very closely, she whispered. "Don't give up on yo'self, my friend, as *I* won't give up on you. Until we make things right."

"Ye'd bes' git," Cretia said flatly, her old dialect coming through for the benefit of the footman. "Befo' yo' dady comes lookin' fo' you."

Cecelia kissed her cheek, paused for a moment, and then went out of the room.

"Another bourbon, gentlemen?"

Her father was asking the question of two men she did not know just as she reached the second-floor landing. He was standing with Anne but entirely attentive to his guests. One was old and slim, with a neat mustache and beard. The other was young and attractive. They were both dressed elegantly, and they looked alike, with their long thin faces, aquiline noses, and the particular taupe-colored shade of their thick hair, which began on them both rather far back on their foreheads.

And then she noticed it, and her heart felt as if it stopped beating entirely. The younger man wore the gray dress coat and white trousers of a West Point uniform.

"I do believe I will. No sense in gon' home sober on a splendid evenin' like this!" The older man chuckled just as she came up beside them. "Yo' home is impressive indeed, Stovall."

"We're comfortable here."

The old man's eyes met Cecelia. "And who is *this* lovely creature?" he asked, his long, bushy mustache entirely covering his lips.

"Where *have* you been?" Anne whispered. Then before Cecelia could reply, her father interjected boastfully, "I declare, if that Negro house gal of ours gets any slower at dressin' you, I do believe we're gon' have to sell her off and find someone decent who can do the job!"

Panic mixed with revulsion inside Cecelia. Had she really ever been like these people, or believed in their ways? Once again, she felt foolish and incredibly dim. She had lived her whole life without seeing any of this.

"This is my daughter, Cecelia. Darlin', do say hello to Mr. Ashford Gardner and his son, Richard."

The old man took Cecelia's hand and kissed it. "You *are* a vision, young lady."

Cecelia lowered her eyes properly.

"Son, say hello to Miss Stovall now." The senior Mr. Gardner slapped a hand across his son's back. "Speak right up there, boy."

Richard moved a step nearer. "A pleasure, Miss Stovall."

"Mr. Gardner." She nodded and forced a sedate smile she did not feel.

"My son is on a short leave from West Point, where he is a second-year cadet, I'm mighty proud to say. Ordinarily, you can't pry them from the place till the second summer. But as he is at the top in his class, they let him go on account his mama has been ill."

"I'm sorry," Cecelia said, glancing at the younger Gardner, whose pale cheeks had flushed, and who looked slightly embarrassed by his father's more commanding and slightly overbearing presence.

The thoughts that ran through her mind at that moment were rapid and many. Did he know William? Could this be her chance—a way to get a real message through to him at last? Her heart was beating so fiercely all of a sudden at the renewed hope that she could hear nothing else at all.

"May I escort you in to supper, Miss Stovall?"

She smiled more broadly now than she had been able to for months. Her face was flushed with excitement; Cecelia took the arm he extended to her. "I do believe, Mr. Gardner, that would be delightful."

Supper in the grand dining room was a long and very formal affair. While Pleasant Stovall sat at one head of the long, elegantly laid table, Marcellus presided grandly at the other. Candles in exquisite chiseled ormolu sconces flickered and glowed from the four marble-topped mahogany sideboards, and from silver candelabra at both ends of the table, as well as from the Hungarian crystal chandelier above them. The window draperies were of silk, with tie-backs of clumps of bronze grape leaves and bunches of white glass grapes. Beneath their feet was a specially woven Aubusson carpet. Two gilt mirrors reflected the light, setting the long room and the bright foil wallpaper, crimson and silver, aglow.

There were four rich courses, first of soup and vegetables, then boiled bass, followed by mutton, ham, and oysters. Finally during the dessert of ice cream, ground nuts, bananas, and sweet wine, the room shook with conversation, laughter, and the clink of glasses and silver against china. Cecelia learned that Richard and his father were from Charleston and that they had met her father there, at a convention of cotton merchants the previous autumn.

"I'm sorry 'bout yo' mother," she said, leaning closer to him as more wine was served by the two liveried black servants who assisted Josiah.

"Don't be. She's fine, just lonely. My older brother, Frank, is up North now, married to a girl from Ohio, and she has fairly well disowned him. So seein' she needed a bit of family around to cheer her, my father finagled a visit from me." He smiled and lay down his spoon. "We brought her over to Savannah for some shoppin', where we met up with yo' father once again."

"And what do our fathers find they have so in common that it brings you to our home this evenin', Mr. Gardner?"

He leaned back and looked at her as he dotted his lips with a white linen napkin. "We have a respectable-size cotton plantation outside of Charleston. Yo' father bein' a cotton merchant here in Augusta, willin' to come to more friendly terms than some, and my father decided to do business together."

She had no idea what else to say to him. She did not find him in the least interesting or attractive. In fact, he was rather mild and weak. So much so that it was difficult to see him surviving the rigors of a place like West Point when her own hearty brother had failed so swiftly. Still, Cecelia was driven to engage this young stranger until she could find a way, privately, to ask about William.

"And will you go into the cotton business when you're finished at West Point, Mr. Gardner?"

"As the eldest, the plantation is my brother's to inherit, Miss Stovall. I'm afraid my life will be one of military service after this year."

"I thought yo' brother had been disowned?"

"Only so far as my mother's current emotions, I'm afraid. In South Carolina, blood, and the loyalty to it, is thicker than anythin' else."

"It's really no different here in Augusta, Mr. Gardner."

Cecelia glanced over at Marcellus and his intended bride. She was lovely, Cecelia thought, carefree and softly laughing. They were in love, with their whole lives ahead of them. And no one was stopping them from being together. How could it have been so easy for him when her own wishes were so entirely forbidden? A new mixture of raw anger and futility shook her, and she thrust back her chair. Amid the great profusion of wine, food, moving servants, and laughter, no one but Richard even noticed the movement.

"May I see you outside for a breath of air?"

Gripping the expanse of her violet silk gown at the sides, she did not reply, nor did she object. He merely followed her from the dining room and out onto the columned veranda that wrapped around the length of the house. The night air was cool and sweet, with the laughter and conversation from the supper party spilling out around them. Cecelia drew in a breath and exhaled, leaning over the balustrade. The sky was very dark and the stars shimmered from it like diamonds on black velvet. She wrapped her arms around herself and gazed up, wondering if William could be looking at the very same sky just now. One small thing to link them, at least.

"Yo' brother, Bolling, told me that you visited West Point last summer."

Cecelia continued to gaze up at the sky, holding her lacy ivory shawl over her shoulders. "Yes."

"I wish I'd met you there."

"And why is that, Mr. Gardner?"

"Because then I would be able to say I had known you for nearly a full year, and you would be obliged to call me Richard."

She finally looked over at him. "And what would be a point to such familiarity?"

"Truthfully, I find you utterly captivatin', Miss Stovall."

"Suh, you don't even know me."

"I would certainly like to."

She looked away, down into the darkness of the garden now. *And what would you think if you knew that my heart could never belong to you? That you have no chance at all of any sort of life with me? That I would fight you as furiously as I am fighting the attentions of Mr. Shelman?*

"Tell me, Mr. Gardner. At West Point, are you acquainted with a cadet by the name of William Sherman?"

"Is he in my class?"

She modulated her tone, knowing how much she needed to make it look like a casual inquiry. "This would be his second year."

In the small silence, he searched his memory. "Sherman, Sherman. Ah, yes, of course! Some call him Cump. Slim fellow, very taut—copper hair and the deepest eyes that remind me of a tiger's."

Just the memory of William was warming. Here, with her suddenly, was a link back to him.

"He was a friend of my elder brother's there," she casually explained before he could ask more questions. But she began to stroll the length of the veranda, not wanting him to be able to see directly her expression. "They were roommates. I met him last summer. He seemed to be havin' a bit of trouble fittin' in with all the regimentation, and I suppose it's only natural to wonder how he's gotten on."

"Sherman? Oh, that's no problem anymore! He's doin' quite well fo' himself. Rarely garners demerits. He regularly hosts illegal little suppers in his barracks room for some of the boys, and he's clever enough never to get caught. If he keeps it up, he'll have quite a military career ahead of himself."

Bolling came outside then. They both turned around when they heard the door click. "Daddy's about to make the toast to Marcellus and Sarah."

Cecelia looked at Richard Gardner. "We should join the others. But thank you for keepin' me company out here."

As she turned to go back inside, he caught her arm. "In case I don't get a chance to ask you later, and because we don't return to Charleston for another few days. I *would* like to call on you."

She needed to establish a rapport—a trust—before she asked him to carry a letter back to West Point for her. And she needed to give him a reason to do it.

"I would like that, Mr. Gardner." She smiled.

Again, it was late. Cretia sat alone on the edge of her bed enveloped by the darkness of her small, cold room. The exhaustion she felt was total. She had not even lit a candle. There was not a part of her body that did not throb or ache for rest. But strangely, she was not sleepy. It had been a grand party for the master's family—and a debilitating foray for her father, for Setty Mae, and for herself as they walked in endless procession up and down the service steps with dishes, serving bowls, and wineglasses.

The men had all drunk too much liquor and eaten too much of Setty Mae's rich food. The women had all enveloped themselves in gossip and tittering laughter while they consumed endless cherry cordials. Earlier, Cretia had even managed to taste one in the warming kitchen before her father brought the tray upstairs. She had known instantly as the liquor had burned her throat, that it was one of the forbidden pleasures of the white man's world.

She glanced down at her own feet, bare now, numb and throbbing, like the rest of her. She could not even manage to move her toes. It could be worse, she reminded herself in that realistic way. And it *was* worse for most other Negroes who had been bought and sold in chains.

Like Josiah. Like her mother, too.

Her mother—that ghostly figure of her earliest memories, who was still somewhere in Georgia, but too far away ever to see again. Cretia's mother was a fading image who neither Setty Mae nor her father ever spoke about now. Enduring family connections were another of the privileges rarely accorded blacks. Like the master, like old dresses and all the backbreaking work, that was just how things were.

She lay back and closed her eyes, daring to torture herself with the image of herself in a gown like Miss Cecelia wore tonight, her hair smoothly curled into rings, and with something winsome in the world that might actually make her want to laugh. She had made the image so real that she did not hear the click of the lock and the door squeal to open.

"You asleep?"

She started, then bolted upright. It was not the father before her in the shadows this time, but the son. Marcellus closed the door but stood at the small distance, not moving closer toward her. "I'm sorry to have startled you."

He was wearing his nightclothes, a heavy, tufted burgundy velvet robe, and slippers. Not knowing what he wanted, she did not respond. But he was a grown man now, about to marry. Setty Mae had warned her that this could happen. Cretia only looked at him and waited with indifference for the master's son to tell her or show her what would happen now.

A moment later, he pulled a letter from his vest pocket and thrust it at her. She recognized it by the writing as the one she had been given by Miss Cecelia to send to New York. She looked at him now, in shadows and the light of the single candle he had carried with him.

"I intercepted this from Old Joe. He was given money to send it to West Point. I know my sister has, most unwisely, taught you to read, so don't bother tellin' me you don't recognize it, or that old Joe was not given it by you. Besides, I gave him mo' money, by half, than Cecelia did to tell me the truth. And you, bein' one, know where a fool Negro's loyalty lies."

Still she did not speak. There was no point in denial. He knew the truth, and he was here with a purpose. He would tell her all of it when he was ready. "I want you to bring to me any mo' letters that my sister gives you."

"Now, why'd I do dat, suh?"

He moved two steps that, in the small room, put him very near her. The scent of perspiration on his skin, and rancid liquor on his breath, were overpowering. The candle he carried flickered. The shadows between them danced wildly on the four dark walls. Then he sank onto the edge of the bed beside her.

"Because, you uppity black bitch, *I* am the only one in this world with the power to get you away from my father!"

It was a sharp blow, partially because he knew about Pleasant's sexual appetite, and also because he had spoken about it so freely. But more than that, because, after all this time, Marcellus Stovall might actually have the power to rescue her—and that meant less than nothing to him.

As she looked into his eyes, at that precise moment in the taut silence, she saw, not the hate she had expected, but rather pure indifference. He was not here to take her, or to help her. Nothing so magnanimous as the latter. He wanted something, and the means by which he would obtain it would be through her.

Simple and cold as that.

He was offering her hope with no more care than a man who, in a softened instant, tosses a scrap of meat to a stray dog. The thought moved across her weary mind. For some strange reason, perhaps it was the lateness of the hour, or how terribly weary she was, but, in that silence, she felt tears suddenly wetting her cheeks. Impossible. It had been such a long time since she had cried. Her glittering eyes met his with an expression that said, *All right. You win. What must I do?*

"Good," Marcellus said. He did not smile. He had known he would find victory with her even before he had come here. "After I am married next week, I will take you with me to our new home, across the state to Rome, and I will do it only on one condition. *If* there are no slipups. And *if* you do precisely as you're told."

She couldn't help it—her heart swelled, then quickened with a glimmer of hope. She fought to keep her tone servile. "Yassuh."

"You will *not* tell my sister that her letter to William Sherman was never mailed. I told you about it tonight *only* to demonstrate the things I am capable of findin' out from far brighter sources than you. She will *never* be allowed to have him, so there is no point at all in you helpin' her sustain *that* particular fool dream."

"What about Josiah?"

"What about him?"

"He *is* the only family I've got."

His face tightened in disgust. "Well, that ain't my fault! Can't you just be happy with what I *can* do for you, instead of askin' me to change the things I *can't?* Good Lawd, no wonder the South is headin' fo' the trouble it is with you Negroes!"

"I ain't askin' you fo' nothin', suh. But please don't ask *me* to do 'gainst Miss Cecelia."

In an unexpected movement, he reached out and touched her, running his long white fingers slowly up the mahogany length of her bare arm from wrist to elbow. Reacting without thinking, Cretia jerked away.

Marcellus smiled. "I don't understand what my daddy sees in you, that's for damn sure. You can rest assured you won't have those same problems over in *my* house. That, at least, should be some comfort to you." Marcellus did not touch her again. He only sat for a moment in silence, gazing at her and shaking his head.

"So then, here's my offer. *When* you bring me any other letters my sister tries to send to West Point, or you report to me any other attempt she makes to communicate with him, I will take that as a show of good faith on yo' part. And you will be rewarded."

"But, suh. What if Miss Cecelia don't send him no mo' letters?"

"Fool gal. You really don't understand the human's nature any better than a dog does, do you?" He stood and walked the two steps across the bare wood floor to the door. He was shaking his head again. "Mark my words, she *will* come to you. My sister is as coltish and stubborn as they come. She won't give up on that Yankee without a fight. Now it'll just be up to you, whether yo' loyalty to her—or yo' freedom from my daddy, matters more. About that, apparently, we shall just have to wait and see."

Chapter Eleven

The approach of Marcellus's marriage to Sarah McKinne, and the complicated preparations for it, took the pressure off Cecelia's own situation, at least for the time being. And once again she was free to pursue her determined goal of being absolutely certain that a message had finally gotten to William. He must know she would still and always wait for him while he finished school.

She had received no reply to the two letters she had sent, one through Marcellus back in London, the other through Josiah that Cretia claimed her father had taken to his free black friend to post. But that was understandable, she knew. If William *had* replied, her family would have made certain she never saw it. All she had now, months after their parting, were her memories of the commitment they had made, and an abiding trust in him. That would have to be enough. The only letters she was allowed to receive were from Charles Shelman.

Richard Gardner was her last hope.

Two days after the engagement party, Gardner drew up before the Stovall house in a very grand, rented carriage with a white driver and two black coachmen, all in dark green livery, who attended him. Cecelia saw her father's face as they watched him through the large bowed parlor window.

"Grandstander!" Pleasant muttered as he scowled, then drew the newspaper back up before his face.

"Now, Daddy. Let's not be *too* harsh 'bout Mr. Gardner. After all, he *is* a proper Southern gentleman, which is what I thought you wanted for me. The Augusta Horse Show is one of *the* events of the season. You wouldn't want me to miss it, would you? Just because Mr. Shelman can't be here."

Anne, who sat beside her husband, embroidering a pale pink rose onto a tea towel, shot Cecelia a sudden and cautious glance. Business at Stovall & Hamilton was still down, and Pleasant's frustration was deepening by the day at the clever ways Cecelia had found to put off the interest of Charles Shelman. A second major influx of capital from him seemed the only way now to keep the family business from bankruptcy. Marcellus's engagement party, and keeping up appearances in general, especially to Sarah's expectant family, had brought an enormous strain into the Stovall house, which settled around them all just now like a funeral shroud.

"Well, you sho ain't marryin' that Gardner boy! So I don't know why you insist on leadin' him on with buggy rides and flirtation!"

She shot to her feet just as the knocker at the front door clacked sharply. "Isn't there any chance at all that I will have some say in decidin' who it is I marry?"

"Not unless you *decide* that it's Charles Shelman!"

"Ha!" Cecelia spun around, her dress of cherry-pink silk edged in satin ribbon swirling about her like fire. "You can be such an incredibly cruel and pigheaded man!"

"Cecelia!" Anne gasped, her embroidery hoop clattering to an uncarpeted part of the wood floor. She had meant to scold her, yet seeing the expression in Cecelia's eyes, Anne had thought better of it, which only deepened Cecelia's anger.

"Maybe it's time, Anne, my father learned that he cannot *force* everyone in this world to do as he wishes!" she cried. "There are some of us—at least whites, anyway, who have a choice—with a mind of our own, who aren't forced by the cruelty of our laws, to give him every last thing he desires!"

As Pleasant thundered to his feet, knowing full well now what his daughter knew, the moment was diffused by Josiah's sudden welcoming tenor in the foyer beyond them.

"Aft'noon, suh. *Do* come in. I'll tell Miss Cecelia you're here."

Not only had Richard Gardner come for their little carriage ride out to Shultz Park, but the father was to accompany them, as well. This new relationship would never lead to marriage because it couldn't see Pleasant out of the debt he was in. But objecting to this proper diversion for his daughter might well lose him a cotton account he sorely needed. And, after all, the Gardners were going to be in town for only a few days more. Keeping Cecelia's mind off that West Point Yankee until Charles returned to Augusta would certainly be worth the small amount of risk involved.

The carriage ride out to Shultz Park, between the shady row of old moss-draped oaks, was cool and pleasant. Changed now into a blue leghorn hat with a black grosgrain ribbon, and a day dress of deep blue taffeta, Cecelia felt the first hint of pleasure she had in months. They sat for a while with a collection of other carriage occupants listening to Bohler's Brass & Cotillion Band playing music in the white gingerbread bandstand in the center of the park. The air was cool, the music was sweet, and Cecelia was away from her family, and from the pain they had brought to her, for at least a little while.

Life here in the South seemed, for a moment, almost as it once had—lovely, carefree.

Cecelia glanced over at the Gardners, both with such silly, wistful expressions on their faces as they listened to the music. She had a job to do now, and she could not return home until she had done it.

Cecelia was at the horse show, and Anne had taken Georgie into town to do some shopping at *Barnes & Turpins*. Bolling and Thomas were fishing on the river. But for the other servants out in the kitchen house and the stables, Pleasant was alone here. It had been a long time, he thought, since he had been here with only his thoughts. And with his anger.

So Cretia had told Cecelia what was between them. Fool Negro bitch!

Cretia had ruined the finely tuned running of everything here in his home. And he had been better to her all these years than she had deserved. She sure as hell had a better life here in this house than she might have had somewhere else. In the cotton fields . . . in the heat of the laundry house out by the kitchens. He had fed her, clothed her, let her off with house work only. Fool ingrate! Now she had gone and ruined it all.

In butternut-colored trousers, jacket and lace-front shirt beneath, he stalked the length of his book-lined library on the second floor. He wrung his hands as his black boot heels clicked sharply over the plank floors. He didn't favor beating slaves. Pleasant Stovall had always found that happy Negroes were far more productive than unhappy ones. Until today.

A soft knock sounded at the closed door, and he turned toward it. His face flushed with anger. There came a time when a man had to set things right. Cretia opened the door and slipped inside.

"Close the door!" he snarled, not turning from the wall of windows to look at her. The door clicked to a close. Outside, a carriage passed by the house, the steady clop of the horses hooves breaking into the silence between them. "Come over here." One heartbeat. Then two. "I *said*, come on over here, gal!"

Cretia complied, and when she had reached his side, in a movement that was as fluid as it was lethal, Pleasant spun around, striking her with such force across the side of her head that she fell in a heap at his feet.

He was unaffected by her small, startled cry. "If you *ever* betray me again, you fool nigger," he said tersely, "I swear to God Almighty, I'll kill you! Do you understand me?"

Cretia rubbed her cheek.

"I asked you, did you understand?"

"But I ain't done nothin', suh."

As she tried to sit up, he struck her again, the blow landing, this time, across the side of her face. "Don't you lie to *me*, girl!"

"But, Massa Stovall—"

"Cecelia knew 'bout us befo' I sent her to West Point, but you went and told her it was still gon' on, to gain her sympathies and turn my daughter against me, didn't you?"

"She figured it all out fo' herself!"

Pleasant drew her up by her shoulders, squeezing her so tightly that she grimaced. "What kind of fool do you take me fo'?" Again he struck her hard across the face. "That daughter of mine ain't smart enough to see the nose on her own face, much less figure out what's between a man and one of his slaves!"

"Please, suh!"

"*Please* won't help you, you tart, if you *ever*, and I do mean *ever*, betray me to anyone in this family again, y'hear?"

She was trembling as she sank onto one of the leather chairs, holding her raw and bleeding cheek where the skin had cracked open beneath his knuckles. Never in all her years here had she ever been struck by anyone, and the moment was as confusing as it was frightening.

"Yassuh."

He loomed over her for a moment, hands on his hips, his chest heaving from the indignation and the exertion. "Haven't I been good to you, Cretia girl? Brought you into my house from out back where the others are? Gave you a room upstairs . . . You aren't outside, or downstairs doin' the washin' or the cookin', are you? . . . Well, look at me, gal! Are you?"

Her voice broke. "No, Massa Stovall."

Once again, he drew her to her feet, though the zenith of his anger had passed. "Now, I'm sorry for strikin' you, girl, I am. But I'll do it again if I have to. You have *got* to learn. And sometimes there just isn't any other way. What my wife and my daughters think means a powerful lot to me, and I'll do what I must to protect that."

Then, in an oddly tender move, he ran his hand along the wound on her cheek and drew a handkerchief from his own pocket to wipe away the crimson streak of blood. When she shrank from him, Pleasant pulled her toward him and, for the first time, kissed her boldly.

"Please, suh. No mo'."

"I'll tell you when there won't be anymo' between us!" he declared, kissing her again, this time more roughly, his mouth open, tongue thrust into her mouth.

"Please, suh!"

"Father, let her go!"

The tenor of Marcellus's commanding voice, breaking the silence, stopped the moment. For that moment, Pleasant Stovall froze. When he turned around, it was with wide, angry eyes. "How the devil'd *you* get in here?"

"Closin' the door is not lockin' it, is it? If you're gon' to go on fornicatin' with the slaves, you'd do well to remember that. I could hear you all the way downstairs."

"Get the hell out of here, son!"

He took a step nearer, not fazed by his father's apparent anger. "Cecelia and her escorts have returned from the races, Father. They are all outside in the courtyard. And I'm quite certain you don't want *them* hearin' what I heard."

Glancing at the tall ebony clock against the wall near the fireplace, Pleasant only then realized that two hours had passed. Everyone else would be back soon. Including Anne. "Go put some cold water on that cheek befo' it looks even worse," he said blandly, flipping a dismissive hand at Cretia and refusing to look at her again. When she had gone, he looked across at Marcellus.

"Father, you can't go on with her like this!"

"What the devil do *you* know about it? You haven't ever done nothin' wrong in yo' whole young and innocent life, have you, boy?"

"What I *know* is that it's wrong, couplin' with a slave!"

"She's *my* property, and I'll do with her as I please!"

"Those days are over, Father. Sarah and I are takin' Cretia with us when we leave, and *you* are gon' to give her to me for my new household as a weddin' present."

"You're out of yo' mind!"

"I've never been more lucid *or* more serious!"

"Well, what if I'm not inclined to be so gracious?"

"Then I expect I'll be sayin' the same thing concernin' a certain upcomin' talk I'll be havin' with yo' wife."

"Don't you threaten me, boy! Besides, Anne knew 'bout Cretia a long while ago."

"But does she know how often it's gon' on still?"

Pleasant paled. He had been beaten. "You wouldn't!"

"Wouldn't I? I want what I want, Father. And you are the one who taught me to stop at nothin' till I get it."

"Cur!"

"*Yo'* cur, entirely. 'Less of course you're accusin' my poor dead mama of havin' behaved as you do."

Pleasant moved to speak. Then he simply stopped. Looking at what his son had become was like looking in the mirror, and he found quite suddenly that what he saw he did not particularly like. He ran a hand behind his thick neck and then moved to leave the room. When he spoke, it was over his shoulder.

"Tell Gardner and that boy of his I've gone up to bed with a resoundin' ache in my head. I can't bear to be in the same room with those ingratiatin' faces of theirs another day!"

In the echo of his victory, Marcellus Stovall chose to keep the obvious retort to himself. Pleasant's eldest son had learned well from his father, and he had already won enough for one day.

Cretia could not escape the images of Pleasant's sudden anger. Her head still burned with the reminder. His had been an expression of hate, meted out at her in a frightening new way. The sting of his hand on her face, his sexual desire for her in the midst of it. Her stomach heaved. If she stayed here in Augusta, things between them could only get worse. And what sort of life was there for her in light of that? He would never let her have a family as she once, a lifetime ago, had dreamed of doing. And how much longer could she avoid carrying a child by him?

But could she betray Cecelia in exchange for her freedom?

Each alternative was inconceivable.

"Oh, Cretia, he'll do it! Mr. Gardner'll take a letter back to West Point fo' me! I tell you, I'm *convinced* that somehow that letter you gave yo' daddy never made it to West Point or I just *know* I'd have heard from William by now! But Mr. Gardner is sure to get the letter through, and everythin' is gon' be all right at last!"

Cecelia rushed into her own bedroom, her wide, hooped skirts swaying like a bell as she ran, tearing Cretia from her own dark, untenable thoughts. Her pale cheeks were flushed with excitement, and her smile was wider than Cretia had ever seen it. Cecelia was like a child again, filled with happiness and hope.

It was unbearable to be confronted by that, today of all days.

"And since there is no danger at all of me havin' to marry him where Daddy is concerned," she went on as she sank onto a stool to let Cretia begin removing her shoes, which was their usual routine when Cecelia returned from anywhere outside the house, "I actually enjoyed myself this afternoon! It was a lovely day, the air off the lake was cool, and the horses were so sleek and lovely." Only then, as she glanced down, did she see Cretia's face, the swollen lip, and the bruise near her eye, hidden by a scramble of black curls, yet deepened now to the shade of a plum, which made it impossible to avoid.

"Dear Lawd God Almighty!" Cecelia shrieked as her expression changed to one of horror.

Cretia stood with the shoes, then turned away. "Ain't nothin'. I took a fall was all."

Cecelia charged into the dressing room after her, a small room next to her bedroom, with a copper bathtub, pegs for some of her dresses, and an iron dress model. "The devil you did! Someone *struck* you!"

Her mouth was trembling. "You only gon' go and make it worse."

Cecelia closed the dressing room door and then pulled her down onto a tufted stool, seeing the sheer panic glittering in Cretia's dark eyes. Cecelia took her friend's hands and squeezed them trying very hard to catch her own breath. "Are you sho'?"

"Yes."

"Because I'll go to Daddy right now and—"

"That'd be the *worst* thing you could do!"

Cecelia felt the full weight of that warning and, for a moment, she could not speak. It was hideous, this new life into which she had been thrust, the knowing of dark things, of dark truths.

"Please just leave it be," Cretia murmured. "Please."

Cecelia, still holding tightly to Cretia's hands, pulled her into a desperate embrace, pressing Cretia's head on her shoulder. "Some day I swear I'm gon' find a way to make it right for you. I promise you, I *will* find a way."

"Promises ain't no way to live a life. I've got to live fo' what *is*. Not fo' the way I want it to be."

Walking into his room that night at the Augusta Hotel, Richard Gardner was surprised to find a lamp already lit and glowing. But he was more surprised to see that it was Marcellus Stovall who was sitting in the dark cane chair beside the bed.

"We need to talk," Marcellus cooly said. Richard closed the door. "I know you fancy yo'self a suitor for my sister."

"And if I were?"

"Well, if you were to be one, there's a challenge to her heart you'll need to vanquish first."

He moved a step nearer. Marcellus had been drinking. Richard could smell the rancid odor across the room as he drew off his West Point cap and regulation cloak. "All right. Who?"

"A Northern sot to whom you've foolishly agreed to bear a love letter."

"Sherman?" He was truly surprised. Richard sank onto the bed in a way that allowed him to face Marcellus directly. "Yo' sister told me that they were barely acquainted. Apparently they shared a dance or two last summer. She said she wished to leave him with no false impression that it would ever grow into anythin' more than that."

"I'm sorry to say that it is you, Mr. Gardner, who have been given a false impression. Sit down and let me tell you the *whole* story of that summer. Then, if we are in accord, you will give me her letter for Sherman, and I will give *you* something to convince Sherman that all hope with my sister is forever lost."

"I *am* sorry 'bout yo' lip, all right?" Pleasant said mildly. He stood in Cretia's small garret room as Marcellus spoke with Gardner, all of it long after everyone else in the house had gone to bed. "I'm sorry about it. I had no intention of ever hurtin' you."

"Yassuh."

She did not meet his gaze, keeping busy by removing her black leather ankle boots and the collection of hairpins that tamed her springy ebony hair.

"Now don't go givin' me that tone. I mean it. I do."

He was not here only to apologize. She knew that, too. Even now after what he had done, he would expect to lie with her. It was too much. She felt old, used, and so weary of it all. He had certainly ruined her for any sort of life with another man. There was no future for Cretia, only survival. But she was weak. There was only one kernel of power she possessed. But to save herself, she must destroy the hopes of the one person in the world who had ever shown her tenderness and respect.

"Please, suh. Leave me be."

His eyes, swiftly hard and full of fury, fixed on her, and Cretia felt a chill shoot down the length of her spine in response. "You givin' *me* orders now, gal?"

"No, suh."

He was silent for a moment, studying her, some of the flaring violence leaving his eyes. "That's good. . . . That's *real* good."

Pleasant touched her bare shoulder, and a cold sense of purpose began to seep through her. A new force was rising to the surface and coming into the light after a very long time. Indignation. Raw, open, and full of its own power. Her heart began to throb with it even before she spoke, because she knew all too well what it meant.

He had moved nearer, and the smell of bourbon on his breath was noxious. "You know what to do. . . ." Pleasant's warbled drawl startled her. "Come on, then. I haven't got all night!"

Cretia stood awkwardly in the doorway, waiting for him to lunge at her. Suddenly she was struggling to free herself from his grip but there was little use in it. He tossed her onto the bed, his mouth pressing down hard and open onto hers in spite of the bruises. *Lawd . . . oh Lawd . . . not again . . .* She felt the indignation now, wild and powerful, spiraling up through her, giving her an odd and suddenly ferocious power. When she lashed out at him with both fists, he grabbed her forearms, the veins standing out in his neck.

"Listen, you darky bitch! Don't you go pressin' my good graces and fo'get! You are *my* property!" he brayed. "And I can damn well do as I please with *my* property! Now get on over here, and do like you always do!"

As she lifted herself over his pale, naked body, straddling his hairless thighs, Cretia began silently to weep, shoulders jerking, tears stinging her cuts and bruises. He fondled her breasts roughly, and his eyes rolled to a close; she made no sound to distract him from his intent. The less she resisted, the sooner it would be over.

As he moaned and moved, she thought of anything, everything, but this vile duty. . . . And then, as he began to shudder, she felt strangely the distant, powerful call of freedom, beckoning her. There had been no choice. Betraying a friend was the only way to rescue her own dying soul. And the instinct for survival was stronger than anything else in the world, she had discovered.

Even loyalty.

In the days that followed the whirlwind of physical violence that had risen up from Pleasant toward Cretia, the incidents of his roughness only increased. For Cretia, it became a sign, and her decision was irrevocably made. So, two days before the marriage of Marcellus and Sarah McKinne, when he made good on his offer to take her from Augusta, Cretia agreed to go.

Josiah knew she planned to leave, because he knew all the workings of the Stovall house. But he and his only daughter had not spoken of it. They rarely discussed anything that would have taken the conversation beyond the business that owned them. Nevertheless, very late that final evening, Cretia drew a cotton shawl across her shoulders and walked next door to her father's garret room, with its locking door, a softer mattress filled with Spanish moss, and a fireplace that glowed with a golden fire as he opened the door to her.

Cretia stood stiffly in the doorway, the sound of deep, soulful singing filtering up from the open windows of the kitchen house outside. Her voice, when she spoke, was low. "Daddy, I know you never got to say yo' good-byes to my mama, so I'm here proper-like, tellin' you direc'ly that I'm gon' 'way."

She was startled into silence when his dark eyes filled with tears. She had never once seen this before. She stepped inside and gently closed the door as he went back to the hearth and sat on a small three-legged stool beside it.

"So, you went on 'head and betrayed Miss Cecelia."

She felt herself stiffen as she remained standing near the door. "You got no idea what it's like. I can't take it no mo'. Everybody's got their limit. Massa Stovall . . . he brought me to mine."

Josiah looked back at his child. The tears were gone now, and his dark face, in the firelight, glowed a rich amber beneath his tight crop of white, nappy curls. "It ain't so bad here, is it, chil'? Least we be together here, you 'n' me."

"How you know it ain't so bad, ol' man?" she snapped. "Can you tell me dat? You ever been raped by the massa?"

"Lucretia, chil', praise da Lawd, you ain't never gon' know *what* been done to me, and dat kind of evil ain't never gon' happ'n to *you*!" His eyes now were a bitter coal black. "You don't work da fields, under a sun dat feels like you already done found hell, nor got yo' backside split clean open for lookin' in da wrong direction. No suh," he sighed. "You is as close to free as a slave round here can be!"

"Ain't nothin' 'bout me dat's free, Daddy."

Josiah took a homemade pipe from beside the hearth and lit it. He was reflective now, staring into the flames. He did not look at her again. In the silence, he drew deeply on the pipe, and the small closed room filled with the scent of sweet smoke.

"I ain't got no way to save you from him, chil'. Dis place is as far as I could take you." He said achingly, "So if it's dat bad, you bes' do for yo'self what you can."

Cretia had always wondered if things might have been different had her mother still been with them. Would that have healed some of his wounds? She wondered so many things about Josiah's life, his experiences. But she had never asked him. To survive, he had closed that part of his life off to her. And she mourned that now, especially because she was going away. As she moved toward the door and opened it, Josiah was still gazing into the fire, rocking back and forth in a rhythmic motion.

"Da good book, it say tings gon' be better over da mountain when we sees da Lawd. Das what I hopes. Yassuh. Das what I hopes."

❧

Out in the corridor, on loose, rough planks that creaked, Cretia saw Setty Mae standing in the shadows. Her flat, dark face was gentle, the expression rich with concern. She was always there nearby, Cretia thought. A friend to her mother after Cretia was born. Then Setty Mae had been a tender refuge when Cretia's mother was sold. It was not unlike Anne Stovall was to Cecelia after the loss of her mother, as she tried to connect with another motherless daughter. Both older women had met resistance from the girls they had sought to love.

Cecelia feared betraying her mother with a replacement.

Setty Mae had never tried to be a replacement.

As Anne Stovall had done through the years, Setty Mae had tolerated the rebuffs, and the anger from the pain of so great a loss as a little girl's mother. She had only ever offered friendship, and a soft shoulder to a girl in need of a woman's tenderness. As she did again now.

"You all right, chil'?" she asked, true concern softening the lines and the years that hard work had etched into her face. She stood in the shadows holding a stack of clean linen, as though she had only been passing by. But she always seemed to be nearby.

"Course I am."

"Den, you's gon'?"

Cretia wasn't particularly surprised that Setty Mae knew. The walls up here were as thin as they were out over the kitchen house, and slaves gossiped just like anyone else.

"I am."

She shifted her weight on thick, tired legs and gave a little sigh. "You gon' be all right wit Massa Marcellus. It be different wit him."

It was what Cretia hoped with her whole bruised and battered heart. It was for that alone that she had betrayed a friend. The two women stood a moment more, together like that, with some odd tension that Cretia could not place bristling between them. Setty Mae seemed to want to say something further. Cretia waited. Suddenly without speaking again, the old woman reached out and drew her into a deep and silent embrace. To Cretia, it was better than any words she could think of.

Chapter Twelve

～ふ～

Something was wrong. The powerful and unsettling sensation was as swift and certain within William as the snuffing of a candle. He knew also, inexplicably, that it involved Cecelia. There had been no letter, no message, no communication of any kind, yet he knew.

He was at a history lecture when he first sensed it. *I love you too*, she had told him. And he believed her. But that had been a year ago. Now, the end of June was approaching, and he must take the summer leave from school he had promised the Ewings, and return to Ohio. It was that same evening, at Benny Haven's, when they had all sneaked out for a drink after curfew, that William met Richard Gardner. The sensation he'd had earlier that evening had been, he believed for the rest of his life, a premonition.

Benny Haven's was crowded, airless, and thickly blue with smoke, as it was most evenings after midnight, brimming with young cadets willing to risk demerits, or worse, for an hour's worth of freedom from the rigid conformity of their Spartan military existence. At one table, a game of dice was going. At another, an animated game of cards. Here, they catered to liquid desires (and desires of the sexual variety, as well), and the place was alive with voices, laughter, and the occasional hoots of pleasure.

William sat at a rough-hewn table with his roommate, Edward Ord, and his fellow Ohioan, Ulysses S. Grant, whom everyone now called Sam. Grant was a watchful sort, set apart from the rest of them, and overly wise for his years. There was something extraordinarily complex about him, William believed. So far in the hour they had been there, Grant had outpaced them all, having consumed four very stiff whiskeys as though they were water. Still he sat, sober-faced and quiet, pleased apparently, to be in the company of upper-classmen for the first time at this West Point institution.

Suddenly, Edward was on his feet, embracing someone William did not know.

"So you *did* go!" Ord chuckled, slapping his own knee in surprise. "I tell you, I never thought you'd get away with it, Gardner!"

"Well, my father's letter made it all sound so dire that the academy actually sent an escort to see me onto the train!"

"You ol' dog! So when the hell'd you get back?"

"Last night, and, believe me, after two weeks of playin' the gentleman, I am more than ready for a bit of what Benny Haven's has to offer!"

"Boys," Edward said, grinning widely. "I'd like you to meet a friend of mine. Richard Gardner, this is Sam Grant, and William Sherman."

"My friends call me Cump," William said, extending his hand.

"Well, well, well." Gardner sank into a spare chair Edward had pulled over from another table. "If that isn't life's irony at work! I'm given to understand that you are acquainted with the girl I am gon' to marry."

"And who would that be?" William asked casually, lifting a glass to his lips and taking a deep swallow of whiskey.

"Her name is Cecelia Stovall."

It felt like being hit very hard in the chest. There was a moment before he could catch his breath and no time to think. No time to breathe. The voice he heard was resounding in his ears. The echo was deafening. Edward was looking at him, his face spiked with sudden shock and concern. Somewhere in the tavern a man was warbling out the words to the old battle song, "Saints and Soldiers."

"You *do* know her, don't you?" Gardner said, with just the slightest hint of upturn at his lips.

There had to be a mistake. A different girl. A different Cecelia. No matter what happened, she would not betray him like that.

"Pretty dark-haired girl, hails from Augusta?" Gardner prodded.

"Her brother Marcellus roomed with us here last year," Edward cautiously revealed, hoping Gardner was wrong.

William's skin was tight with gooseflesh.

Lord, it hurts . . . more than I ever could have imagined.

"Well, I am a lucky sot to have won her." Richard Gardner beamed. "Cecelia is beautiful, spirited, and she certainly knows her own mind."

William stiffened, trying to rein in his emotions, yet still he could not speak. Edward sensed it and leaned forward toward Gardner. "Have you set a date?"

"Not yet, no. Our fathers are workin' out the details, I imagine, as we speak. But since our family's cotton plantation is one of the Stovall's biggest accounts, I shouldn't imagine there would be any great impediment."

The door rattled. Someone else came in. A cold blast of air followed. Edward's eyes darted from Richard to William, then back again. "Miss Stovall must have mentioned Sherman to you."

"Of course. She found her meetin' with her first Yankee a pleasant diversion and, if I saw you again, I was to wish you well for her."

Edward held his breath a moment. "Was there any message for him beyond that?"

Richard Gardner cocked his head as though he were actually considering the question. The laughter and clink of glasses swelled around them. Then, very swiftly, he swallowed the remains of his own drink. When he looked at Edward again, there were the slightest fragments of a smile turning up the corners of his mouth. "A private message, you mean? Oh, no. There was nothin' at all like that."

Guilt was a curious thing, Cretia thought as Cecelia embraced her tightly to say good-bye. It crept through your body like a black poison, but it didn't kill you. It only made you feel like you *wanted* to die. Maybe, she decided, that was its true, lethal quality, that you were forced to live forever with what you'd done. Cecelia cried softly into Cretia's shoulder before she left for Marcellus's wedding. There would be no time, no period of adjustment, before they sent for her. Cretia was going with them tonight. Sarah felt she needed a girl to attend her exclusively now that she was a wife.

"You take good care of yo'self, you hear?" Cecelia murmured. "And if that brother of mine so much as lays a hand on you, I'll come straight up to Rome and kill him myself!"

Cretia managed a grim smile. "Thanks. Fo' everythin'."

"Now you and I both know this wasn't *my* idea. I still can't bear you leavin'."

The knife twisted. "I meant, thanks fo' what you've done all my life, teachin' me to read . . . and speak, carin' 'bout me . . . treatin' me almost like I wasn't a slave."

"Cretia, you have *always* been mo' to me than that."

The guilt seeped further down, seizing Cretia's heart. She tried not to think of the name William Tecumseh Sherman, and how very much Cecelia loved him. How much she had trusted *her*.

"Look," Cecelia said. "We don't have much mo' time, so I want to give you somethin'." She drew forth a small bound stack of currency. "I know you didn't want this befo', but I won't sleep a night from now on if you don't have this with you."

She was stricken as the black poison of deceit hit its target, the center of her heart. "I can't do that."

"Oh, nonsense. I can't watch over you, beyond Augusta. I can't do anythin' fo' you fo' a while. And now that I know the horrid things men are capable of, I need to know you're safe. I want you to come and live with William and me after we're married. But since he won't be finished at the academy for two mo' years, you'll be safer with Marcellus than here."

Cecelia drew Cretia against her once more. "You'll be back with me one day. I'll find a way to make that happen. But until then, that money is yo' insurance."

Cretia took the stack of bills reluctantly and then turned away. She could not bear the trust in those bold black eyes a moment longer. A thought moved across her mind: What would it do to their friendship, she wondered, if Cecelia discovered that her happiness with William Sherman had been the real insurance for a slave's freedom?

William was going home to Ohio for summer leave. Everything had been arranged. The Ewings were expecting him. Phil had written that his mother had planned a party to celebrate his arrival. But the last thing in the world William felt like doing was celebrating anything. Not until he saw Cecelia. Not until he heard the truth of her marrying, directly from her. Two days before the end of term, Ord and Van Vliet found a way to make that possible. They had taken him to Benny Haven's, and there over a very stiff drink they had given him enough money for a train ticket. The Ewings were sending him to Ohio. But, they said, before that, he must go to Augusta.

"I can't take that," William protested, half-drunk now and possessed by his despair.

"You can't *not* take it!" Edward chuckled. "It's like stopping a book before the end! I, for one, will never be able to rest until I know how it turns out."

"Not every story has a happy ending," William blandly reminded him.

"Well, this one sure as hell should!" Van Vliet countered. "You love each other."

"Sometimes love just isn't enough."

Edward leaned forward, clutching his own drink. "Do you truly believe she is going to marry that unbearable dullard, Gardner, so soon after knowing *you*?" He shook his head. "For my money, somehow Marcellus put him up to this."

"But why would he? And Gardner definitely knows Cecelia. That much was clear."

In unison the other two chimed, *"Marcellus!"*

Noise in the small, cramped tavern had crescendoed, and their laughter simply melted into all the other deep, masculine conversations, singing, and laughter. But even so, William had taken their point.

"Thank you," he said simply. "I *will* pay you all back."

"We never doubted it." Van Vliet smiled. "Now, go claim your Southern belle!"

Augusta was not as he had imagined it. At the head of the Savannah River, it was a center of commerce, and steamboats moved along the river toward Charleston and Savannah, as if it were an open road. Warm wind blew up off the water, rustling the grand shady evergreens. Its streets were broad, and there were green lawns, and everywhere were elegant private homes surrounded by trees and gardens with parterres full of flowers.

Stately and grand as Augusta was, he saw quickly how the debilitating heat settled in around it during summer. Heat brought hordes of dangerous mosquitoes, and sent its wealthy residents to their homes up the hills in Summerville. William stood on an Augusta street corner and mopped the back of his neck with a handkerchief.

The train from New York had been stifling, and the carriage trip after that unbearable. Only the steam train down the river had offered any sort of relief from the heat and humidity. But he was here now at last, in Augusta, on a broad, elm-lined street called Telfair. The young ladies strolled in groups together, or with young men. They wore the finest, most expensive-looking outfits he had ever seen anywhere. Elegant hats over their long, tight curls, dresses with wide skirts made of silk and satin, and they looked quite perfect, all of them. It seemed to William, at that moment, as if Augusta were actually the center of the world.

He had asked when he arrived, and so he knew that the Stovall family lived on Broad Street. "It's da corna' house, suh," a neatly dressed black man in a checked suit and black bowler hat had politely told him. "You can't miss it, suh. It da one wit' da columns and dat wide veranda. Grandest house on da street!"

William paused a moment more, collecting himself, standing tall and magnificent in his dress uniform coat, neat white trousers, and cap. Yet his heart vaulted into his throat, and his mouth had gone dry. He had no idea what he would say to Cecelia when they saw one another again.

William faced her house for a moment, gazing up at its stately white mass, the wraparound veranda, and long, brick walkway leading up several steps to a wide front door.

The house was as understatedly elegant as Cecelia herself had been.

He moved forward toward the front door, determined yet unsure of how to force them to let him see her. But he had traveled all this way, and, after all they had promised, he must hear it from her directly that she meant to marry Richard Gardner. He would not leave until he did so. After two firm clicks of the lion's head knocker, a house slave wearing a black suit and a cream-colored vest of brocade velvet, opened the door. His hair was a steely silver, his eyes tired, and his oval, mahogany-shaded face bore the lines of a life that said not all of it had been easy.

"Yassuh?" Josiah said.

Both of William's hands became involuntary fists. "I've come to speak to Miss Cecelia."

"Oh, she ain't here, suh. They is all off to da church already, suh."

"Church?"

"Yassuh, fo' da weddin', suh."

Wedding. It was a word that crept swiftly through his mind, moving down over his heart, squeezing it. Since he had met Richard Gardner back at West

Point, it was the one word he had feared hearing on the long and tedious train rides, the carriage rides, the waiting, and the walking to get here.

"And Mr. Gardner?" The name choked him as he forced it out. "Is *he* gone, as well?"

Josiah chuckled. It was a gravely, shocked sort of response. "Oh, he be there by now, course, suh. Rode over in dat grand carriage of his wit' Miss Cecelia."

Devastation cornered him; then it bloomed up from his chest, exploding in his brain. It clung to him like powerful, meaty hands, making it difficult to breathe or to think. William saw that there was a black girl in the shadows, another servant, staring at him behind the man. But she moved back into the darker recesses beneath the staircase alcove, disappearing from his view. What was there to do now? To say? Words fluttered on his lips but he could not speak them. For a moment more, he was too stunned even to move away from the door.

"Is it too late for me to get to the church? Can you tell me where it is?" William finally asked in a choked, uneven tone. "And if the ceremony would be over by now."

"Yassuh, it sho'ly be done. Bride 'n' groom be off to dey new house over to Rome way, by now."

Through the large parlor window, Cretia had watched the handsome, copper-haired stranger, cap in hand, his face blanched, lips tightly parted, as he had faltered at the bottom of the wide stone steps once Josiah had closed the front door on him. She had watched him linger a moment more, then finally go out into the street, and disappear very slowly around the corner. And, Lord help her, she had not gone after him.

That surely had been Miss Cecelia's William in his military uniform with his giveaway Northern accent. Yes, he was exactly as Cecelia had described him. Especially his eyes. Yet all the while, she had stood there behind her father, only half-packed for Rome herself, and let Mr. Sherman believe what she knew he must have concluded. He believed that the bride today was the love of his life . . . and that his chance at a life with Cecelia Stovall was over.

Reality, Cretia thought, was a bitter pill. She felt the ache from it now, sharp and defining, and she hated herself for letting him walk away without the truth. But there had been no choice. She had made her decision, and she would need to live by its consequences.

Cretia was wearing a new dress today, a red-and-white cotton that Miss Sarah had actually bought for her in a store downtown. It was the only new dress she had ever owned, one not made from the remains of another. And more important even than that, it was the only dress the white master had not touched or sullied. This dress represented a cleansing to Cretia, a chance at taking back the shreds of the life Pleasant Stovall had stolen from her. Cecelia had no notion—none at all—of the violation of trust, and then the desperation, nor would she. Friendship or not, Cecelia would never be black, never be a slave. She would never be property. Cretia glanced down at her new shoes, sturdy black leather, soft and fitted well to her feet, then lifted her gaze to the top of the stairs, determined to force away the guilt. Maybe Cecelia would never have her William now, but it was a different world for Cretia, a world with different rules.

And there would be other fine suitors for Cecelia. Other chances, other loves.

Leaning against the banister for a moment, Cretia squeezed her eyes as if that alone could stop the shivering that had taken her over. She had done a great wrong in her silence today, and her whole body ached from it. But if she had done anything at all to bring him together with Cecelia, Master Marcellus would refuse to take her with him. Her only chance to get away from here would vanish as quickly as it had come. *Sweet Jesus, help me, but I'm just not that noble,* she thought, trudging slowly back up the two flights of stairs to her room.

Chapter Thirteen

In the sepia shaded light of a stifling late afternoon, William walked down Main Street in Lancaster, Ohio, with a heavy heart. Almost from the time he had left here to begin at West Point, he had ached to return to the predictable peace of the life he had found with the Ewings. And yet he was not that idealistic and grateful boy he had been when he last left here. And he wondered how anyone could change so entirely in two years' time.

Nearing the Ewings' large, stately white corner house, shaded by grand oak and mulberry trees, William stepped more slowly past what once had been the Sherman family home. It had been a charming, well-kept house then, and his life had been simple and happy. Now, the paint along the eaves was chipping, and a small pane of glass was broken out in one of the second-floor windows. He felt a little squeeze when he looked at the small area of bare earth where his mother once had planted roses and those lovely little English violets. It was neglected now. The house, once so loved and alive, felt dead to him—a thing of the past.

He walked on toward the Ewings' larger, corner house. The little white gate at the point of the sidewalk was unlatched and open. It was a welcoming gesture, and yet William felt a surge of unease. He willed himself to move forward as the front door opened. Maria Ewing came out and stood on the wood-plank landing, hands on ample hips. Her full face softened with that lovely wide and motherly smile that always welcomed him. She, above all the others, with her smile alone, could make him feel like he was almost a Ewing.

William broke into a run as Phil came out beside her. Seeing him, Phil, with whom he had fished for tadpoles in the creek and hunted rabbits, took the stairs two at a time. As they heartily embraced one another, William saw that Phil was taller and more filled out. He, too, had changed in two years' time. His face had a more angular, masculine quality. They had both grown up.

"You were supposed to be here two days ago, you old dog! Where the devil have you been?"

"There was some business I needed to take care of."

Phil slapped him on the back and led him back toward the steps. "And did you?"

"It's finished," William said sadly, revealing nothing more.

Maria Ewing came down the stairs toward him in a red-and-beige checkered dress, with her auburn hair pulled up into a lace bonnet. Ellen was beside her. *Ellen.* She looked so grown up, William thought. An image from long ago passed him like a whisper. She was barely six and running after him and Phil, absolutely determined to be a boy, and to be accepted by them. He saw now that there was nothing of the boy in her any longer. Sixteen now, she stood beside her mother, smiling quietly in a pretty emerald silk dress that accentuated a tiny waist and matched her bright green eyes exactly.

How many times had he looked into that face, the pale dusting of freckles across her nose and cheeks, the small rosebud mouth? Here she was at the crest of womanhood, changed entirely, her hair darker, her body more shapely, but he hugged her as if she were still the child he had left behind.

"Hello, Cump," she said quietly.

They looked at one another oddly for an instant before he drew her, like the others, into his embrace again. "I almost didn't know you, Ellen! You're practically a grown woman!"

That seemed to please her, and her tentative smile widened. She would be a pretty adult, a fine catch for someone one day. "Thanks, Cump."

"Well, do let's get ourselves inside," Maria said in her warm, singsong soprano tone. "It's beastly hot already. And you must be exhausted and famished after your long journey!"

"I don't know which I feel more." William found himself smiling.

"That surely was the right answer for mother," Phil whispered into his ear. "She's had the servants baking and cooking for your arrival for nearly a week!"

They all laughed and moved up the neatly painted white steps, then into the house that was so familiar and comforting to him, with its carpeted foyer, two chandeliers, watered silk wallpaper, fragrance of flowers, and family portraits lining the walls.

I am home at last, he told himself as they moved into Maria's favorite parlor, with the ornamental plaster cornices and silk brocade wall coverings, dark teakwood furnishings and European wall tapestries, which fronted Main Street. *Home. The place where I am meant to be.* But even with so great a welcome as this, William knew what they said was true, that you really never could go home again.

Her heart was beating so wildly, thumping against her breast, that Ellen could barely breathe. And yet she was certain he had not even noticed her. Not really, beyond the kind, brotherly acknowledgment he had given her. She watched him now, in his dashing uniform, sitting on mother's blue cushioned divan, that last pale bit of afternoon light streaking across his square face. He had a glass of lemonade in one hand and a fresh slice of gingerbread in the other as everyone sat gathered around him. She thought Cump seemed overwhelmed. Tenderness for him welled up inside her. It must be different to be back here after two years.

It made her wonder what it was like to grow into a man, what trials they faced while girls worried about their hair, the latest dress fabric from Paris, and playing the piano well enough one day to please them. And she even wondered if he had yet known a woman. She was not supposed to think like that. Even contemplating such a question was a sin, Mama said. Father O'Beirne would have her saying Hail Marys for the better part of an hour if she confessed it. But she did not care. Since last summer, when she had discovered the whole truth about love between men and women, it had been difficult to stop imagining herself being kissed passionately by Cump, lying with him and, yes, even more.

There was nothing she would not do for him, or with him. Nothing. Ellen realized that at the root of her emotions was a childhood fancy for a boy who had always been slightly beyond her reach. But knowing that changed nothing. Looking at him now, while everyone else pummeled him with questions about life at West Point, Ellen felt as if she were balancing on the precipice of a steep ledge, and she was about to hurl herself, knowingly, into a black and endless void. Since, to love Cump, *really* love him, when she knew she was like a sister to him, would bring her the same uncertain end.

He had never given her any encouragement or the slightest reason to hope that he would ever love her. But Ellen could not help what she felt. Nor did she wish to do so. In part, it was the look of him. The way his mystical eyes crinkled at the corners, the devilish grin, and, mostly, that penetrating expression that made her feel she couldn't breathe when it fell upon her.

"Ellen? Ellen, darling, what on earth is it? Are you all right?" Maria asked, and everyone was looking at her, suddenly, even Cump. "You're not coming down with something, are you, dear?"

She was flustered by everyone's sudden attention.

"Really, mother." Phil laughed. "It's just old puppy love rearing up again, quite as expected."

Ellen felt the white heat rush into her cheeks before she drew another breath. It entirely took her over. Everyone in the family knew he had meant Cump. Except, perhaps, Cump himself.

"*Really*, Philomen!" His mother gasped. "You can be so entirely thick!"

Ellen felt herself flush red; then the tears began rushing down her cheeks and she had no way to stop them. "Excuse me," she said softly, her voice cracking as she dashed from the parlor, the emerald bell skirt flying out behind her.

"If your father were here, Phil, I do believe he would box that very thick head of yours himself!" Maria cried, her kind face changed now into a disapproving scowl.

"Really, Mother, you know perfectly well, I haven't been a whipable child for ages."

"Then what a disappointment you are to us both that you continue behaving as one!"

"Where is the senator?" William asked, feeling an odd, familial tension that had always excluded him. He knew there had been expectation on the father's part before he'd gone to West Point. But he had always hoped Ellen would find someone more suitable on her own in his absence. He was surprised now to consider that she might feel something for him beyond an ordinary girlhood infatuation.

But Maria's voice stilled the thought and took him from the question. "He's gone back to Washington, dear," she said proudly. "At the request of Mr. Harrison, who we all pray shall win the presidency this next time around."

"Father is involved deeply in the campaign, and if William Henry Harrison wins in '40, he's been promised a place in the administration."

"That's wonderful," William said, yet his thoughts now were scattered.

He could still see her, small and waiflike, running after him and Phil, yet mightily determined to keep up. Then her ginger-brown hair had been bound by pigtails, blowing out behind her, and her small face glowed red with fury. Ellen could not have been much older than seven or eight. But even then, she had been determined to get what she wanted in life. He had never really considered that, or its implications, until now.

"I'm coming with you!" she had shouted after them, their day of fishing and smoking a stolen cigar all but ruined by a little girl who meant to meet her goal unconditionally.

"Go home, Ellie!" Phil had declared over his shoulder, picking up his pace.

"I will not! I *like* fishing!"

"So do we! Alone!"

"You are a truly horrid brother!" she had cried out at him in her high, tinny voice.

"Then stay home and sew, and you won't be faced with me!"

William remembered marveling at how she kept up with them after that as they dashed around the corner and then took a purposeful detour through the cemetery, the haunted place that most everyone feared, even in the daylight hours. This one time, however, she did not fall away but stayed close behind them, which drew secret admiration from William.

"Cump!" she had finally called out in a panting, defeated tone. "Please . . . wait for *me!*"

He had not thought of that incident for years, the expression on her child's face as she finally stopped running. He had caught one last view of her as he turned back around. She had looked shocked. In spite of it all, she had really believed William would not abandon her. And yet, of course, he had. How many other moments had there been like that since then? How many signs had he not seen? *Puppy love, quite as expected;* Phil had said, as though it had gone on forever. And perhaps, thinking back now, it had.

But what was he to do about it, if anything at all? He loved her, yes, but as one loved a sister. He did not return any sort of feeling beyond that. His heart was bound up too completely by Cecelia, and the loss of her.

Even so, if there had been no Cecelia, this was Ellen—his family. His dear sister—well, nearly his sister. And there seemed something sinful about even contemplating what everyone else apparently already knew she desired.

Later, after supper, he and Phil stood on the front porch, looking out across the street and beyond, at the way the sunset faded from gold to fiery orange over the thick copse of evergreen trees. William was still in his uniform. Still awkward. And now, weary.

"Why didn't you ever tell me about Ellen?" he asked, without taking his gaze from the familiar surroundings.

"I *assumed* you knew. For heaven's sake, man, she's felt like that forever!"

"Your father talked about us a long time ago. . . . But that she—no, I didn't know."

"I see that now."

William drew breath. The sweet, familiar night music of the crickets began. "She's grown up a great deal since you've been gone. Gotten—I don't know—actually rather pretty, I suppose you could say."

The words of confession were on his tongue. He and Phil had always told one another their most private thoughts. But suddenly, when he considered speaking of her, he felt Cecelia a more sacred thing. Not a part of this place or these people. And to share her felt, somehow, as if it would be dishonoring that. He would probably never know why she had done it. Why she had broken her promise, betrayed him. And he was not quite certain yet that he could live with it.

"It's difficult for me to think of her in that way, Phil," he finally hedged. "To me, Ellen is still that little girl with the pigtails, always running after us."

Phil laughed. It was a friendly sound that brought William back more firmly to this world—the one that held assurance and familiarity with the Ewings. "I haven't thought of that for a long time." Phil leaned forward on the porch banister, the hair on his forehead ruffled in the balmy evening breeze. "So, do you feel nothing for her, then?"

"Of course I do. I'm very fond of her."

"Beyond that, is there nothing?"

William met his eyes squarely. "I know what you all hoped, but not like *you* mean."

"Well," he sighed. "She is in love with you, that's for sure. You know, Cump, Ellen's not like other girls. There's something fragile about her. Some man—a stranger, could really take advantage of that. And, I confess, as her older brother, with Father away so much, I feel responsible for her. And really, no one would ever be more devoted to you than—"

"Stop!" William held up a rigid hand. "I appreciate what you're trying to do for her, and, yes, I knew it before I went away. But I'm just not ready to settle down! I haven't even finished the academy!"

"Of course. I know that. No one would expect any sort of announcement today or tomorrow. And Ellen's young yet. But you should know, Father is still counting on it, even if Mother has her doubts. And if there could be an understanding perhaps, among the family, at least—"

The sudden tension crawled up around them like a heavy blanket, and they stood awkwardly with one another for a time as Phil's enthusiasm trailed off into silence. A moment later, he rethought his direction.

"All right. So you're not ready," he finally declared, acknowledging the hunted expression on William's face. "But at least say you'll think about it when you go back to West Point."

"How could I *not* think about what you've just put before me?" William replied, knowing he could not possibly give any of them what they wanted in this. This was little Ellie, after all. And if that were not enough all by itself, the rich and haunting shadow of Cecelia Stovall would always be there between them.

Part 3

❧

Gone—glimmering through the
dream of things that were.

—LORD BYRON

Chapter Fourteen

MAY 1841

Cecelia had always loved new dresses, yet she would have given anything in the world not to be wearing this one. Gaunt-faced and hollow-eyed, she looked in disbelief at her own reflection in the long, oval mahogany mirror in her dressing room. She could hear the church bells of Saint Michael's begin to toll. Today her eldest sister Maria's daughter was being buried. She was the youngest victim so far of the yellow fever epidemic that had devastated Augusta.

The new black silk mourning dress with a mantle of white crepe showed Cecelia's nearly skeletal shape. The weight she had lost over the past two despondent years was impossible to hide. When the seamstress could no longer alter her stepdaughter's dresses, Anne was forced to sell a Sèvres vase of her grandmother's to pay for new mourning dresses—for both of them. There were enough problems for the family, Pleasant had grumbled, without having to deal with this now, too. But Anne had taken her husband's anger in stride, tried to help the now long-suffering girl in the only way she knew how. Even so, nothing could erase the last five years for Cecelia. Nor could anyone change Augusta's fate, and the worst did not appear to be over yet.

Tears welled in Cecelia's eyes as she thought of the last four sleepless days and nights, the family taking turns at a vigil, praying for a miracle to save the bright and pretty little girl. Her death now was like a punctuation mark on a horrid six years for Augusta and for the Stovall family.

The slowdown in her family's cotton merchant business had been a signal of something far worse, they now knew. The Stovalls' great prosperity of the early thirties, when Pleasant Stovall had so firmly established them in Augusta society, was followed by the nationwide depression and a succession of local misfortunes, including his own.

Three years ago came a devastating crop failure, notably cotton, followed by a massive flood the following spring. Business after business closed their doors. Cotton warehouses stood vacant, and many of Augusta's wealthy families lost their fortunes altogether. Pleasant Stovall had, until recently, hung on to part of his, due only to the largesse of a man Cecelia had not seen in over a year.

Charles Shelman had given Pleasant an initial cash infusion five years ago, during his original negotiations for Cecelia's hand. To keep his suit for the uninterested girl alive, and to vanquish his rival Richard Gardner he had twice since lent Pleasant good sums of money to keep his business afloat—with the understanding that one day he would indeed take Cecelia Stovall as his wife.

But today, a gray and humid day, that threat seemed very far away to Cecelia as she moved from the mirror across the small shaded room to let Setty Mae help her with her shoes. The thickly set black woman, murmuring her Bible quotations like music, had been moved up from the kitchen house and into the main house to replace Cretia. Everyone knew Anne herself had selected the old woman, determined to avoid the same impropriety as before, and Pleasant had not argued the point.

Since Marcellus's marriage, Cecelia had seen her childhood friend on three occasions, always when she went up to Rome to visit her brother and his wife. Today was the first day in four years that Cretia would be back home in Augusta. Even knowing what temptation it might rekindle, Anne had arranged it, gently telling her that she hoped the comfort of an old friend could rock her from the downward spiral that had held her since her return from England.

Back in her bedroom, Cecelia sat on the corner of her bed, hugging a goose down pillow to her chest as Setty Mae heated the hair tongs.

"Oh now, you ain't got no mo' time fo' dat, chil'!" Setty Mae huffed as she came heavily toward her with the hair tongs, her wide brown face possessing a kindness Cecelia knew their family did not deserve. "Everyone, dey is downstairs waitin' on you."

Too much sadness. She did not want to attend a child's funeral, and yet she must. It was how things were done. And she had been going through the motions for such a long time. She drew in a breath finally and let Setty Mae heat the remaining sections of her hair into tight ringlets as the pillowy gray clouds just beyond her window moved across the sun and darkened the room. She could hear her own heart beating in the silence as a small knock sounded at the door. It took Cecelia a moment to realize it was Cretia who came to her at the bed and held her tightly.

"Oh, it's so good to see you! Tell me, old friend; how is it over in Rome? And how is my brother's wife treatin' you?"

"It's like any other place. I have a duty to white folks there."

"But surely there is freedom there of a sort you did not have here."

For a moment, Cretia was distracted from her shock at seeing the change in Cecelia. "That much is true."

"And do Marcellus and Sarah still treat you well?"

"Leave us, Setty Mae, will you?" Cretia asked. "Miss Cecelia gon' be downstairs direc'ly."

The older woman, whose face in this light, Cecelia thought suddenly, looked strangely like Cretia's, gathered up the heating tongs and silently complied. She padded slowly out of the room, closing the door behind herself. When they were alone, Cretia's expression changed to one of great concern.

"What's been happenin' here? You're thin as a rail! Are you sick?"

Cecelia could not look at her. "I'm fine. Thin perhaps, but healthy as a horse."

"You don't look like any Stovall horse I've ever seen. You've seen the doctor?"

Cecelia moved to the window, her black dress swishing in the strained silence. She gazed out at the changing sky. The gray clouds were dark now, and there would be rain. Fitting, she thought, for a grim day like today.

"I'm not in need of any doctor."

"Then what *do* you need?"

"The one thing I am not meant to have is the only thing I have ever *needed*."

Dark fingers splayed out across her mouth, once again. "That Yankee still?"

"It always will be."

"But it's been near to four years! I thought sho'ly—"

"I have lived every day of that time missin' William, and I'm truly tortured by the question of what happened to him, what changed his mind after—"

The silence—things unsaid, things not fully known—settled between them. "I had no idea it would last so long."

Cretia's last words were murmured, yet still Cecelia heard them. She turned around, her face so gaunt and pale in the shadowy light. "What did you say?"

Cretia stammered, stopping herself from the thing she could never reveal. "I only meant, what ever happened to that nice Mr. Gardner who was callin' on you fo' a time?"

"Father said he wasn't suitable, which meant he wasn't rich enough."

"I had no idea," Cretia said thinly, shutting her eyes.

And she hadn't. The ramifications of a desperate action, one moment in time, lived on with disarming power. In Rome with Marcellus and his wife, she tried not to think of what she had done. It would pass, she had told herself. *Cecelia has a lifetime to forget that one summer. That one Northern boy.*

"I know I shouldn't ask," Cecelia whispered, desperation washing out from her in a flood of words. "But you are the only one I *can* ask!"

"Oh, Miss Cecelia . . ."

She moved away from the window and crossed the room. Her face etched with desperation. "Send one mo' letter fo' me. I'll never ask again. I promise. If he doesn't answer this time, I *will* move on with my life. *Please*. Do this one final thing for me."

Cecelia's words, the pure desolation in her expression, rocked Cretia and stirred the guilt, so deeply buried beneath old excuses. "You know I'd do anything fo' you, Cecelia," Cretia finally said.

After the family had gone to the funeral, the old house was quiet as the servants took a rare break to eat and rest. Josiah was alone in the warming kitchen when his daughter came to him with the letter. The room was warm with two low-burning fires and small windows.

"I want you to get Theo to try again to send a letter fo' me," Cretia told him.

Very quickly his pepper gray brows merged as he frowned. "Chil'," he snorted, and then spoke on in a rusty tenor. "*Together* we ain't got 'nough luck fo' a ting like dat to work. And I is *too* old, and *too* tired, to be sold off back to da fields."

Cretia shook her head, then looked back at him. "I ain't never in all my life asked fo' anythin' from you. Not protection from danger, not affection . . . and I sho' ain't never asked fo' any favors!"

"Den you bes' not be doin' it now. Especially when it ain't even fo' yourself."

She squared her shoulders. Her lips were pursed. "Well, I *am* doin' it now, ol' man. You owe me dat much! And who's to say *who* I'm doin' it fo'?"

He looked up at her, his sad, lined face etched with so much more than age. His face bore trauma even she would never fully understand. "You is in dis fair deep, ain't you?"

"Deep as you can get," Cretia answered.

"She gon' hate you one day."

"I expect so."

He glanced at the letter, rolling it around in his callused hands. "How she knows where to send it? It been four years time since she be in New York."

"She's sendin' it to da family who cared fo' Mr. Sherman as a boy and askin' dem to send it along. Ain't no reason *dat* family should stand in dey way like dis one done." Her old dialect was coming through again.

He shook his head and looked away from her. "I don't know 'bout dis, Lucretia girl. I don't feel good 'bout it fo' *you*."

She leaned across the narrow table used for arranging meals on trays to take upstairs to the master and his family. Here, in the kitchen, racial lines were never crossed. "It's good now with Mr. Marcellus and his wife. Ain't no harm gon' come to me no mo'. And I owe Miss Cecelia fo' what I done to her." She took Josiah's hand.

"Seem to me, da price you owe is powerful high."

"Only if she finds out what I done in da first place. With da good Lawd on my side, she never will."

A look of incredulity spiked his tired, raisin-dark eyes. "You thinks da good Lawd is *ever* on da side of slave folk, Cretia girl?" He shook his head again and gave a little huff, but the sound was dry and bitter.

"I know—" she keened, squeezing his hand more tightly. It was the first burst of connection she had felt with him in a very long time.

"When you look at what happens to us," he went on with a shuddering conviction. "Seem to me, dat ain't 'tall likely. The good Lawd watched my back breakin' all dose years, under de burnin' sun. Den He done let da massa have his way wit de only chil' He give me. No, Lucretia. I don't 'spect, where ever He is, *that* Lawd care much at all 'bout us folk who He done put in colored skin."

"Daddy, what if there weren't any mo' slavery one day?"

"That's fool talk! Talk to make you crazy! Make you *hope*!"

"You know, Mr. Marcellus was tellin' his wife they is folks up North talkin' 'bout that very thing! Makin' us all free Negroes! He says they could come to war over it!"

This time he did not answer her. He only sat staring blankly across the table before he said, "Dat ain't never gon' happen in my lifetime, chil'. Too many white folks down South here wants to keep tings jes' as dey is."

"And Mr. Marcellus says there are just as many Northern folk who want to fight against it!"

Josiah paused for a moment, ran his thumb over her hand in a way she did not remember him ever doing. Her heart swelled with love for him—for the man she wanted him to be, but that he never could, for the tenderness of a mere touch.

"Sweet Lucretia chil' . . . ," he sighed. His eyes were dark orbs of bitter intensity as he looked deeply at her now. "Don't you go pinnin' yo' hopes on a ting dat'll sho'ly never be! *Dis* is our life! Good as it gets. And fo' an old man like me, it's *got* to be good 'nough."

"Well it ain't good enough fo' *me*!" She bolted back to her feet, a spark of pride in her that those early backbreaking years in the fields had snuffed out in him. He was glad for her—and frightened at the same time. "I want mo'. I *want* hope!"

"Oh, dey is a world of hurt in *dat* word," he softly warned.

"Maybe so. But I can't give it up. Least not yet."

A small, injured expression worked up the corners of his mouth into something very near a cautious smile, just before it faded back into the expressionless face he normally kept. "Jes' you be careful of yo' dreams, chil'. Dat dey don't end up destroyin' da rest of yo' life while you is chasin' after dem."

It was real advice, she thought with a jolt of surprise. Like any father might offer. It was the first time in her life she had shared a moment like this, a family moment. But a real family would have included a mother that hadn't been sold away.

So many times through the years, she had wanted to ask Cecelia to find out who had bought her mother. Cretia had longed to write to her mother—but it was rare for slaves to be able to read, even if she had. Thanks to Cecelia, Cretia was the exception. Who would read a letter to her mother, even if she did send it? And how angry might that person be for the imposition? So she had never asked. But that had not diminished the longing.

"I hope, wherever she is, they are good to her," she softly said. "And I hope one day I see her again . . . I hope dat most of all."

He knew who she meant. And he seemed undone by it. Though he made no sound, Cretia saw tears stream down her father's leathery face. "Oh, Lawd. I is sorry, chil'," he said haltingly. "Fo' so many tings."

After the funeral, Cecelia stood in the crowded parlor in her black dress, amid all the other black dresses, dark suits, and a sea of somber faces. Guests and family spoke in low tones, creating a dismal hum. She watched Georgie across the room, almost eleven now, and extraordinarily tall for his age. No longer was he the little boy she had tended like her own child. She had never known a boy who wanted to grow up more desperately. He despised childhood and its limitations. He wanted to be a soldier, he always said. Fight in some exotic foreign war for a wonderfully just cause. She had always felt a bad omen in that. But she could never bear to examine her fears for the future.

Then she saw someone else across the room, talking to Father, and all other thoughts vanished. It was Charles Shelman, of all people, at a family funeral. Cecelia felt a swell of anger rise up. She was rid of that ineffectual Richard Gardner. But Charles always seemed to be turning up, like a bad penny, inflicting himself on the family with that annoying air of expectation.

Certainly the money he had given father bestowed a certain level of entitlement upon him, she knew. Nothing in the world, not even a loan, came without a price to be paid, and Cecelia was quite certain that price—even after all this time—was still her. She wrinkled her nose at that thought and turned away. He was not a bad man, nor disagreeable particularly, nor ugly. But he was not William Sherman.

Perhaps when enough time had passed for William to receive her latest letter she might finally extricate her heart. Even now, she recalled each word of her missive as if she had only just written it, and remembered, too, the stab of longing that assailed her as she committed each to the formal slip of white vellum.

She knew that Cretia had seen to its mailing. Now if the fates would see that the letter got to William, she believed that he would finally come for her. The only thing in the world that had kept them apart until now was her family. And perhaps enough time had passed that neither Father nor Marcellus would think to be vigilant. So now she was of an age to take a stroll in the park each day to be available to a messenger, or a message. In the company of a servant, of course.

Charles stood across the room near the fireplace hearth beside Pleasant Stovall, both of them watching Cecelia. She stood alone near the window, gazing out. She must be deeply affected by her niece's death, Charles thought, his genuine concern for her growing at the idea

In the beginning, he had thought it an advantageous match. Cecelia was an exotic sort of beauty and Stovall was an influential cotton merchant who would only increase his wealth if their two families merged. But very quickly after meeting her, it had become something more. Cecelia was unique, beautiful, fiery, and, most important to him, not quite attainable. It was that quality most of all, the challenge in it, that had first drawn him.

Always young ladies had clambered for him. They had come to him, laughed a little too quickly at his jokes, made themselves available because he was a wealthy man. Their hopeful smiles had left him cold, in spite of what he might well have gained from an alliance with a number of their families. Then in London to get away from all of it, he had met Cecelia.

It sounded foolish, to say that meeting her had changed his life. He was a man now of a certain age, never married, never involved in any serious *affaire de coeur*. And yet here she was, making him feel like a boy. Unsure. Foolish. And even a little desperate to have her. So desperate for that promise, in fact, that, over the past four years, he had already given Pleasant Stovall in excess of forty thousand dollars. And no matter what assurances were made, she was not yet his.

He watched her carefully now, delectable in her melancholy. Flawless, blanched skin, small delicate mouth, eyes as round and dark and indecipherable as a doe's. He felt his loins stir. God, how many years must he wait to possess her? To draw her, with his great passion, from that melancholy? Certainly she would be worth whatever length of time it took. But for now, the wait was excruciating.

Marcellus noticed him watching her. "My sister gets more lovely each time I return home," Marcellus observed.

"And each time I visit Augusta," Charles agreed, neither of them acknowledging how thin she had become, or speculating on what might have caused it.

"Tell me. Is my dear sister still managin' to string you along without a promise?"

"Like the handle of a fine silk purse." He smiled.

"Well, don't be too disheartened." Marcellus chuckled. "You have made great progress in her affections. She has told me so herself. And quite recently, as well. Today is simply not a day for displays of that. She was hit quite brutally by our little niece Anna's passin'."

There was no argument to be made against that, Charles knew. The death of a child—while all too horribly frequent these days—was still a devastation. Especially when one had reached the age of seven, as this child apparently had. He had never met the little girl himself, but he knew by Cecelia's face, the pallor and the melancholy there, that she had been special.

As he watched her, a thought came to him, startling him into a dull groan. Charles found himself considering what it would be like to have her grieve for something of theirs—a child, a favored pet, perhaps—after they'd had years and moments to bond their lives the way he still believed they one day would. If only he could remain patient.

"Somethin' wrong?" Pleasant asked as he stood beside his eldest son, anxious to keep the bond alive between them.

"She just seems so sad. If there were only somethin' I could do to help, somethin' that would matter to her."

He silently watched Pleasant's eyes focus on something in the foyer, out beyond the crowded parlor. A very pretty slave girl stood by the door talking in a low tone to the old black houseman. A moment later, the man turned from her and went out the front door, leaving the girl alone to linger awkwardly for a moment, her expression caught on the crowded room, before she moved toward the back flight of stairs and was gone.

"If you gentlemen will excuse me," Pleasant affably said, almost, Charles thought, in response to the girl's disappearance. "I shall leave you both to decipher an appropriate little token to bring the color back to our dear Cecelia's rather pale cheeks."

Marcellus caught his father's arm as he turned. "Father, don't." His tone was harsh and brittle, changed completely from a moment before. His eyes, too, had gone dark and different from what they were.

For a moment, everything stopped. Until, suddenly, Pleasant smiled.

"Why, Marcellus Stovall, I do believe I brought you up better than to use that hostile tone with me. Sho'ly, son." He narrowed his gaze. "It is the emotion of the day, and nothin' any more wholly unsavory than that!"

Pleasant nodded politely to Charles, then moved across the room in the direction the Negro girl had gone. It was only then, in the silence, that he remembered the girl was Cecelia's maid. As he looked back at the stricken expression on Marcellus's smooth-featured face, the pieces came together, and Charles understood.

Good Lord, the old bastard was capable of a good deal more than he had ever guessed. And with a slave! Then he remembered more. Of course. The girl was Cretia. Cecelia had spoken to the Queen of their friendship, and again shortly after the slave had left Augusta to live with Marcellus and his new wife. The girls had grown up together, she had told him, and he remembered his surprise at the thought. It was the moment she had become complex to him. Her bounty, richer because she was not only beautiful and unattainable, he had discovered, but the open kindness of her heart was a powerful draw, as well.

"Is there anythin' I can do?"

"It's a family matter, Charles. But thank you."

He rocked back on his heels, carefully choosing his words. "Since I hope to be part of yo' family before too long now, and I recall how fond yo' sister was of that Negro, the matter concerns me."

"I didn't mean to offend you, Charles. You know how fond we all are of you. It's just not somethin' a gentleman speaks of."

"How much?"

Marcellus lifted a brow. "How much what?"

"The Negro *is* yours now, isn't she?"

"Oh, Cretia's not fo' sale. She was born to our family."

"*Everythin'* in life has a price, my friend. The game is merely to find it."

Marcellus's face began to redden. He was uncomfortable. "I couldn't sell her, Charles. I am—" He stopped, then began again. "It's complicated. But what I *can* say is that I am honor-bound to protect her."

Charles glanced back at the foyer. "Seems to me she isn't all that protected when she comes back here," he dryly observed. There was a small silence.

"All right, then." Marcellus exhaled a breath and looked directly at Charles. "Ten thousand dollars."

Charles audibly gulped. "Fo' a slave?"

"Fo' the precise chit to secure my sister's hand."

"Extortion?"

"Business."

"Out of the question!" Charles scoffed.

"Then, in all likelihood, so shall Cecelia be."

"Good God, no woman is worth that!"

"Cecelia may well be worth it to someone else."

Charles glanced around the room, trying to get his bearings. His heart was racing. He was feeling panicked by this unexpected volleying, and might well lose it all if he lost control now.

"You know what great sums of good faith money I have already given to yo' father these past four years!"

"I do indeed. And you're quite right, you have been generous to a fault. But this has nothin' to do with that. I am makin' my own deal with you." Marcellus leaned in more closely as several of the guests, having sensed the intensity between them, had begun to turn around. "No matter what you have given my father, he has not managed to deliver you a wife. I believe you can see how this will."

Charles had regained his composure through sheer determination. "And where will you be, Marcellus, if you push this golden Savannah goose before you just a touch too far?"

"Poorer, certainly. But happily married still. Which is a sight mo', I suspect, than I shall be able to say about *you*."

Game, set, and match.

Charles glared at him. "Ten thousand dollars, and not a single cent more. And for that, I expect you to allow me to reveal the terms to yo' sister, in my own time and my own way."

Now it was Marcellus who was thrown off his game. "My wife is certain to tell Cecelia once she knows."

"Then I shall remain sadder certainly, but richer still," he slyly parroted. "Which is a sight more, I suspect, than I shall be able to say 'bout *you*!"

The surprise spiking Marcellus's eyes was a kind of balm on Charles's dented pride. He was paying too much—taking this all too far for a woman. All he could hope now was that Cecelia Stovall would one day soon prove worth the effort. Charles was careful not to let any of the triumph he felt show. Knowing he had, at last, found the way to Cecelia's heart would be more than enough. Especially once she finally agreed to become his wife.

Chapter Fifteen

✢

SPRING 1841

"Mama! It's a letter for Cump! And the handwriting looks like a girl's!"

Charles Ewing slammed the heavy front door and bounded into the foyer of the home on Main Street in his gray, corded trousers, camel-colored vest, and ivory shirt. Ellen cut the boy off at the bottom of the staircase with her pale hand extended.

"Mail, if you please," she commanded with a dry and well-feigned indifference. Ellen held out her hand to her ten-year-old brother, cutting him off at the third step. As the daughter with four younger siblings, she had developed an instinct, now that her own mother was away in Washington so often with Father, who was now President William Henry Harrison's Secretary of the Treasury. This afternoon, in fact, Mama was preparing once again to return.

When her brother hesitated and stood on the step looking at her, Ellen scowled and snatched it from his hand. "Mama is upstairs packing, and she will thank you not to disturb her with minutiae!"

"Then I'll at least go tell her the mail has arrived. Maybe she would like to send the letter to Cump herself with a little note of her own or something. We haven't seen him in such a long time."

"No!" Ellen burst out in a sudden tone of alarm. "I mean, Mama is late as it is, and if she misses that last coach out of Lancaster, she will never make the train connections she needs to for Father's party!"

That seemed to register with the apple-cheeked boy, who studied her for a moment before his expression softened into one of full compliance. Ellen responded with a sedate smile.

"Thank you. Now get yourself back outside and play. You don't belong indoors on a splendid morning like this."

"Well, you're in here," He challenged her suddenly, loitering as he focused on her tight grip of the little stack of letters.

"*I* am a girl of marriageable age, Charlie, and you know perfectly well that we are not meant to tousle about like boys for all the world to see!"

Angry at her tone, he glared at her. "And I'll bet the someone you would like to marry is Cump!"

"Don't be ridiculous!" She did her best to scoff. "Cump is like a brother to me. And to you, for that matter."

"You're still sweet on him," little Charles taunted.

"Oh, for heaven's sake! I've had quite enough of your foolishness for one morning!" she swatted at him. "Now, get back outside and look after Marian, before I *do* call Mama down from her packing and she takes a switch to you herself for the interruption!"

They were both out in the carpeted foyer as the last word, so grandly delivered, leapt from her lips and he disappeared, like a shot, back outside. Ellen smiled to herself, watching him through the little panel of etched glass beside the door.

"Would you like *me* to take the mail up to Mrs. Ewing?" a young maid asked.

"That won't be necessary," Ellen tightly replied.

As she walked alone back into the parlor, whose elegant furniture and heavy velvet draperies pooled on the plank floor, she saw her older sister, Angela. She sat in a high-backed chair, covered in blue velvet, looking up at her with a judgmental glare. "He is going to find out if you keep it from him, you know."

"Only if *you* tell him!"

"What if it's important?"

"Then *I* will see that he gets it."

Angela lifted a single brow. Ellen's sister was a pretty girl, plump and sweet-faced, with a kind of maturity Ellen was not yet fortunate enough to possess. "And if it's the ministrations of some love-struck girl left behind, you shall, I suspect, be only too glad to dispose of the missive for him?"

"There is no one in this world," she said with calm confidence as if she were speaking to a child, "who will ever love Cump more."

"You cannot possibly know that!"

"I do! Yes, I absolutely do!" What she felt for William Sherman went beyond love. It was history and years, and understanding of the childhood he had, the disappointment he had known, and how those things had shaped him.

"I still think you should give the letter to Mother. Let her decide."

"And if I don't?"

Beyond the parlor walls, they could both hear the clatter and footsteps of two of the male servants and their mother, with all of the luggage, descending the twisted flight of mahogany stairs.

"Then the consequences of that will be yours to bear."

In the end, Ellen had not been able to help herself. The curiosity had been too great. And, she thought, it was bad enough that Cump had scarcely even noticed her yet. She would never win in doing battle with an unknown rival. Better, she decided, to know her competition, to be able to vanquish it speedily.

Ellen sat alone in her bedroom overlooking High Street. The door was closed and locked, and her mother had left for Washington. A soft breeze was blowing maple branches against her window in a soft, brushing rhythm, and the sky was full of billowing white clouds. She had gazed at the small ecru envelope for a long time, studied the thin, sloping hand with which Cump's name had been written. She had even pressed it to her nose half a dozen times to see if a hint of scent from whoever had sent it still remained. Because she knew in her heart it had been sent by a woman—a Southern woman.

Yet for the better part of the day, it had remained unopened. Curiosity did battle with her fear, because once she opened it and read the words inside, there would be no turning back.

She touched it, pressed it to her nose again, then held it up to the light, tempting herself until she could bear it no longer. Then, alone with only Cump's letter and her conscience, Ellen broke the seal with her thumb, and opened a message never meant for her to see.

Tears pooled in her eyes and she made a soft, pained sound, from the first words. "My darling William . . ." This stranger, this Southern woman, was no casual acquaintance. They knew one another, well. They had expressed feelings for one another. As her tears fell, Ellen brushed them away with the back of her hand, determined to read every word. She must know what she was up against. She must know everything, in order to win.

My darling William,

Even after this very long four years without a word from you since our cruel parting at my brother's hands, I cannot help but believe with all my heart, a heart that still bears the greatest commitment to you, that you have tried to see me, or write to me, if only to tell me that you no longer bear the sentiment you once so strongly expressed. It would not be in your nature simply to break a promise.

To that end, and that which has kept me strong, all this time, I know well of my family's commitment against you, and so I am driven now to find my own way to a resolution.

I know that you have graduated from West Point a year ago now. Even not knowing it as fact, I am as certain of it, and of you, as if I had been there at your commencement myself, because I still believe in you. I know not where you are stationed, nor how difficult it will be to come to me once you read this. But it seems the only way to bypass the great forces against us. From now until summer, when we move to our home up in Summerville, I will be at May Park each day from two until three o'clock in the afternoon. If you cannot come to me yourself, please send someone with a message, for I crave nothing in the world so much as a resolution of the things we expressed, the promises we made.

With my love to you forever,

Cecelia

"*The things we expressed . . . the promises we made . . .*" Ellen's heart wrenched in shock. There was an expectation that Cump might actually come all the way to Augusta to see this . . . this—? Ellen glanced down at the signature as her own tears spotted the elegant velum. *Cecelia.* Her name was Cecelia.

The lump that had formed in her throat grew now, nearly choking her. This woman loved Cump. She had signed the letter in a way that lovers do and, at some point, he had returned that love. Ellen sank back onto her heels, hearing only the pained beating of her own heart. Right now it felt fragile and broken— so wounded by this shock. But she was determined not to be undone by it now. She had waited too many years for Cump. He had been hers first.

And, by God, I will not give him up!

She went to the candle at her bedside as if in a trance and lit it. She took the let- ter and the candle to the fireplace hearth. Holding both inside the soot-blackened hearth, she lit the tip of the letter to the flame and watched it quickly curl to black.

A moment later, the flame had hungrily taken possession of the paper, and Ellen let it slip from her fingers, a flaming ball, onto the pile of ashes. Her tears dried with resolve as she watched the paper burn. There was solace, she thought, in the destruction of this letter. Besides, it never would have been right—Cump and a Southerner—those folks with their oddly formal ways. And their strange beliefs about colored people. Southerners determined to possess other human beings as if they were no better than cattle. It could not last . . . nor could a romance between Cump and one of them.

In truth, she was doing Cump a favor. He was not like that, and he never could be. He was a decent, caring man whose allegiance to family, and to the Ewings, defined him. Mother would see one day how perfect they were for one another, how great and powerful and wealthy he one day would be. She glanced back at the pile of harmless ash in the hearth and sighed with relief. Yes, one day everyone would believe in a match between them. Everyone, including and especially William Tecumseh Sherman.

No matter what he tried, he simply could not get it right. William tossed his pen down, wrapped a hand behind his neck, rubbed, and then groaned in frus- tration. His gaze moved again to the window above his desk and the vista beyond. Why was it that the act of sketching always brought him back to Cecelia? He hated that. He hated the longing. And he hated thoughts of her when she was so far gone from his life.

Picolata, Florida, was a world away from West Point, and the changes in his life had come so quickly. A cadet one moment, and a lieutenant in the Third Artillery the next. Five years ago still felt like yesterday. It was still too wrenchingly easy to remember moments, feelings, as though they were not well buried in the past with a mountain of circumstance atop them.

It was easy to remember because nothing like it, or Cecelia, had ever come again.

He had accepted this commission to a desolate, uninspired locale, like so many other things, against his better judgment, but out of duty and in recompense for his education. For West Point. And to live up to the faith of those who had helped him along the way.

William looked back at the sheet of paper that lay before him, feeling his stomach constrict. The sensation was like a flower too long without water or the nourishing effects of sunshine. But this was his life, his duty. He had meant to sketch the vista from his desk, the seacoast near Saint Augustine. But like a phantom, her face was before him again, and the haunting, passionately dark eyes, refused to let go of him.

He crumpled the sketch into a tight ball and tossed it across the room over his shoulder, cursing his own weakness. *She is gone, damn you! Another man's wife. And she can't come back to me!*

Life in Picolata was lonely and disconcerting. It made him miss his connections with those he cared for. That must be the problem. It had been too long after graduation; the cadets, his friends, had scattered like birds. He had been stationed first at Fort Pierce, on the east coast of Florida. Bragg, Ord, and Van Vliet had been posted nearby. After a year, William had received a promotion to first lieutenant, a move that usually took five years to attain.

With the promotion, his post was changed to Picolata, Florida, where the mosquitoes he swatted seemed as large as sparrows, and he spent the bulk of his time perspiring and trying to remember the fanciful pages of *The Spanish Cavalier*, the sweepingly romantic novel that had driven him toward the daring life of importance he long had hoped to find as a soldier.

Phil wrote to him often of Senator Ewing's career. After President Harrison's untimely death a month into his presidency, Phil's father had resigned his cabinet post, but he remained deeply entrenched in politics. William also heard from his brother, John Sherman, an attorney now, who had begun to have political aspirations of his own. And, of course, he heard from Ellen. In his years since leaving Ohio, it was she, now a grown woman of nineteen, who had been his most consistent connection to the past. She wrote every week, telling him about everyday life in Lancaster. Last year, for his birthday, she had even sent him a picture of herself. Since he had not been home for nearly three years, once again, he marveled at her appearance: the little pixie had matured, with darker, fuller hair and soft, kind eyes. The woman before him was difficult to reconcile with the little mousy-maned girl and her skinned knees and elbows or the flustered sixteen-year-old. But she was still like a sister to him. A touchstone with the past, that of a simpler time before he had known love and then lost it.

After the mysteriously empty envelope posted in London, William had never heard from Cecelia again. In the beginning, during those last West Point years, he had made many excuses for her. Married to Richard Gardner or not, he had believed that she was honor-bound to send him at least one letter of parting to explain. But there had been nothing. No letter, no word, no message. Now she was a wife. Perhaps a mother, as well. And the promises between them had long ago lapsed.

Here, in this godforsaken place, there was refuge only in his drawing. It was the one thing that had kept him from remembering lost causes and vanished hopes. He glanced at the landscape out the window again, looking keenly at what he had *meant* to sketch. Why did Cecelia still haunt him so?

William shivered and put away his small, leather-covered sketchbook.

"Lieutenant Sherman, sir?"

The call brought him out of his thoughts, and William swiveled around, still seated in his desk chair. "What is it?"

"A message for you, sir."

Would it ever stop? A gut-wrenching knot of hope still seized him by the throat every damn time someone sent him anything. And anguish always followed. Bitterly, William pressed the hope away. "Who sent it, Sergeant?"

"It's from Washington, sir. From former Secretary Ewing."

In spite of President Harrison's premature death, Phil's father was still a very powerful man in Washington circles. Everyone here in Picolata had ribbed Sherman endlessly, saying that his first lieutenancy promotion had come out of family loyalty, not by any merit of Sherman's own.

"That'll be all," he said flatly, taking the letter and then dismissing his aide with a wave of his hand.

The sun came in on a warm breeze, and William sank into his chair to read.

Dear William,

Here in Washington I have heard endlessly from our Ellen at home that you are quite miserable and unchallenged there in Florida. Your own letters show nothing of the kind. But then perhaps that is due to your fine and honorable instinct to finish what you have begun and not to complain about it. I had hoped, my boy, that the first lieutenancy would have been enough of a challenge to get the military out of your system, now that you are suitably trained and educated. I hear from Ellen that such is not the case. It is therefore, with pleasure, that I am writing to inform you that you are being transferred, effective immediately, to Fort Moultrie on Sullivan's Island near Charleston, South Carolina. Your rank will ensure you a multitude of duties and, I hope, a challenging stay that one day soon will bring you to your senses, and back to the family in Ohio.

You owe a debt of gratitude in this, not to me, but to our dear Ellen. I trust the form of payment of that debt shall be made apparent to the family, forthwith.

A father's love to you,

Thomas Ewing

William walked out of his office and into the humid, dusty daylight of a Picolata afternoon. Imagine it, he thought. Little Ellen had done this for him. He was going to the South—into Cecelia Stovall's world. He was surprised and even a little pleased with Ellen's ingenuity, and a tired smile tugged at the corners of his mouth. Was there something there, after all, to help him heal the pain of the past? Something he had refused to see? In the years since Cecelia, there had been more than a few dark-eyed Picolata beauties who had caught his attention, and with whom he had come to understand the power of full physical passion. And yet, within that awakening, he had also learned that sex without love was an empty expression, as fulfilling to him as eating a meal or bathing. Images flashed across his mind—things he had done here in Picolata, women he had followed into bed—and he physically cringed. That was certainly not the life he wanted.

But the one he wanted, he could not have.

He thought about Ellen and Cecelia, and how entirely different they were. Ellen, he realized here so far from her, was fiercely devoted to what he wanted. He knew that she would never turn away from a promise made. At least not without an explanation.

William felt an unexpected rush of peace. *Ellen,* he thought. *If it cannot be Cecelia . . . why not Ellen?*

There was only one way to know for certain. He must take a leave and go home to Ohio. He must see Ellen. Spend time with her, not as a childhood friend, but as a man courting a young woman to see if there was a future there. Her mother would not approve. Maria Ewing loved him like a son, but he possessed one grand flaw: he was not a Catholic like the rest of the Ewings, and he had no desire to become one.

Then he thought of Thomas Ewing and the leading nature of his letter. Ellen had always been the senator's favorite child, and whatever she had wanted through the years, he had helped her get. Phil, William's best childhood friend, his confidant, had established his feelings on the matter years ago. But what would Phil think if he knew a part of Cump's heart would always be tied to another woman?

Of course, he was getting ahead of himself. He must see Ellen first. They would need to spend time alone, to explore the possibility of a future together. But above everything else, William would have to discover if he had enough heart left over to make a life with a woman who was not, and never could be, Cecelia.

Chapter Sixteen

MAY 1844

Cecelia sat on a bright green bench in May Park, trying hard to read the newspaper she held open in her hands. This marked her fourth spring of coming here for a few days to wait for William. The headlines that day were of "Oregon Fever" still sweeping the country, and the thousands of pioneer families under President James Polk, still following their dreams out West along the Oregon Trail. While others pursued their dreams, she merely waited.

Every moment, every carriage, the shape of every man coming across the park in silhouette against the noonday sun, brought anticipation, then disappointment. Cecelia despised herself for compulsion to do this, to come here beneath the shade of a venerable old oak tree each afternoon with Setty Mae until the family moved to the relative cool and safety from illness of Summerville.

"He ain't gon' come, you know, dis spring any mo' den da last."

Cecelia glanced over at Setty Mae, startled by her thick voice in this sweltering heat. "Who?"

"Whoever you be waitin' on here every day to lead you away from dis place."

She thought, for an instant, of lying. But Setty Mae was a wise woman, full of a serene kind of insight she had never seen in the other Negroes they

owned. Setty Mae was the epitome of kindness and wisdom, who spoke only
when she had something to say. With Cretia gone for so long, Cecelia needed
someone in whom it was safe to confide. Cecelia felt the familiar tingle of
tears in her eyes at the thought of giving up William and their dream. She
gazed off across the small shaded green park and heaved a shallow sigh. "Oh,
Setty Mae. I do suppose I know it's no use," she said thinly. "I've just wanted
him fo' such a long time. I don't know how to stop."

"You jes' does it, chil'. Like blowin' out a candle. You jes' decides fo' yo'sef
you ain't gon' go on wit hopin' no mo'. And you blows out dat flame. Setty
Mae say dis gone on *long* enough!"

Cecelia put a hand on Setty's knee for a moment and then settled back
against the bench. "It's the lettin' go that's so hard."

Now it was Setty Mae who gazed off across the park and was silent for a
moment. "Well, chil', like da rest of us in dis' ol' worl', you jes' do what da
Lawd calls you to do. It be easier if you got faith."

And as the sage words left the black woman's thick, full lips, Cecelia knew
then with a sudden ache of compassion that Setty Mae had meant that the
losses of family—of children, separated parents, sisters losing brothers,
fathers, mothers, sons . . . her own pain, the losses she had known—went far
beyond the loss of a first young love in a life rich and complete by any other
standard. Suddenly, Cecelia was ashamed. Her cheeks burned with the embarrassment of it. The very fabric of her life and her beliefs had been changed by
one young man in a single summer, already so long ago.

She looked at Setty Mae, who sat proud and strangely regal in a dark, exotic
way. Cecelia found herself wondering if she might not, in a faraway native
country, have been some kind of Negro princess, meant for a life of greatness
she would never know.

"I'm sorry," Cecelia said softly. "So very sorry."

"Now what is you gon' on 'bout, chil'? Ain't no reason to go sayin' sorry to
ol' Setty Mae 'bout nothin'. I jes' sees life from a different side dan white folks
do. And you's a good girl, not like da rest. Josiah and Cretia, and me, we all
jes' wants you to be happy, chil'."

She wanted to tell this dear, rich spirit beside her that, at this moment it was
not her own life at all that caught her mind and heart. But she could say nothing because she could do nothing to help them. At least not yet.

As she sat in the warmth of a springtime afternoon, Cecelia caught sight of
a tall man with a strong gait coming toward them across the length of the

park. He held a walking stick, moving it with each stride, and he wore an ivory felt hat so that his hair, both color and style, were obscured. Press it back though she tried, a spark of hope exploded in her chest, leaving her heart to hammer so that she could hear nothing else but a heavy, relentless pounding.

Do not hope, her mind bade her. But her heart had a very different purpose. She came forward on the bench, her spine stiff with anticipation. After so long *Could it actually be?*

"Oh, chil' . . ." Setty Mae glanced at her, then across the lush, green expanse to the silhouette of a man who neared them.

Charles Shelman came from the shadows of the park like an apparition. His face brightened as a shaft of sunlight shone down upon him between two shady trees.

"Your mother told me I might find you here." Charles nodded a greeting to Setty Mae, and the weight of disappointment settled forcefully on Cecelia's heart. For a moment, she was certain it had stopped beating altogether.

"It's good to see you, Mr. Shelman," Cecelia thinly managed to utter as she sank back onto the bench, feeling weakened by a moment's hope.

"Why, Miss Stovall, you don't look well. May I get you some water?"

Setty Mae was fanning Cecelia now, as concerned about her mistress as Shelman.

"I'll fetch my driver at once to take you home! God willin', it's not the swamp fever this early in the year!"

And with that, he dashed back across the park, sprinting as though he were in a race. As soon as had he gone, Cecelia felt her heart crumple. A great flood of tears rushed forward into her eyes. Setty Mae saw it and drew Cecelia into that big, warm, and protective embrace.

"Oh, chil', you sho' push dat heart of yo's into a heap of hurt!"

"I thought it might actually be him this time."

A moment later, the firm arms that had caressed her held her at arm's length. "Now, you listen to ol' Setty Mae. Dry dem tears, y'hear? Massa Shelman, he been sweet on you fo' near as long as you been pinin' for dat ol' Yankee boy, and he done waited fo' you, too!"

Her wet eyes looked like chips of black glass. "But I don't love him, Setty Mae! I know I could *never* love him!"

"Dat be fool talk, chil'!" she said, squeezing Cecelia's thin arms with hands that were firm and certain.

"Look at ol' Setty Mae direc'ly now! I tell you dis one mo' time: Dat Yankee—Lawd, you gots to know he ain't never comin' fo' you, after all dis time. And why you gon' waste dat pretty face o' yours on a dream dat ain't never comin' true?"

Charles Shelman came dashing back to them before Cecelia could reply. His smooth face was tense and stricken as he stood before her.

"My driver is movin' the carriage across the park nearer to you. He won't be another moment. Can you walk just over there, to the curb, do you think?" he asked, taking her hand from Setty Mae and helping her to her feet. You should know better than to sit out in this heat."

"I tried to tell her dat, Massa Shelman. But she be one stubborn gal, Miss Cecelia, when she set her mind to somethin'."

Charles smiled as he held her arm at the elbow, leading her toward the elegant black-and-gray carriage that had just stopped at the edge of the park. "One of the qualities in her I have long admired," he replied with a patronizing smile as they walked together out of the park, away from her dreams, and toward something she could no longer avoid.

Chapter Seventeen

❧

The details of a marriage had at last been worked out to Pleasant Stovall's satisfaction, and the date for a wedding was set. Cecelia had finally consented to become Charles Shelman's bride on November first. While her father was moved by money, Cecelia's acquiescence was due to a single, intangible factor: to her surprise, Charles had bought Cretia from the Stovall family. Cretia would come to live with them at their new home of Shelman Heights, a mansion he had been building for her along the banks of the Etowah River.

Charles was not only giving Cecelia the one person she had long desired to protect, he was also giving her a path toward serenity that had evaded her since losing William.

Cecelia spent the sweltering weeks of August at Summerville in relative peace as a woman at last betrothed, and Charles worked to complete their new home. To wait out the intense summer heat, her father and Anne hosted card parties in the cooler hours of early evening, and intimate little suppers during which every aspect of her impending wedding was discussed and decided upon. Through most of it, Cecelia sat among them, a bystander in her own life. She wanted to care for Charles, and she was trying her very best, but her heart—fool thing that it was—could not be coaxed. She would marry Charles Shelman, but she did not love him. Pray God, she thought, that would come in time. For now, all she wanted was a future she could count on—something over which *she* had some bit of control.

Cecelia opened a book of Tennyson's poetry as the high-pitched voices of her sisters and Anne trilled with quick excitement. At that moment she felt a desperate desire to escape.

"Oh, don't distract her from wearin' our own mother's weddin' dress!" Maria droned haughtily. Maria was their eldest sister, the first to have married, a fact she wore like an arrogant badge of honor. "It didn't fit either of us, but Cecelia would look a positive dream in it."

"I only hoped she might wish to consider mine," Anne cooly offered, fingering a glass of lemonade, but refusing to rise to the debate. "The decision, of course, is hers."

Maria sat beside their other sister, Caroline. Both of them turned their lighter eyes, brown with flecks of green, on Cecelia. She sat removed from their discussion, fingering the leather-bound volume of poetry.

Nothing is as it should be. Mother should have lived. She, not her replacement, should have been here helping to decide these things. Not Anne. I should be marrying William. She felt her heart twist and the pain rise up as her sisters condescended to Anne.

"It's a lovely offer, Anne dear, especially considerin' how close you and Cecelia have become this past year," Caroline interceded in her thin, high tone, as if Cecelia weren't even there. "But one of us really should wear *our mother's* dress."

As Cecelia closed the small volume, she tipped it on end and, in so doing, something fell, like feathers from its pages. It was the dried bit of fern from West Point, now in bits and chips. Seeing it brought a sharp pain that stabbed at her heart. It opened a wound she had thought almost healed. Tears swam in her eyes. Maria noticed first.

"Oh, what the devil is it *now*, Cecelia?"

"Only weddin' jitters," Anne calmly offered, her kind smile a sudden balm. "They happen to us all, you know. It will pass."

"Not before the weddin' night!" Caroline chortled. And Maria began to laugh, too, until they were both cackling like a couple of fat old oblivious hens.

"Don't mind them," Anne said calmly, glancing back down at a yellow needlepoint she was near to completing on a square of white linen. "The weddin' night can be what you make of it—rather like marriage itself."

"Will you wear Mama's dress, then?" Caroline prodded.

Cecelia wanted that. It would be, she thought, like having her mother there with her on a day when she knew she would need strength.

"I know she would approve," said Anne, smiling kindly.

"Oh, you don't know anythin' of the sort," Maria cruelly shot. "You married her husband before she was cold in her grave! *That* certainly can't have been what she wanted."

"Maria!" Cecelia gasped.

Caroline said, "Now, sister. You needn't be cruel about it." A half-smile turned her lips. "True or not."

Maria and Caroline were mirror images of one another. In their looks, behavior, and in unquenchable ambition. Cecelia glanced at Anne, who looked stricken by the sudden blow. It was true she had married Father soon after Mother's death. That much she remembered herself. But in all her years as Pleasant Stovall's wife, Anne had shown all of them only patience and kindness.

"If you would let me, Anne," Cecelia smoothly said, surprising even herself. "I would be honored to wear yo' weddin' dress."

"You *can't* be serious!" Caroline cried.

"I'm quite serious."

"What would Mother think? Good Lord, Cecelia, she would be turnin' over in her grave!"

"On the contrary, sister." Cecelia glanced up. "With her unique and heavenly perspective over us all, I'm certain Mother has grown quite fond of Anne these last years fo' how she has turned the other cheek to our indifference and still tried to care fo' all of us."

"You go ahead and nurse that fantasy." Maria bounded to her feet indignantly. "You were too young to remember Mama, anyway!"

"I remember enough of her to know she would be well ashamed of you two!"

Caroline glared at her. "It's little wonder no one but a potbellied old man like Charles Shelman wants you, Cecelia! You are such a hateful girl!"

With that, Caroline stood in a swirl of yellow taffeta. Together with her sister, she stormed from the small parlor, their dresses billowing out behind them.

"I'm sorry about that," Anne said softly once they were gone.

"*You're* sorry? You haven't the least thing fo' which to be sorry. They said cruel and unnecessary things!"

"They said, finally, what has always been in their hearts toward me, and I am grateful for the truth out between us."

Cecelia had never felt closer to Anne than she did now. "You don't deserve that."

"Perhaps I do," she sighed. "They're right, after all, 'bout Pleasant and me. I did take up with him far too soon after yo' mama's death, and they remember that. They were old enough to be powerfully hurt by it. But my father insisted," she said, laying her head back against the cane rocker. "I was too young to think of a way out of it."

"Bein' powerless about yo' own life is the worst thing." The sudden jolt of understanding was painful. "May I ask you somethin', Anne?"

"I'd say today you've earned the right to ask me just 'bout anythin'."

The tick of the mantel clock broke the silence.

"Not wantin' to be here in the first place. Then havin' my father—" Cecelia floundered for an expression that would not wound Anne too much. "—become somethin' of a disappointment, how do you make yo' peace with a life like that?"

This was painful territory, Cecelia saw. But there was a new trust there. After a moment, Anne leaned forward, drew up Cecelia's hand, and gripped it tightly. "Oh, my girl. It's still that Yankee, after all this time, isn't it? Even two days before you marry someone else."

She looked away. "I'm sure he's long since married by now. There was a girl back home who wanted him even then. Her father had great importance in his life, and I'm sure he has seen to it."

"Well, they say the best way to heal an old love is with a new one."

"That's just what Setty Mae said."

Anne lowered her gaze, still full of such kindness. "She is a wise old woman, Cecelia," she said gently. "And Charles *has* waited a long time fo' you."

"Will you feel you must tell father 'bout any of this?"

Anne was still smiling, her beautiful face bearing only a shadow of age and time in a few fine lines near her eyes. "Yo' secrets shall be safe with me. But if I may offer one small piece of advice from my own misfortune?"

"I would welcome it."

"Don't dwell too much longer on how things might have been. You'll only be eaten alive by that, and you have such a long and glorious life ahead of you. After all my years by yo' father's side, one thing has most definitely happened fo' me. I've come to want *you* to be happy, almost as much as if I were yo' real mother."

"Thank you," Cecelia said as they embraced. "I'm certainly tired of the hurt, and I do intend at least to try to be happy with Charles."

Setty Mae came heavily into her dressing room, carrying the gown Anne had worn on her wedding day to Pleasant Stovall. Mother would approve, Cecelia was certain. It was such a beautiful embroidered thing, with melon-colored thread and small ivory-colored rose petals. She had forgotten how beautiful it was. She fingered the brocade and lace. It would be nice to wear something so lovely. Perhaps it would give her luck, as Anne's friendship had.

"Is you ready, chil'?"

Cecelia let out a small sigh. "As ready as I shall ever be, I'm afraid."

Her maid's rusty voice rang with kindness. "Give Massa Charles a chance."

A floorboard creaked, and they both glanced back at the door. It was Cretia, standing in a new green dress and bonnet, and she was smiling. A wave of relief washed over Cecelia. She went to her old friend, and they tightly embraced.

"I'm so happy you're here!" Her eyes darkened, remembering things. "But you know you should not have come. I asked my brother to wait and send you to *my* new house, not back to this one."

"I wouldn't miss this day fo' the world!"

"It's too dangerous for you with my father around!"

They came into the room, and Setty Mae closed the door. Cretia drew off her shawl and sank onto a small brocade stool near the empty copper bath. She was still smiling. "Not after today, it won't be."

Cecelia glanced back at Setty Mae, who stood at the door, her blue-black hands poised on ample hips. She, too, was smiling. "We keep her busy and tucked away till after the weddin', Miss Cecelia. Then she gon' be safe with you."

"It *is* a dream come true." Cecelia laughed, dancing Cretia around the room, their arms outstretched between one another. When they stopped and Cecelia's eyes fell on Setty Mae, she felt a sudden and sharp prick of guilt.

Almost as quickly, the old woman reacted to it. "Now you two, don't you go thinkin' what you's thinkin'. Ol' Setty Mae be jes' fine here wit' Josiah. Jes' like always."

Cecelia got to her feet and went back across the room. I'm gon' ask Charles to bring you with us, as well. I simply cannot be without either of you!"

"Don't you go doin' any such thing, y'hear? Dis is my place. Fo' a slave woman like me, it's a good life. Better 'n' most."

But Cretia isn't gon' to *be* a slave, Setty Mae! If Charles truly wants to please me, he will see that you and Cretia are made my *free* servants as soon as possible!"

Setty Mae was shaking her head. "Chil', you be gettin' yo'sef in a heap of trouble tryin' to hep Negro folk in times like dese."

"What other people think is none of my concern," Cecelia declared in a sudden show of determination that surprised all three of them. "You both are what I care about. I want you to be free. To stay with me because you *want* to stay. Not for any other reason besides that."

"Oh, chil'—I 'spect soon enough dem gon' be fightin' words. No. Now you and Cretia go on to dat pretty new house of yours over near Rome, and you don't, neither of you, give ol' Setty Mae another thought. 'Sides, somebody gots to stay here and look after Josiah, don't dey?"

Cecelia and Cretia exchanged a glance, surprised at the sudden tears that clouded Setty Mae's eyes now, too. Cecelia felt there was something more to what the old woman was saying, but for now she was late for her own wedding.

After the wedding ceremony, they all entered the ballroom back at the Stovall home, a collection of cheering guests bent on revelry and congratulations. Garlands of rosemary and white roses hung from banisters, mantels, and chandeliers. The servants had been decorating everything while the wedding party went to the church, and now the wood and brass and silver shone like new coins in the silvery afternoon sunlight through the wide expanse of parlor windows.

Cecelia stood beside Charles, near the fireplace hearth, triumph making his face shine in the room bursting with guests. He received the parents first— mainly Pleasant, who rocked back and forth on his heels like a crowing rooster, proud and happy, and made wealthy once again by this long awaited day.

The afternoon wore on into evening. The grand house was crammed with guests, laughter, chatter, and music that filled the parlor hallways and smaller rooms. Cecelia smiled, sipped punch, and danced, watching Charles, who stayed near the magnificent black and white marble hearth, deep in conversation with her father and the most influential guests from around Augusta. It was not until late in the evening that she and Anne moved toward their respective husbands and linked arms with their men.

"As I stand here lookin' at you, they're gon' bring this thing to an all-out civil war," her father said loftily to the other men. "Imagine somethin' so absurd as that Dred Scott fool Negro clottin' up our busy court system with his crazy notions."

"Well, he does believe himself to be free, dear," Anne cautiously interjected.

"Lunacy! He's a Negro, and the courts already said slaves are inferior bein's," Charles defended. "So I fail to see how that troublemakin' slave can waste the time of those very busy and honorable gentlemen with his pointless rabble, by takin' this to the Supreme Court!"

Cecelia flinched at the viciousness. Their hateful tones were worse somehow than even what they said. *Inferior beings . . .* She thought of Cretia, Josiah, Setty Mae.

"What do they say of Mr. Dred Scott's plight in the North?" she asked of everyone, including Charles, who looked at his new wife as if she had just asked the most trivial thing in the world.

"Dearest," he said in a surprisingly smug tone. "I don't suppose proper folks *anywhere* speak of somethin' so vulgar in polite company."

"No, they don't," Pleasant harshly seconded. "And I declare, those fool abolitionists won't rest until they have entirely succeeded in destroyin' our entire way of life down here!"

"There *will* be a war befo' that ever happens!" Charles snorted.

A cough sounded among the men. The air was thick and strained. Cecelia looked at Charles—this stranger, her husband, and her heart vaulted into her throat. Good Lord Almighty, she thought as a panicked chill shot up the length of her spine. *What in the name of heaven have I just done by marrying this man?*

Of course, she had known his view of slavery before she had agreed to become his wife. It was on par with that of every other Southern man. And yet— She drew in a breath. It did not matter. She had married Charles Shelman, his beliefs, his biases, and all the rest.

This was to be her life now. He was to be her life.

But that could not possibly be all there was for her. The thought alone was painful.

"May I have this dance?" Georgie asked, coming up behind her and taking her from the horror of her thoughts. Georgie was still gangly, she saw, and yet dashing at the very same time, teetering on the verge of manhood.

Relieved, she smiled back at Anne's boy. Nearly fourteen now, Georgie was sweetness to her, innocence and good. The things Marcellus had been— before that West Point summer.

"I would be honored, kind suh." She smiled at him and took his hand, grateful to leave the overheated parlor for the cooler and far larger ballroom across the foyer.

"You're so beautiful today, Cecelia," he said awkwardly. "I sho am proud to be yo' brother."

He had always felt that way, and showed it, she thought, touched by his devotion. Anne's son, Georgie was the most connected to Cecelia, and she loved him as much as if they had shared both their parents, not only the one. More now perhaps, too, with the newly tightened bond between herself and Anne.

"Are you frightened 'bout tonight?" Georgie asked her as they danced.

She knew instantly what he meant and blushed a bit at the surprise of so blatant a question. But she would not tell him he should not have asked. He had always been able to ask her anything, and with so much in her life changing, at least one little piece of it—Georgie—should be allowed to remain wonderfully the same.

"Yes," she answered with a weak smile as they twirled to the music and her dress danced around her like a silken bell. "I am, a little. But everyone in this life has duties. And I suspect I shall grow accustomed to all of mine, sooner or later."

"I don't want him to hurt you," Georgie declared with such awkward sincerity that her heart swelled with love for him. "Truthfully, I can't bear to think of that."

"Then don't, sweet boy. Think of me only as happy and smilin' at my new home, with Cretia back beside me again."

"Cretia?" he asked in genuine surprise above the chatter and music.

"Charles managed to convince Marcellus that I needed her more."

"Oh, that's heaven!"

"Isn't it?" They were both smiling. The music ended, and they came to a stop, still holding hands in the center of the parquet wood ballroom. "I'm gon' miss you terribly, you know," she said.

Their faces both changed, and she embraced him. "I'm gon' come and see you the moment you say I may."

"Would you?"

"Just try and keep me away! I love you, Cecelia," he confessed, more like a suitor than a young half brother who had been following after her for his whole life.

"And I *adore* you, my Georgie."

Cecelia stood in the foyer with Anne, Charles, and her father, saying good-bye to all the departing guests as they left through the wide and grand front doors. As the last guest left them, his tie and lapels stained with wine and food, she was feeling almost too exhausted to be frightened by what lay ahead. It was too late now to leave on their wedding trip, and so they had decided to stay the night and leave in the morning. The one thing she had seen to before the party was over was that Cretia would spend the night out in the slave quarters, not in the main house as she had always done. Cecelia knew her proud and arrogant father would never seek the woman out there among the male slaves. At least there was a bit of peace for her in that, until she could get her away from here for good.

When Cecelia and Charles were alone at last with the door to the large bedroom closed, Charles glanced at her for only a moment, then went to the bedside to light a second lamp. He seemed nervous, she thought with a little burst of surprise she had not expected, and she was glad of it.

Before Cretia and Setty Mae had left her for the night and closed the door, sealing her in with her new husband, Cretia had brushed her dark hair out into a shining plate of black onyx. Then they had helped Cecelia out of her wedding dress and into a new nightdress of ivory French lace with long, bell sleeves. There were pink ribbons at her wrists and a sash of pink satin at her waist.

"It was a lovely party," Cecelia said tentatively, wary suddenly of moving any closer to her husband.

Charles had remained at the bedside and was pouring a second glass of brandy from a crystal decanter into one of the two glasses that had been left there.

"Lovely."

Suddenly, when he still did not look at her, the thought occurred to Cecelia that he regretted his noble show of patience. "Perhaps the wait fo' a wife has not lived up to yo' expectations?" she asked into the still quiet that fell between them.

Charles looked at her. "Whatever do you mean?"

"Only just that I know I am not the loveliest, by far, of Pleasant Stovall's three daughters."

When he looked at her, it was as if he could not quite believe what she had said. "Oh, but you are."

"My nose is too long, and my lips are——"

"Mrs. Shelman, I've always found the totality of you quite remarkable."

He crossed the room and took her into his arms. Charles smelled, she thought, of bourbon, wine, and cigar smoke as he held her to his chest and kissed her roughly, as if there were some sort of anger nested within his desire. It scared her. As he picked her up and carried her to the grand maple canopy bed across the room, her fear deepened to panic. Charles set her on top of the bed, pressed her back onto it, and arched over her. He was drunk, foul-smelling, and she knew instinctively that he would not be patient this night.

Cecelia felt herself stiffen against the fear, against the sensation of Charles kissing her now, his mouth open, his tongue pressing between her lips. It could not be more different than when William had kissed her. *God help me*, she was thinking wildly as her heart slammed against her ribs, *but I still remember how it felt . . . how he felt. Tell me how to forget that?*

She tried to turn away, but Charles would not be denied now. Not after all the liquor, and all the years of waiting. He was pressing himself against her bare, trembling thighs and murmuring something angrily against her neck about submitting. Cecelia felt the nausea rise like a wave within her as his saliva clung hot and wet on her neck. He kissed her throat; then his rough face was scratching her breasts as he moved to kiss her there. She squeezed her eyes against the tears as he moved over her. There was no point in crying any longer.

Charles waited until Cecelia's breathing changed and he knew she was asleep before he rose, put on a black velvet robe, and went downstairs. Just after midnight, they were waiting for him, let in by Josiah and collected now in Pleasant Stovall's first-floor parlor, drinking brandy. Several of them had been guests at his wedding earlier in the day.

"You're late, Shelman," one of them said in a lazy Southern drawl as they stood in the shadows clutching their hats. "We've all got wives to go home to, as well, you know!"

"Take it easy, Cyrus. You knew very well this was my weddin' night when you called this meetin'."

"It couldn't be helped. Things are heatin' up," said a barrel-chested man dressed in a chamois-colored frock coat and brown trousers, who slouched in a high-backed chair. His jowled face was dark and menacing in the shadows of the spare, golden lamplight.

"The talk up in Washington is growin' for endin' slavery," he said. "Damn Yankee politicians seem to talk of nothin' else! Seems there are abolitionists everywhere!"

"End slavery, and it's the end of me!" said another man, a plantation owner from South Carolina. "How would I ever pick all my cotton without them?"

"Some fool, a former senator named Ewing, is involved up to his ears! Anyone like that is just one cog in a very powerful and well-oiled machine. I don't know that we can fight them all."

"We'll do what we can. Fight them with all we have," Charles decreed. "And even so, secession may still prove the only answer."

"They sure as *hell* are talkin' 'bout it over in South Carolina, forming our own damn Union!"

In a weak moment yesterday, Charles had nearly given his new wife's Negress the freedom Cecelia lobbied for; he was proud now of his stalwartness. What message would that have given these men, his friends, his compatriots with whom he shared a vision and certainly a common goal to keep the South as it was.

He lowered his voice and glanced back at the staircase. "Fo' now, gentlemen, let's keep our focus on getting Franklin Pierce elected as the next U.S. President! Without him at the helm, we might as well say good-bye to our ways down here in the South, and all in the world that is sacred to us. So are we all in fo' ten thousand? I'll send a draft to Washington first thing in the mornin' if we are."

"I'm in," said one of the men. "I have no other choice."

"Count on me," said another. "I consider it my sacred duty to defeat his challengers, and those fool abolitionists who support him!"

Chapter Eighteen

He saw her in the shadows, more beautiful even than before. Her loveliness startled him. Her dark hair was loose and long, flowing out behind her as if moved by a gentle wind. Her eyes were wide, but he saw suddenly that they were full of tears. He ran toward the image, but each time he reached her, she would slip farther away. He could not bear the way she looked at him, her expression full of such helpless panic. She had called to him. She needed him. And yet he could do nothing to help her. Nothing at all.

"Cecelia! Wait! Oh, God . . . Cecelia!"

William catapulted forward in his bed, his mind dream-soaked, his body bathed in perspiration. She was so real. *It cannot be a dream.* And yet it was. That was all it was.

The bedroom door crashed back against the wall, and before he could think or even see clearly, Ellen was beside his bed, her green eyes filled with panic. "What is it, Cump? What's wrong? Are you ill?"

She was standing beside him, her hair braided down her back, and she was holding a candle lamp. Her hand was trembling so wildly that the candle shot dancing shadows and light onto his face and across the bed.

"Dear Lord, you've a fever! You're burning up!"

"I'm perfectly fine! Just leave me be!" he snapped, his mind slowly embracing the reality of the moment, and the notion that he had lost Cecelia once again. "Look, I'm sorry," he said more evenly once he focused on her hurt expression. She loved him. He knew it. They had an understanding now, an intention to marry one day, as soon as William could afford to be a husband. He had given her that hope. Yet what held him back had nothing to do with money and everything to do with dreams. But dreams were foolish, powerful things. Each time he had tried to let go of the past, the dreams had come at him again.

"I didn't mean to be cross with you," he grudgingly said.

He watched her expression slowly soften. "Was it that same nightmare again?"

He shook his head, unable to look at her, unable to acknowledge with words the details of something so sacred and close to his heart.

Wanting honesty between them, he had tried a dozen times this past year, in a dozen different ways, to tell her there had been someone else. She deserved to know it. Ellen was a decent, caring woman who had waited a very long time for him, and was worthy of better than a man who could never love her as fully as she deserved.

With her father and mother away in Washington, and only the servants left now on the other side of the house, he thought how Ellen felt no need for the propriety that defined her life. She sank freely onto the bed beside William and brushed the damp, tousled coppery hair back from his glistening face. The bodice of her nightgown was loose, and seeing the shape of her full breasts spilling out against the silk aroused him.

"Let me take the trouble from you," she murmured in a deep, seductive tone. "Let me be to you what it is you need—what you desire."

William stilled her hand on his cheek. It was clear what she was offering. "This is your father's house. It wouldn't be right."

She kissed his cheek tenderly, then his lips. Her mouth was warm and open, and it felt good to be desired in this way by a woman after so long. "But my *father* isn't here just now," she said. "And it's what I want, Cump, to be a wife to you, a comfort in any way that I can."

"But you're *not* my wife! Not yet." His heart was racing. His loins ached. "And it would be a sin to treat you in any way other than that!"

Ellen stiffened and set her hands properly back in her lap, her spine stiff and formal as she remained beside him on the edge of his bed. "You don't desire me?"

He ran a hand behind his neck as he looked at her. "It's not that."

"What is it, then? I so want *that* with you. I want to become yours. And we're alone here in the house—no one would ever know."

"But *I* would know, Ellen! I would know! And you *are* mine already, in a manner of speaking, aren't you? We've promised ourselves to one another."

Her full lower lip turned out in a little pout, and for a moment, she studied him. "Promised, but not yet engaged."

"I have nothing to offer you, not yet. You know that. I'm only a lowly lieutenant in the army. I earn only seventy dollars a month! Lord, I can barely afford to live myself on that pittance, much less support a fine woman like you!"

"If you would give up that silly military fantasy of yours," she shot angrily. "And allow Father to find you a *real* job—"

He was defensive suddenly, his entire body rigid, reacting to what was wrong with this liaison. "I like the army, and I don't want any more of your father's charity!"

"He loves you, Cump. So do I. We're your family. Why must you be so pigheaded about that?"

"I want to make my own way, Ellen! I allowed him to support me through West Point, and before. I do have *some* small bit of pride, you know. And if that's not good enough for you—"

"It is!" She leaned toward him and tried once again to kiss his mouth in a seductive way that might make a difference to him. "*My Dearest William . . .*" words from the intercepted letter haunted her.

Perhaps it was the lateness of the hour or the shape of her breasts through the thin silk fabric of her nightgown—or how he had awakened so desperately desiring Cecelia, but, even knowing how wrong it felt, this time William kissed Ellen back, opening his own mouth to her. He tasted the innocent honey sweetness and quickly felt himself aroused again.

A moment later, she was bound by his arms, pressed deeply into the bed linen, her face and neck covered with his rough, desirous kisses. He felt her shiver beneath him and was spurred on all the more, his tongue exploring her mouth once again, and his body taut with desire.

"*My Dearest William . . .*" Ellen fought the sound of a voice she had never heard, one she knew belonged to Cecelia.

"*I* love you, William! *I'm the one!*" she murmured as he felt himself pulled powerfully toward pleasure and release.

And as the words moved through him, he felt their shock like a wave of icy water. Ellen had only ever called him Cump. The only woman who had ever called him William—had been Cecelia.

How could Ellen have known—and did she?

William sagged against her and rolled onto his back, sealing himself off from her.

"It can't have come as a surprise after all this time," she softly said. "After we've been promised to one another."

"No. It's not that." He struggled with deep enough breaths to steady himself before he said anything that he would never be able to take back.

Ellen rolled onto her side next to him and propped her head with a hand. "Can you not tell me?"

"I *want* to tell you—I need to tell you," William said with a very sudden edge of unsettling desperation. "If we are ever to make a life together—possibly a marriage, there needs to be honesty between us. You deserve that, no matter what you might think of me afterward." He exhaled deeply again, trying to gain strength from each new intake of breath. "Then, if you still wish to marry me, once you know about the past—"

"With my love forever, Cecelia." The words, and the woman's name, moved through Ellen like an icy chill, and she sat up moving very swiftly away from him. Her arms were wrapped around herself in protection from her phantom rival. The woman Cump dreamed, longed for . . . waited for. If Cecelia became more than a phantom, if she were real between them, Ellen could lose what little power she held.

"I don't think this honesty is such a good idea, after all."

"But I have done things—There have been people—women." He struggled. "*One* woman."

Ellen shot to her feet. "Stop! Please, Cump! A wife shouldn't know *everything* about her husband's experiences, before. You're a normal man," she said, her heart racing. "And I know men have certain—needs." Her expression was grim, but she was trying desperately to appear more understanding than she felt. "What you did before we were promised to one another, it's simply of no consequence."

He looked bereft, lost. "Some things are different, some experiences."

"Nonsense! They are all the same in one way. No matter whether we like it or not, they are all in the past, aren't they?" He drew in a ragged breath and then released it. Ellen took it for the reply she wished. "Then that's all I need to know. To me, the past is in the past. Shall we not just let it lie and try our very best to go forward from here? It truly is the thing I desire most in the world." She said softly, seductively, "That, of course, and you."

The summer of 1847 fell swiftly, and the air was thick, not only with mosquitoes, as it had been in Picolata, but with the increased talk of a secessionist movement. More and more politicians had begun to speak of ending slavery and, like many in the South, William was concerned. While he had always abhorred the notion of physical bondage of one man by another, living here in the South, among its people, he also realized how tightly they held on to their way of life. The events of a July Fourth celebration at his new post, Fort Moultrie, on Sullivan's Island near Charleston, brought those ideas home with a vengeance.

On that steamy Southern summer day, a breeze whipped up onto White Point Gardens Park from the river beside it. William stood alone with a cup of lemonade in his hand. Around him was a large collection of people there to celebrate the United States' independence. Children scuttered around the oaks, roses, and holly bushes, little girls in pinafores, their hair in neat, long ringlets and bows, little boys in their knee pants and caps. The din of their laughter and chatter was a rich, happy sound. William watched with a detached contentment.

Their history was long and deep, as was their love for this land, and here in Charleston, they had embraced William as one of their own. He had been particularly welcomed by Lyla Anderson, the kind and spirited wife of his commander, Capt. Robert Anderson. A stout, middle-aged woman with pale brown hair and quick gray-green eyes, Lyla had been instrumental in arranging invitations for him, and in having William accepted in her circles.

William smiled as she approached him now, dressed in a flouncy apricot silk dress, hoops beneath, and a wide peach-colored ribbon under her chin, holding a wide straw hat in place. She came across the spongy green lawn, the ruffles of her parasol fluttering in the breeze.

"There you are! I declare, Lieutenant Sherman, you are as elusive as a fox! There is a string of eligible young ladies over by the bandstand just dyin' to have a dance with you!"

He kissed her hand and bowed formally to her, but the familiar smile never left his face. "Now, Mrs. Anderson, you know perfectly well that I am promised to a girl back home in Ohio."

She lifted her brows, her lips tight with a slim and clever smile. "And has that young lady a ring from you and a date to be married?"

"No, ma'am, she hasn't."

Lyla asked him the same question monthly. It had become a game between them. "Well, there, you see? There *is* hope for the young ladies of Charleston yet!"

He drew her arm through his own, and they began to stroll along the edge of the park, her wide-brimmed hat also shading a part of his face from the afternoon sun.

"Very well, then." She smiled over at him. "Tell me about yo' young lady back home. What is her name?"

"Ellen," he said carefully as they passed a group of boys crouching near a large holly bush, playing marbles.

"Ellen. Why, how charmingly provincial."

"We've known one another since we were children. I owe her entire family more than I can ever repay."

"Do you owe her the rest of yo' life, as well?"

"I expect I do."

They walked another few steps before she said, "Pity. Unless, of course, you're made fo' her." She looked directly at him and then stopped until he was forced to meet her forceful, honest gaze. "And are you? I mean, do you love her?"

"I love them all. They've been family to me, Mrs. Anderson. My own scattered like autumn leaves after my father's death, when my mother could no longer provide for all of us. Mr. Ewing was the one who took me in."

"Secretary Ewing is yo' Ellen's father?" Suddenly, she began to understand. "The man who saw you into West Point, out of Picolata, and here with us?"

"They have—each one of them—changed my life."

She turned to face him, looking straight up into his eyes. "And did you know, all along, there was so high a debt to be paid for their . . . *generosity?*"

William began walking again, unable to look so closely at the honesty in her eyes. He had not spoken about it—or of Cecelia—to anyone since leaving West Point. But suddenly a bit of confession seemed as if it might be good for his soul.

"Everything in life has a price," William said. "Besides, one beautiful

Southern girl in a lifetime to break a man's heart, I have found to be quite enough."

"And I will wager I could say who was the one who got away."

William spun around, gazing headlong into the rough face of a dark-haired man he had not seen since West Point. The man whom he had battled that first night for a dance with Cecelia Stovall.

"Why, Bragg," William said tartly.

"Major Bragg to you—*Lieutenant*," he shot back with an ingratiating little nod. "Imagine us finding ourselves here together all these years later."

"Yes. Imagine it," William repeated with a carefully amused smile.

Bragg slapped William's shoulder with spirited affection. "So, how are you, Sherman?" he asked, beaming broadly. "I ran into Ord a few months back, and he told me you had an unenviable post with the Third Artillery over in Picolata. I never expected to see you *here*."

"I was reassigned here last spring, I'm happy to say."

"It does pay to have friends in high places, doesn't it?" Bragg sneered, remembering William's connection to Thomas Ewing.

Looking at William's shocked expression, Lyla Anderson said, "Really, Major Bragg. We Southern ladies expect mo' from our gentlemen than such an indelicate volley."

"Ma'am." Bragg nodded with such great charm that William nearly believed him. "I assure you, I meant no insult whatever to the lieutenant. I merely remembered one evening, long ago, when a girl—one of our own lovely Southern daughters—came as gently and yet as boldly as a wave on a beach, into a moment in *both* of our lives, and there was an incident of—shall we say, spirited competition between us."

"Do go on."

"She was beautiful and unique and the good lieutenant here was enamored a bit more than the rest of us. Truthfully, Lieutenant Sherman, I thought you had married the girl by now. What was her name?"

He had never much cared for Bragg, and the way things were going, he didn't see that changing any time soon. The only single thing in his favor at this moment was that this oddly arrogant man could make the memories real again.

"That is in the past, sir. Long since. I can't actually recall it now."

"She was Stovall's sister, wasn't she? Whatever became of her, I wonder."

"She's married now. Or so I heard a couple of years back."

"Well, I *hope* it's to a good Southern gentleman." He leaned forward on his toes as an afterthought, and his smile crested like a summer sun. "No offense, of course, Sherman."

The afternoon went on from there, with a meal, games, and music. Through the hours, William and Bragg, in their dashing summer uniforms, made uneasy companions for Lyla Anderson as they rose in turn to fetch her another lemonade or a sliver of sweet cake. She seemed to have some odd agenda, William thought, in keeping them near one another, but what she had in mind escaped him. Still, she was a smart woman whose sense of perception was acute, and, as always, he would need to be on his toes with her.

"So, tell me, gentlemen," Lyla began, sitting on a park bench, her apricot-colored dress fanned out around her. "I would so love a soldier's perspective. Politically speakin', do you suppose there is enough of this sentiment toward secession to be a danger?"

Bragg and William exchanged a glance as they stood before her. Bragg spoke first. "I dearly hope not, as there is only one place that sort of move can lead."

"There's just so much talk of it these days that the prospect is dizzyin'." She shook her head. "And I fear I am too much a creature of comfort to endure war. For surely that *is* where it will lead if South Carolina breaks from the Union, as they are threatenin' to do."

"I can't imagine my own North Carolina would be far behind. People *do not* like the way those abolitionist sorts are tryin' to change our lives. But I just can't see it."

"What about you, William?" Lyla asked. "Where do you stand on it?"

"Well, well, well," said a young, gaunt-faced stranger who came upon them at that precise moment as the three stood together beneath the shade of a full magnolia tree. "How perfect this is!"

"I beg yo' pardon, suh?" Lyla remarked, glancing up from beneath her wide-brimmed hat.

"I couldn't help overhearin' yo' two military companions," the man said glibly. "One from here among us. The other a Yankee."

William felt himself stiffen. He knew a challenge when he heard one, in spite of the man's smile and affable bow. "Allow me to introduce myself. I am John Stuart, editor of the *Charleston Mercury*."

The title had been unnecessary after the name. Everyone in Charleston knew Stuart as a rabid secessionist intent on stirring up trouble anywhere he could. "I couldn't help overhearin' you, and with the strength of sentiment fo' secession and nullification 'round these parts, as it is, I've always wanted to interview and get the reaction of a man who hails from the useless strip of land that lies between two other great and honorable states."

He had meant North Carolina. Stuart had been spoiling for a fight for weeks with anyone who had voiced a pro-Union sentiment. It appeared now he had his man—and in this very public forum.

In response, William saw Bragg's posture change and his jaw tighten. "Come on, Bragg," William murmured. "He's only trying to start a fight."

Bragg was as rigid as a straightedge. "Well, I do believe he has what he wished fo'. Suh, I do not take insults to my homeland lightly!"

"I am sorry, *suh*, if plain speakin' offends you."

"Insults, Mr. Stuart, are what offend me, and I assure you they shall not go unpunished. I challenge you to a duel, suh, tomorrow evenin' after dark, in Rope Maker's Lane."

Rope Maker's Lane, the cobblestone alley beside Saint Michael's Church, was legendary. The little lane had been hosting illegal duels for over a century. William felt his own body constrict. "Bragg, no!"

"What's done is done, Lieutenant."

Lyla Anderson shot William a stricken glance, then tugged at his arm. "Fo' heaven's sake! You cannot permit him to go through with it, William!" she said desperately. "If that foul Mr. Stuart fights as he writes, our Major Bragg will be dead by an underhanded shot befo' mornin'!"

William moved a cautious step nearer the men. "Gentlemen, please. Now there really is no need to let this get out of hand."

"It *is* out of hand, Lieutenant! The major here has challenged me to a duel. Archaic, but powerful, nonetheless. I am honor-bound, it seems, to meet his challenge."

William trudged on, wrapping a hand around the newspaper man's shoulder and leading him a few steps away and toward the band box. "Look, Mr. Stuart," he said in a low, surprisingly moderate voice. "Tempers are high just now with rumors of secession. That much is certain. I fully understand that, as does the major over there. But *I*, having been witness to this, feel honor-bound myself to tell *you* that I was at West Point with the major, and he won two citations, my plebe year alone, for marksmanship." William let the comment settle between them like dust, along with his own affable, concerned tone.

When Stuart turned to him, William saw the marked changed in his expression. "But I've taken up his challenge!" he whispered hotly with wide eyes that revealed the first evidence of panic. "I can't back down now! I'd be a laughin'stock!"

"Are you married, Mr. Stuart?"

"I am! I've a small son, as well!"

William glanced around, then looked back at the editor. "My father used to say a successful gambler knows when to walk away, Mr. Stuart. The way, I see it, you gambled here today, and you lost. Having seen Major Bragg shoot on more than one occasion when we were both at West Point, it would be my utmost plea to you that you refuse the duel and not make your loss one of the permanent variety."

William had spoken with a deadly calm, and in such an unchallenging manner that he gave the combative writer the leeway to back down. A moment later, Stuart did precisely that.

"I won't fight you, Major Bragg," he finally announced in a voice full of contrition. "But I *will* extend my apology fo' my unwarranted insult. I cannot ask you to accept it, but I will ask you to let me walk away in peace in the name of my wife and young son."

Surprised glances shot back and forth between Lyla Anderson, Bragg, and William. "All right, go, Mr. Stuart," Bragg finally decreed. "Befo' I change my mind."

"My, my," said Lyla Anderson after Stuart had gone. She was shaking her head. "If I hadn't seen it with my own eyes, I'd never have believed it. William, you were positively brilliant just now. You can rest assured that Colonel Anderson will hear 'bout *this!*" She was smiling so widely and flatteringly that William had to bite back his own bemused smile.

"I assure you, I did nothing."

"You only saved a man's life, is all," she chuckled.

"I'm not so certain whose that would have been."

"What did you say to him, Sherman?"

"I simply told him that you were cited twice my first year at West Point for your marksmanship."

Bragg's sudden laughter rolled between them like a clap of thunder. "Oh, I was singled out, all right! I pulled mo' than *one* tour at nighttime guard duty fo' missin' the target altogether!"

"William, you *are* brilliant—fo' a Yankee." Lyla Anderson laughed, clapping him on the shoulder. "I do believe it was the major's life here you might well have saved! There must be some reward in this fo' you. Although I have no idea yet what it would be."

True to her word, Captain Anderson's wife did tell her husband about what had occurred, and how William had saved a man's life. But the "reward" was something he could never have anticipated. Even the commander himself could have had no idea the grandness of the gesture. Six weeks after the Fourth of July festival, William was sent by the commander to make peace among a collection of squabbling officers. The destination was the Arsenal in Augusta, Georgia.

Chapter Nineteen

For months, Cecelia had thrown herself into decorating the new house Charles had built for them on the Etowah River. Cretia had taken over as housekeeper. It was her task to bring up a suitable butler from Mr. Shelman's collection of slaves, as well as a new house cook. Cecelia trusted Cretia implicitly with the task that was generally the domain of the home's mistress. It was essential to her that Cretia feel as needed as she could make her, until she could one day convince her husband to set Cretia free.

But with the new level of freedom, something had changed in Cretia. There was a kind of intensity there, not visible before. On Mondays, her one day free from duties, Cretia left the house early in the morning and rarely returned until late. No explanation was ever offered or given.

Cecelia hoped that perhaps there was a man, a freed black, with whom her friend might make a life in a way she knew had been denied to her father and her mother—wherever she was. Finally, one warm August day, when they were far from the house, and from the threat of Charles's wrath, Cretia told her the truth.

"I help with the Underground Railroad." The expression on her face almost dared Cecelia to object. The commitment to help black slaves escape their bondage for a life in the North was deeply etched into the angles of her smooth brown face.

Cecelia drew in a breath, then let it out fully. "What can I do to help you?"

Cretia did not answer for a very long time. "It's too dangerous. Master Charles'd have yo' head!"

"And what is the danger fo' *you*, my dear friend?" Cecelia squeezed her hand tightly.

William Sherman had been the first person to make her think about slavery as an evil. But what she watched Cretia endure had made the most impact on Cecelia. This was her friend, and she would be loyal to her.

"I want to help if I can."

"Do you know I break the law every single week! They'd hang you—snap that slim, pretty neck of yours, just like they're gon' break mine once I'm caught."

Cecelia clutched her own throat, recoiling at that thought. "Aren't you and yo' group careful? I am not at all prepared to lose you, Cretia, no matter how worthy the cause!"

"And that's why you can't help me," she said in a forceful tone. "Because I *am* fully committed to lose my life, to see as many of my people as I can free from the bondage they have here."

Cecelia felt her heart begin to pound. "There are too many slaves. You will never lead them all to safety!"

"Then I'll die tryin'!"

It hit her heart like a great weight, the enormity of the difference between them. Their experiences, their mere existence. Cecelia could dress Cretia up in all the fine dresses she wanted, proudly make her a companion, not a slave, and their lives, at the heart of it, would still be worlds apart.

"Have you heard of Frederick Douglass?" Cretia cautiously asked her. Cecelia had. Only just recently, after a dinner party, the men had returned to the parlor to smoke cigars, sip port, and boast about a runaway slave they had seen lynched off the road outside of town.

"I tell you," Charles had said pompously. "It's the fault of that arrogant Negro inciter, Frederick Douglass, this fix we're in down here."

"Niggers stirrin' up trouble all over the North. Fool Yankees have no idea what a powder keg they're settin' off!"

"Can you boys just imagine anythin' so pathetic as a darky up there preachin' to white folks—and them listenin'?" Charles heaved with ugly laughter. The incident had changed Cecelia as she stood, undetected, outside her own parlor door. She associated the name Frederick Douglass with her first real sense of loathing for the man she had so foolishly married.

"Yes," said Cecelia, looking back at Cretia. "I've heard of Mr. Douglass."

Cretia leaned closer, lowering her tone. "There's a rally tonight, at midnight, when it's safe, and all the fools will be drunk or asleep. One of Mr. Douglass's aides is here to raise money fo' the cause. He'll be speakin' to us 'bout the underground movement, and the progress we made so far. Come with me, Cecelia, if you are serious about helpin'."

"Charles would know I was gone! I could ruin it fo' all the rest of you!"

Cretia unexpectedly smiled. "You a wise woman, Cecelia Stovall. I trust you to find a way."

But there was no way. Six months after their marriage, she understood her husband and accepted the bleakness of her marriage. Charles would do with her as he pleased, and only fate could intervene beyond that. He still took his pleasure with her nearly every night, and it seemed more a habit, like combing his hair or washing his face, than any sort of act of commitment or love. But she reminded herself, her marriage had bought Cretia's freedom, and had helped her family's business out of debt. And, after all, no one else had come to claim her.

"I'll try to be there," Cecelia finally said. "But I can't make any promises."

"These ain't no times fo' promises," she said sadly. "All we have is hope fo' tomorrow. It's all my people have *ever* had."

Suddenly, Cecelia felt guilty for her halfhearted pledge. She needed to try to explain. "Charles is takin' me to a party tonight, at the armory. Some lieutenant there, a friend of his, is havin' a birthday. If I can get Charles to drink enough . . . I'll come with you."

Cretia's smile was careful. She understood.

"And if I can't get away, I'll leave money in the library, behind the blue leather volume of Plutarch, fo' Mr. Douglass's cause. I wish I could do mo'," she said sadly. "But this, at least, will be a start."

Her dress was periwinkle blue. It reflected her dark eyes and made them shine. Her sleek, dark hair would be done in the latest fashion: ringlets pulled back and held with a gold clasp. Around her neck, Cecelia wore a pearl strung on a gold chain from China, which Charles had given her after they were married for a month's time. They represented the few fleeting days of her marriage before she realized fully to what sort of man she had joined herself.

Cecelia had no desire to go to the armory tonight. Cretia and her involvement with the Underground Railroad was too pressing. And the times into which the country was steadily heading did not feel at all right for a party. But Charles had insisted.

"You be careful tonight, hear?" Cecelia urged as Cretia helped her from her bath and into a blue velvet dressing robe.

"I'm *always* careful."

"Maybe. But things we don't plan *can* happen."

"Don't I know *that!*"

"I simply cannot bear to think of any harm comin' to you."

"My own life'd be a small price to pay if there was an end to the nightmare of slavery someday."

"Now, you stop that! I don't want you to go on like that! It's bad luck, talkin' 'bout dyin'!"

"I knows you depend on me," Cretia said tenderly as she sank onto a tufted stool beside her and draped a mahogany arm across Cecelia's thin, ivory-colored shoulder. "But you are stronger than that—much stronger than you know."

"*You* are the strong one, Cretia," Cecelia corrected her with a loving, sisterly smile.

"You're not the only one who's been changed by the years." Cretia gazed up for a moment, as if gathering strength; then she looked down again. Her eyes were focused and sharp upon Cecelia. "I know how much you want to think of me fo'ever here with you, as we are now. But I don't have fo'ever to give anyone."

Cecelia put a hand to her abdomen. She was feeling ill, and had been for most of the afternoon. The queasy sensation in the pit of her stomach made her impatient. "What *are* you gon' on about?"

"I'm not white, Cecelia! And no matter how I speak, or how you dress me up, I'm never gon' be nothin' to other white folks but yo' trained little Negro monkey!"

"Cretia!" she gasped. "I have *never*, ever thought of you like that, and you well know it!"

"But you are only one soul in a great big sea of heartless, insufferable bigotry!"

"That could change! But you've got to give it time!"

"Time's not gon' change it. Not without a revolution—no, ma'am." She shook her head. "And with how folks feel down here in the South, I wouldn't put a penny bet on my kind *ever* bein' completely free."

Her stomach was souring quickly. "Then why help with the railroad? What's the point?"

"I ask myself that nearly every day. And the only answer I can come up with is, so I can look myself in the mirror."

Cecelia was incredulous. "And do you actually believe you have to *die* to be worthy of yo' people, somehow?"

"Yes," Cretia replied. "I expect I do."

The ballroom at the Augusta Arsenal was impossibly crowded and airless as Charles and Cecelia went inside, amid hooped skirts and ribboned head-dresses, and men's fine frock coats. She planned on staying only so long as it was absolutely necessary before she could feign a headache and still perhaps have time to go with Cretia to the rally. The curious changes in Cretia had concerned her for most of the afternoon and evening, and Cecelia was thinking about that now as she came inside, and saw him.

A hot scarlet flush rose up from her neck and blossomed on her pale face as her eyes settled on a young military officer standing near the door, beside Captain Krieger. It was so sudden. So shocking. So impossible to comprehend. The officer, the last person in the world she expected to see, with a face she could never forget—it was William Sherman.

As her husband and the captain she had met only once before shook hands and exchanged pleasantries, Cecelia felt her heart beating heavily against her breast, resounding in her temples, so that she could not think what to do. William?—here in Augusta? The blood left her face in a rush.

"So *you're* the young lieutenant everyone is talkin' about." Charles smiled, extending his hand. "It's a pleasure to meet you, Lieutenant Sherman. I'm Charles Shelman." There was a brief, awkward silence before he said, "And may I present my wife, Cecelia." He paused, then shot a sideways glance at his wife.

"An unexpected pleasure, Mrs. Shelman. I was under the impression your life had taken a decidedly different course," William said, his eyes dark with intensity as they settled on her.

"My dear," Charles looked at Cecelia. "You two know one another?"

"A long time ago," William replied evenly when he saw that she was at a loss for words. "But for a moment I was not certain it was she, as the woman I remember was very different."

"The harshest of life's disappointments has changed me, Lieutenant."

She had been unable to stop her tart reply. Looking at him now forced the misery back—all of it. She was dizzy. Her heart leapt and then pounded with fast, heavy beats. The small band had begun to play again. She felt like a wild animal, caught. Full of panic and confusion.

"Mrs. Shelman," William said, as though the extension of his hand and the offer were nothing more than a courtesy. "Perhaps you would permit an old acquaintance a dance?"

Cecelia had waited so long, hurt so deeply—dear God, how it had hurt—that this did not seem real. And yet, with reality before her, the hurt was overtaken by anger. Here he was, and she knew the fates were taunting her. She was married to someone else. The agony in that seemed almost too much to bear.

How can he possibly be here—now—so suddenly like this? Can God truly be so cruel? "I really don't think—"

"Nonsense, my dear." Charles was smiling proudly. "You dance so rarely, and yet you do it with such grace. Do show the good lieutenant here yo' skill. Perhaps a turn or two will put a bit of color back in those very pale cheeks of yours. Go on now. I insist!"

William took her hand and led her through the press of skirts before she could object further. "I don't *want* to dance with you!" she declared through gritted teeth. "I *hate* you!"

He held more tightly to her hand as they walked. "Don't say that."

Her anger was a shield for her heart. "You suddenly walk back into my life *now*, after all this time? Good God! What the devil would you have me say?"

As they reached the other dancers, William put his hand to the small of her back, but she was rigid against him. "I don't understand that, Cecelia. I've done nothing since last we were together but try everything to find you, only to believe you'd married Richard Gardner, and now tonight to see it was someone else altogether!"

The music began. It was a quadrille. As they passed one another in step with the dance, William added, "If anyone should not wish to dance this evening, it should be *me!*"

She stopped at the sound of the Gardner name, but William gripped her hand and pulled her back into the movements of the dance, desperate not to lose their moment. Cecelia turned to him with pure pain making her eyes glitter in the blazing lamplight.

"I didn't marry Richard! What on earth would have led you to believe that I did?"

"*He* made me believe it! Gardner himself told me that summer after he returned to West Point that he had proposed to you!"

The couples around them had begun to stare at the steadily heating exchange, and William drew her close. They stopped again. The feel of him beside her like this reopened her wounded heart.

"You might have come to Augusta back then to see fo' yo'self that I did no such thing!" she said in defense. She stoked her torment with raging anger.

"I *did* come!" He glanced around, squeezing her arm and he felt her desire to bolt from him. "I did come to Augusta—on your wedding day! It was July, 1838. Your own butler told me you and Gardner had already left for the church! He told me it was too late to stop you!"

"It wasn't *me* who got married that day!" she whispered urgently as the other couples danced around them. "Good Lord! Richard came to Augusta to see Marcellus married! Back then *I* was still hopin' fo' *you* to come and claim the foolish young girl who had given her heart to you back at West Point!"

William washed a hand across his face, entirely stricken. "Oh, God—"

Tears filled her eyes, spilling onto her cheeks as the anguish took control of her. "I trusted you!" she whispered desperately. She could see Charles approaching them across the crowded floor. "After what was between us that summer, how could you not have gone on believin' I would never marry *anyone* until I knew you had given up on us?"

"Cecelia, you must believe me, there were no letters! I had no idea!"

"Well, I waited! I gave you a part of myself back at West Point that should have assured you I would wait for you *fo'ever!* Of course, I waited! On a bench in May Park for more than one spring! I wrote to you and you never answered my letters! I pleaded with you to find a way to come to me! When you didn't, I married Charles!"

"Ah. There you are, my dear." Charles smiled in a reserved, yet suspicious way. "Is everythin' all right?"

❧

The shock had been so swift and lethal that William still could not breathe. He knew his face had paled, and he felt his jaw slacken. He was at a complete loss.

Everything raced through William's head in a deafening roar. Anger. Shock. And the reality—may God help him—that he had walked away from her house, from Augusta, on a day when he still might have made Cecelia his wife. Pure, raw agony crested within him like a wave, and he stumbled back against the wall.

"Are you all right, Lieutenant Sherman?" A deep male voice he did not recognize suddenly asked as Cecelia walked quickly away with her husband. But he could neither speak nor think. He would never be all right again.

Outside, near the rose garden, Cecelia vomited behind a low hedge, then sank trembling against a mossy brick wall. She had felt it coming from the moment she had seen William's tortured face. Since she knew he had come for her, after all.

Oh, this infernal nausea!

Lord, how she had waited. Believed in him. Then, at last, she had let go of the dream. Only to learn that he had sought her, after all. Cecelia couldn't think, couldn't feel. Escaping Charles for the moment with an excuse about needing a breath of air was all she could manage under the shocking circumstances. *Circumstances . . . bloody hell but they control everything!* Her life, her marriage—her heart, had been bound by circumstance! It was mired in them. And just now she was choking.

"Here," he said. "Perhaps you could use this."

Cecelia looked up with a start, seeing William's chiseled face as he held out a handkerchief to her, just as he had done ten long years ago in front of the West Point chapel. "Now, the color is coming back to your cheeks."

"I can't imagine how," she weakly mouthed. "I've never been so . . . *bereft* is the word, I suppose, in all my life." Cecelia looked into William's eyes, kindly set upon her now, adoring. As if no time—no separation had passed between them at all. "I had no idea you had ever come. I waited, William. I waited. God, I sent so many letters to you!"

"I never got them!"

Her expression was twisted with anguish. "How is that possible? I gave the last two to the woman I trust most in the world!"

He let out a great sigh and gazed up at the cloudless, star-filled sky. "I swear to you, I *truly* had no idea."

They were silent for a moment, both reeling. Finally, William took her hand and very gently said, "I told you once that I would ever love and protect you."

She could not look at him. "After so long a time"—her breath caught on the words—"I gave up believin'."

"I'm so sorry," he murmured achingly.

"No mo' than am I," she replied, and it was said softly, too. The music rose up, along with a burst of laughter, as someone else came out onto the terrace. Light spilled onto the bricks, and Cecelia shot to her feet. "I must go back in! Charles'll be lookin' fo' me!"

William clutched her arm desperately and drew her back against the building in the safety of the shadows there. "Come away with me, now!"

She laughed a bitter, tear-choked laugh. "And live where? Here, a mile from my family? As a military concubine? What you ask is impossible!"

"Nothing is impossible, *if* you still love me! If you do—if you want me— I will leave the military and make a life for us anywhere you say!"

"But you *love* the military! It is what you've worked fo'—what you've always wanted!"

"I want *you* more!"

She tried to break from his grasp, but he only held her more desperately. "Tell me, Cecelia, that you love me!"

Tears stood in her eyes as he held her. "I have a husband! I can't love you now!"

"Has marriage to *him* changed what we felt that summer?"

She cupped a hand sorrowfully around her mouth. "You're too late!"

"Tell me that you love me, Cecelia, and together we will find a way! *Please* . . . tell me! That's all in the world that matters!" Tears stood in his eyes too as he waited for her to speak.

"I cannot love you!"

"Cecelia!"

"I am another man's wife!"

"I don't care about him!"

"You will!"

"I won't!"

"Will you care that I carry his child?"

A strange kind of horror, a thing unspeakable spread suddenly over them both. "No . . . ," he mouthed.

"It's true! God help me fo'ever, but it's true!"

As if by some strange, involuntary reflex, he looked down at her belly, which seemed smooth and flat—and girlish to him. No different from ten years before. It seemed impossible, now that he had found her again, in spite of her marriage, in spite of the years apart.

"Well, it doesn't matter! Nothing does! Let me raise the child *with* you, as my own!"

She spoke barely above a whisper. "I wouldn't do that to you."

"Even if I wanted it—wanted to love your child as my own?"

"It would be a burden we would never overcome, William. Another man's child. And Charles would never let that happen, even if I were selfish enough to try."

Devastated, at the finality of this moment, at the absolute tone of her assurance, William gazed at a woman who had become, even in her absence from his life, more precious to him than she had been that one summer. Cecelia did not move, but stood, tears running down her face in long ribbons, pooling on the white lace collar of her bright blue dress.

"I suppose I have to wish you every good thing with the child," he somehow managed haltingly to say. "And with the life you have made for yourself. You *will* make a wonderful mother. I know that you will."

"Thank you, William." She choked on the words, wanting to run into his arms and let him rescue her from her life.

As he turned to leave, she called out to him one last time. "William? Tell me. Did you ever marry yo' Ellen?"

"I've never been able to think of marrying."

Her smile was slight, forced. Her heart broke. "Now perhaps that can change."

He looked at her for one final moment, trying to drink in and capture the image in his mind—to make a picture that would last forever. "Perhaps," he said finally, to ease her guilt. It was, for William Tecumseh Sherman, the defining moment of his life—and a moment that had absolutely nothing to do with the military.

❧

God help me, William had told himself for months after bidding Cecelia good-bye, *but I will never be able to endure this . . . the horrible knowledge that I could have had her, and would have . . . if I had only taken one last step that final afternoon.*

He could not work or sleep, and the dreams began again. Taunting and unending, they sent images of Cecelia to him—her beautiful face defined by sorrow. *It is your fault, this fate we bear,* she seemed to say. *You did not come fo' me . . . and yet I waited. . . . I waited fo' so long. . . .*

He spent the nighttime hours drinking, chasing her from his mind. And when that did not work, he took to women's beds. Many of them. It mattered little who they were. An unhappy military wife, a young widow, and even a pretty raven-haired prostitute who, in the dark of night, and beneath a whiskey haze, *almost* made him believe he was holding Cecelia once again in his arms.

But he could not go on tormenting himself and survive, as he must.

The next autumn, William Sherman was sent from his peacemaking assignment in Augusta to a recruiting post in San Francisco, far from any action for which he had trained and long had sought. On his way to California, he took a brief leave and went home to Ohio to see Ellen. There was no reason to avoid it any longer. He would never feel for her what he had felt for Cecelia. But he knew—as if by some curious deep-rooted instinct for survival—that the loss, the longing, and especially the guilt over not going on to the church that fateful summer day would eat him alive if he did not begin a new life.

Ellen was a good woman. She loved him. He cared for her. That would be enough to make a life together. It would have to be.

At last, they became officially engaged.

As time passed, Zachary Taylor was elected president. Ellen's father, who had been considered for vice president, was named, instead, as the new president's cabinet Secretary of the Interior. His political power in Washington had returned with great force.

Ewing's pressure on William to marry his daughter followed suit.

William let go of the last vestiges of a fading dream. He returned home on leave once again and, in a grand ceremony, attended by the president of the United States himself, he took Ellen Ewing as his wife.

They honeymooned at Niagara Falls before William returned to his post.

Exactly one year later to the day, they christened their first child—a daughter they named Maria. Two years after that, Ellen became pregnant with their second child. Fatherhood, obligation, and commitment had at last driven Cecelia Stovall from William's mind and heart.

Or so, at least in those early days of his marriage, he made himself believe.

Chapter Twenty

Her marriage was a sham.

After five years, it was the first thing that came to Cecelia's mind—an all-too-frequent thought lately as she sat on the wide white-planked veranda of the Shelman Heights plantation, with its Doric columns, bold and sculpted, before her. The sweeping vista and the cool breeze up off the rushing Etowah had captivated her and Charles both. Where once there had been a knoll of celery-colored grass, there now stood a long and orderly brick carriageway leading up from the gates of filigreed iron to a lovely, flat plateau where the grand white house regally stood. And on their third wedding anniversary, Charles had surprised Cecelia with this new white-columned manor, more grand than anything she could have imagined on the spot of land she loved. But it was never so much a gift for Cecelia as it had been a show of prosperity to his associates, and Charles had said as much when she had not wanted to leave their first home, nearer Augusta.

"We are people of means, dearest," Charles had drawled in a syrupy, condescending way she was coming swiftly to despise. "Shall we not behave like it? Success, after all, does breed success!"

But Charles Shelman's measure of success had never become her own. She looked out across the vast, magnolia-framed vista with Margaret, their daughter, who was three and a half. Cretia held Lelia, the new baby, on her lap, bouncing her gently with a soft, snap-rock of her knees to soothe her, as little

Cleo, nearly two, her head a riot of dark, bobbing curls, played with a pull toy at Cretia's feet.

Yes, Cecelia thought, she knew all too well about breeding. In the five short years of her marriage, she had given Charles three daughters. And though she was weary and restless, spending her days in a kind of busy, exhausted limbo, Charles was straightforward about wanting a son and intending quite forcefully to keep Cecelia pregnant until he got one.

Cecelia lay her head back against the white wicker rocker and closed her eyes. It was a merger, not a marriage, as calculated as any business deal. Now that he had successfully won her, Charles seemed incapable of tenderness or true understanding. Days for him—years even—were attacked and managed, never savored. Nor was she.

He was not a bad husband, she still tried her best to reason. Rather, Charles Shelman was the impeccably dressed and well-mannered shell of one. There was an emotional void, a space she could not fill. Not with her devotion, or her nightly acquiescence. And so there was a void in her own life, as well.

Certainly her children were a comfort, and yet there was always something missing—a part of life she had never experienced, and never would. Love and adventure were replaced by duty and obligation. She was a Southern wife. Any chance she once had to escape the privileged empty hypocrisy of her life had ended with William Sherman.

She glanced now at Cretia and felt the same tight, squeezing fright she always did when she thought of losing her friend now, too. As the whispers of secession and War Between the States grew to shouts, Cretia's involvement in the Underground Railroad movement escalated, as did the risks she took. Cecelia's fear for her became paramount.

"I cannot protect you if you insist on riskin' yo' life like this!" Cecelia had pled with her not long ago.

"I'm not askin' fo' yo' protection!" Cretia had bluntly returned. "Only fo' yo' indulgence, as a friend . . . and a woman who says she can't imagine the horror of bein' the property of someone else!"

And so she had left it alone. But it had never gone away. The fear, the horror at an image she could not vanquish from her mind: Cretia hanging by her neck, as so many countless others had.

Spare her, Lord, she had pleaded in silent prayer. I am a selfish woman. I need her. Her friendship. Her constancy. There must be one thing in my life that does not change or vanish when I need it most . . .

It was that urge, and those dreams, that led her the next morning on a visit home to Augusta—not to see her father and Anne, but to speak expressly with Cretia's father, Josiah.

"Darlin'!" Pleasant said, all open arms and welcoming smiles as she stepped down from her neat black carriage in the carriageway behind the house. He had aged, she thought. He was stooped now, his silver hair thinning and his paunch wide and blubbery beneath his elegant vest. "Should you be travelin' in yo' condition? Charles wrote to me that you are expectin' again."

Anne smiled and drew Cecelia into a deep embrace. "Now, Pleasant, dear—do leave her alone. We see so little of our girl these days, and I'm quite certain she's had enough of childbirth to know what she can and cannot do."

Protectively, Anne wrapped an arm around Cecelia's shoulder and led her toward the stone steps, up to the house. "Now, tell me everythin' about those beautiful grandchildren. I hope you brought plenty of stories for ol' Granny Anne."

As they moved into the foyer of the house, their petticoats swishing, and the scent of magnolia blossoms around them, something sudden resonated with Cecelia. The way Anne had said it, the word *old*, had shaken her. There was a change in Anne, somehow subtle and yet startling. Something was wrong; she could feel it like a coming summer storm, the way it made the hair on the back of her neck stand up just before the first crack of thunder. Anne smiled at her, and Cecelia pushed away what felt like a premonition.

She tried to shake it off as they walked arm in arm through the grand foyer, made more exquisite than when she last was home. Pleasant had not suffered his period of poverty well, and he reacted to that with a startling display of ostentation. The wooden banister had been replaced with scrolled, gilt iron from Italy, and now there was a pretentious marble bust of Cicero drawing the eye. How alike were Father and Charles, in their need to impress. How understandable it was that Charles Shelman had been chosen for her.

"How long can you stay?" Anne asked as they settled into two wing chairs covered in crewelwork. A door onto the veranda was open, and the breeze was cool. She exhaled, surprised by how lovely it felt to be home. It was predictable here. Not demanding, as it was at Shelman Heights. She felt an unexpected frisson of delight mix with the peace.

"Only till tomorrow," she finally replied. "The children need me."

"Yes." Anne smiled. "How well I remember those years."

"Where is Georgie?" Cecelia asked suddenly, leaning forward and missing the bounding way her half brother so often had entered a room like an overgrown puppy when he knew that she had arrived.

"Yo' baby brother is growin' up." Anne declared. "And he has rather an eye now fo' Margaret Winters, that lovely young girl who lives down at the end of the street."

"Georgie?" Cecelia smiled, incredulity lighting her dark eyes. "It can't be!"

"It has been fo' a good while. Now he talks only of Margaret Winters, and of findin' a way to convince yo' father to arrange an appointment fo' him to West Point so that he can finish what Marcellus began, in hope of impressin' her."

It happened every time she heard the place spoken of aloud. It always had. It likely always would. The mention of West Point rocked Cecelia, and for a moment, she could not speak at all. *Nothing is impossible, my darling, if you still love me . . . If you do—if you still want me, I will leave the military, and make a life for us!*

"Darlin' girl," Anne said suddenly and with such sincerity that it startled Cecelia, made her sense the premonition again. They had become so close these past years that she could hide little from her stepmother, behind her practiced, cool veneer. "If we have so little time together this trip, let's not tarry with other things. Talk to me of you, of Charles—of how things are between you."

She could not speak of it. She never had. But Anne, dear Anne. In an odd way, her face, the smiling gray eyes, made her want to confess. But to do that—even with Anne, whom she loved and trusted—would have unraveled the most fragile part of herself.

"Charles hopes for a son this time."

Anne leveled her eyes on Cecelia. Her smile fell. "That wasn't at all what I meant."

"I know," Cecelia sadly sighed. Cecelia met her gaze. For the first time in their lives, they were true equals. Women. Wives. Mothers. Freed of their dreams. Bound more tightly than she had ever believed possible by Southern convention.

"Do you ever think of that Yankee," Anne asked haltingly. "The one you met all those years ago up at West Point?"

An odd question, yet not unexpected after the first mention of West Point between them. "What made you ask that?"

"I was thinkin' only yesterday of a boy I knew once—one I loved." Anne stopped, began again. "That is not the truth. I think of him nearly every day still, and wonder what became of him."

Cecelia was moved by surprise. She studied Anne's face, searching for a trap hidden somewhere in her eyes. "Who was he?"

"His name was Nathan. We planned to marry almost from the time we could consider such a thing. And I think we both felt destined to be together even befo' that."

"What happened?"

She smiled. It was an odd, bittersweet expression. Anne lay her head back against the chair and, for a moment, was silent. "Pleasant Stovall happened," she said. "Once my father met him, he decided there would be no turnin' back."

The poignancy, the similarity of their lives, brought a new, raw kind of pain. "Why are you tellin' me this—now?"

"I wish I knew." She stopped again for a moment. "Of all yo' father's children, it is you to whom I feel the greatest connection."

Cecelia smiled. "I have felt it, too."

"And confession is good fo' the soul. They say that, too, don't they?"

"They do."

"If I were gon' to confess . . . you would be the only one in the world, I think, who would understand."

She felt tears she had not expected, ones she could not chase away, prick the back of her eyes. "Thank you," she haltingly managed to say. Their eyes held one another.

"And so, does it grow easier with time?" Cecelia asked.

"Perhaps duty clouds it a bit. And the moments of joy. But it never truly leaves. Like a haunting reminder, I suppose, of what we never wanted fully enough to choose with abandon. I do think nearly every day of the road I might have taken with Nathan, if I had only known how."

Cecelia looked at her, eyes dried by the unalterable path she had taken. "I wish I would have known that, too."

"Someone once said that youth and age are equally a burden."

"Plato, I believe. And I would agree."

"Yo' West Point cadet," Anne asked then. "Did he never try to come fo' you?"

"He did," she sighed, and gazed off across the room to a very wide window and the trees in the garden beyond. "But what he faced was a woman who had not believed their dream quite so much as he had."

❦

It was difficult to find a moment alone. Josiah was kept busy with the running of the Stovall house and Cecelia's welcome-home supper. It would include a collection of well-chosen guests, like the mayor of Augusta and several wealthy plantation owners. And yet it was why she had traveled all this way, especially now when she may be carrying the son who might well set her free from the constant and determined mauling by Charles.

She thought back to how her sister had laughed. How everyone had laughed. *You'll grow accustomed to it. . . .* But she never had. Cecelia despised the act. Each time had chipped away more memories of William's tender and caring touch. And some part of her wanted—needed—to hold on to those memories, to know she had once been a part of something pure and beautiful.

She found Josiah finally in a calmer moment, out in the warming kitchen, with its worn pink-brown floor tiles and whitewashed walls, softly yellowed by grease, soot, and time. In this simple, timbered room, he was overseeing the preparation of the elegant silver platters for supper.

"Sho' 'nough, Miss Cecelia," he replied, wiping his hands on a white cotton cloth and following her out the back door and toward the henhouse when she asked for a few minutes of privacy between them. "Is dey a problem? And, if I might say, it sho' is good to have you back here in dis ol' house again!"

"Thank you, Joe." Cecelia smiled, but the expression was fleeting. She was not certain at all how to ask him—how to get the information she needed to save Cretia from the dangerous future she was so determinedly nearing.

"Please sit down," she said gently, directing him toward a cane-back chair as she sat down beside him. "I've come about yo' daughter."

He looked concerned. She was relieved to see it. She drew in a steadying breath. Released it. "She be aw'right over dere at yo' place?"

"I want you to tell me the name of Cretia's mother so I can go to my father and try to buy her back."

He rubbed a hand behind his neck, and then grimaced. "Now, Miss Cecelia. Why you gon' go and stir dat all up?"

"If it were possible, wouldn't you like to see her again?"

"Miss Cecelia, you don't know what you gettin' yo'sef into. Bes' leave it lie. *Please.*"

She was taken aback. It was not a response she had expected. What she *had* expected was emotion, surprise, even anguish at stirring it up. Not fear.

"I'm sorry, I can't do that. Cretia needs me. She needs us *both*."

"I thought trouble was over once you got her 'way from Massa Stovall."

"It's not that kind of trouble. Fact is, she doesn't care anythin' 'bout her own life. She spends all of her energy on the Underground Railroad."

"What gon' be da difference if she sees a mama she don't even remember, to change dat?"

Thinking of her own mother, of living without that source of strength and guidance that might have changed so many things, she looked at Josiah squarely. His dark face was defined by an odd fear.

"She will be made different by it now. Hopefully, care mo' fo' herself. I certainly would have been."

He shook his head. "Sho'ly ain't mo' difference possible 'tween da two of you, Miss Cecelia. You can't know it'd change a ting!"

"I *do* know because I know Cretia—better apparently than her own father does!"

"Chil', you is stirrin' a pot dat's long settled!"

Hands outstretched, Cecelia pleaded with him. "How can I make you care 'bout her?"

"I care plenty fo' Cretia and fo' Setty Mae!"

"What in thunder does Setty Mae have to do with this?" she asked angrily. And then, before the answer came, she understood. *God!* It couldn't be! Cretia's mother was sold so long ago! Looking at his face, Cecelia knew it was true. "Setty Mae?"

"Yassum, it be da truth."

"But why did you never at least tell Cretia?"

"Too much risk as a chil' she might've called Setty Mae *mama*."

She gripped her forehead, the story becoming clear now. "You got my father to send someone else away when she was to be sold . . . so you and Setty Mae could stay together?"

"Wasn't hard." He smiled a bitter smile that was fleeting. "White men say we all looks alike. Back den, yo' daddy had so many of us darkies I 'spect it didn't much matter who he sold. Ester was a good woman, loyal as da day to my Setty Mae. Ester hepped Setty Mae when Cretia come—doin' most of Setty Mae's cho'es when she was feelin' po'ly so da massa wouldn't mind neither o' dem." He raised a challenging brow to her and continued. "Since no white massa care which Negro woman births a baby and which don't—so long as it don't belong to him, foolin' Massa Stovall was easy. He sold his darky, made his money, and I kep' my Setty Mae."

They had somehow outmastered the master. The slaves had outfoxed Pleasant Stovall. "I'm glad," Cecelia said softly, meaning it. "But what an incredible sacrifice Ester made fo' a child who'd be raised not knowin' her mother was with her after all, or knowin' the fine woman who made that possible."

"Well, you gots what you come fo'," he said ruefully. "And I prays da Lawd it be worth da price others gon' pay fo' it now."

Cecelia could not move. The shock hit her full force. Then a terrible rush of guilt flew through her for having pushed him. "I wouldn't tell a soul!" she sputtered, choking on the words.

"Truth be like water, chil'. You can try to keep it out. But, in time, it a'ways find a way to seep on through."

He was out of the chair turning away from her, but she followed him. "Tell me what I can do? I'm so desperate to stop Cretia from movin' any mo' deeply into this, like nothin' matters but this cause of hers!"

He scratched his head and sighed. A moment later, he turned back to her. His dark eyes were full of the pain of too many difficult years. "Jes' maybe she's right."

"You can't be serious!"

"Slavery *be* an evil, Miss Cecelia. Ain't never gon' change if young folks like Cretia don't find ways to work against it. I can't have her live a whole life like I done. Dat ain't no life fo' a man—and it sho' as *hell* ain't no life fo' a young woman. She be better off dead, da way I sees it, fetchin' and doin' fo'ever."

It lay heavily between them—bare and ugly, full of its own resentments and its truths.

"I'm good to Cretia," she said defensively, her back stiffer suddenly.

"Man good to his dog, too, Miss Cecelia. Less o' course he get out o' line. Then da differences shine through jes' like da sun."

Cecelia shook her head. She could bear it no longer, this inequity that seemed greater and more heinous to her every day. At its root lay the memory of William Tecumseh Sherman and the conscience he'd awakened in her.

The facts had changed everything. "But please understand, Joe, I have got to try to give Cretia some reason to care 'bout herself!"

Exasperated, Josiah lashed out at her. "Why, when she sho' as *hell* didn't care 'bout you and yo' Yankee man!"

She fell against the back of the bench at the mention of William. "What do you know of it?" she demanded.

He was uncomfortable suddenly. His face changed, and his body went rigid. She knew he had spoken some piece of the truth. There was silence then, a standoff. "I don't know nothin."

"Tell me."

"I can't."

"Damn you, tell me what Cretia had to do with it!"

"You ain't gon' like it."

She lunged at him. "Tell me!"

"Cretia never mailed yo' letters to the Yankee like she tol' you she did! It was da price she be made to pay by Massa Marcellus fo' her freedom from yo' father!"

"Marcellus?" She snapped with blazing, incredulous eyes.

"He had as much reason to want you married to Massa Shelman as yo' father did!"

Cold shock nearly strangled her voice. "Cretia . . . betrayed me, too?"

"Us ol' slaves do all sorts of tings to get by, Miss Cecelia," he bitterly replied, defending himself, his daughter, and every other slave who ever had to deal with the devil just to survive. "Ain't no other way sometime."

"That's fool talk, and you don't mean it!"

"From where you sits, as a rich white woman, wit' everythin' in the world there fo' you, never knowin' hunger, or bein' beaten . . . or raped—maybe it is."

"You don't know a thing about my life!"

"I know you ain't no Negro gal, and dat's knowin' one hell of a lot!"

Cecelia shot to her feet, her face pale with shock. Her words were breathlessly spoken. "Cretia *knew* how much I loved William!"

"Yassum, she did."

Cecelia snatched up her skirts and shot him a last blazing glare. There was a crushing weight on her chest, and she knew only that she had to get away from this man and his truths. "I trusted her! I have *always* trusted her!"

"We jes' da slaves, Miss Cecelia. Ain't right to treat us like we was white. We do what we gots to do fo' our *own* kind. And tell me—ain't dat jes' what da white men say 'bout dey side of tings?"

"God, that is vile!"

"So is dis powder keg we all be livin' in down here in da South. Sometin' gon' give way. It sho'ly got to. Ain't gon' surprise me none if a wah come over dis."

"I hope slavery ends," she sighed, losing some small bit of the horror she felt for herself. "But I pray God you're wrong about a war. This country could *never* survive it. Nor, I think, if it came to it, could Cretia and I."

Chapter Twenty-one

❧

Raised to be the embodiment of Southern hospitality, Cecelia went through the motions at the welcome-home supper that night, smiling politely and asking all the proper questions of her father's guests. She wore a costly new dress from Paris, made of rose-colored taffeta with white organdy ruffles at the wide hem. From her earlobes, chips of diamond and sapphire glittered. But inside Cecelia, a tiny spark of hope for a better future—the thing she had lived on these past years—was dying. She could not go home to face Cretia. Not yet. And she was so tired. Here in Augusta, she realized how weary she was of the pretense of her life, and the emptiness of purpose. And perhaps worst of all, a new secret to keep from her family.

Charles, too, had become a tremendous source of torment. The shock of discovering an all-too-public affair he'd been having with a wealthy widow in Savannah had at first brought heartbreak, then embarrassment to Cecelia, as it slowly became common knowledge to everyone they knew. She did not love Charles, nor did he love her. But worse than that, he did not respect her enough to keep his affair a private matter. She had wanted to leave him a dozen times already, but he was still the father of her children, and the man to whom she was bound by God and the law.

As the quartet that Pleasant Stovall had hired for the evening played, Cecelia sipped iced water from a Venetian crystal goblet. "I'm tellin' you,"

Pleasant declared in his deep, bellicose Southern drawl. "We'll be only too glad to fight fo' what is ours!"

"And I'll fight right alongside you, Father!" Georgie chimed beside him to a crowd of bemused older men, whose condescending chortle turned him instantly pale. Georgie had grown, Cecelia saw, his face now was fuller and his jaw sharply defined. The deep black, soulful Stovall eyes he'd gotten from Pleasant sparkled with the hint of manhood so near now. She cringed at the men's insensitive reaction. Georgie's calm dignity, in response, made Cecelia want to weep.

"Good Southern boy you've raised there, Pleasant," declared the stout, balding mayor, with another horrifyingly condescending chuckle.

"You expect anythin' less? I tell you, we'll kill every last one of them Yankees if they try comin' down here! Squash 'em like the bugs they are!"

Talk of war, killing, betrayal, and the memory of deceit were too much for her. And wasn't the room stifling with all these people drinking, eating, and laughing, in their heavily scented skin? *Someone should open a window. . . . I need some air . . .* The room began to tilt, subtly at first, then more strongly, like a carousel someone had spun too fast. It moved faster and faster so that Cecelia could not think beyond the nausea and the mind-numbing spinning. Chandelier glass turned into jagged shards of bright color, the reflection piercing her eyes, cutting into her mind. *Got to get away from here. . . . Cretia . . . Charles . . . William . . . From everything! Can't think! Can't think!*

It was the last thing she remembered before everything went black.

We're calling fo' Charles now, darlin'," Anne said soothingly as she moistened a fresh cloth and then laid it across Cecelia's brow.

"He's the *last* thing I need! Where am I?" She struggled to sit up. Anne stopped her.

"Up in yo' old room."

Setty Mae was standing over Anne's shoulder, concern wrinkling her flat, brown face, the round dark eyes so full of love and concern.

"He's yo' husband, chil'."

"I saw to that." Cecelia closed her eyes and sank back.

"Tell ol' Setty Mae now—what *was* you tinkin' comin' on a trip like dis in yo' condition?" Her prodding was sweet, and Cecelia found she didn't even mind the tone in which it came. Until she remembered that Setty Mae was the mother Cretia didn't know she had.

"I don't *think* much at all, lately. It's too painful to do anythin' but follow the motions of my day. And still there are traps everywhere."

Anne settled a hand over hers. "Dearest girl," she said gently. "You lost the baby last night. The doctor was just here."

Cecelia felt nothing. No sense of loss, no disappointment. The words should have brought devastation, but she was simply empty, losing Charles's child. Empty, of every other emotion. "Please leave me," she mouthed. "I would like to sleep now."

What she meant, as she closed her eyes, was that she would just as soon not ever open them again.

"We have got to do somethin', that's all! She hasn't eaten a thin' fo' days!"

"Yassum, Miss Anne. I try sometin' else. But she won't take it. Don't matter none what it is."

Anne and Setty Mae whispered, but Cecelia could hear everything. Especially the tone of their concern.

"Ain't you written to Massa Charles yet?" Setty Mae helplessly asked.

"I haven't told him that she's lost the baby, if that's what you mean. What she needs now is a few days away from everythin'—Charles and her girls included."

"The good book say da secret tings belong to de Lawd," she said, softly spouting her biblical verses again. "She be needin' da Lawd."

"She *needs* to get away!"

If I could have just a bit of time alone to think . . . to make sense of things . . . But of course it was impossible. She had a family she loved and missed. Obligations. There were circumstances beyond her control. Circumstances once again. They still ruled her life. Damn them! Quick anger dissolved to hopelessness.

Cecelia slept again then, because it was easier. Because there was some small freedom in it. And when she woke, she found morning just beginning to break, and the pale pink and orange coming up in a long, muted streamer through the casement windows.

Suddenly, the door clicked open, and Setty Mae lumbered through carrying a large, heavy silver tray, clattering with an array of blue and white china.

"Mo'nin' Miss Cecelia! Lawd, if it ain't fixin' to be a fine day out der!"

Cecelia tried to sit up, but her mind was still clotted with dreams she could not remember. She wanted to sound happy, rested by sleep—she wanted to say something happy. But her heart was as empty as it had been. She had nothing left to give.

"Well, now. If you ain't jes' a sorry sight, dat pretty face gone all pale and sunken." Her big, brown hands were at her hips.

"I'm sorry about that."

"Is you, now?" Setty Mae was smiling suddenly, that warm melted butter smile that had always reassured her. "Well if dat temper of yo's was showin' itself at last, even in a glimmer, I'd say to Miss Anne, praise da Lawd! Dat be 'bout the bes' news we had 'round here in a *long* while!"

Cecelia sat up and folded back the bedcovers. "Don't be alertin' the authorities just yet, Setty Mae."

"Look, chil'. You do ol' Setty Mae a favor and eat a few bites of dis here breakfast, and I tell you a secret."

"One bite fo' a *morsel* of yo' secret?" Cecelia bargained.

Setty Mae's smile wandered, and she rocked back on her heels. "Two bites."

"Oh, all right. Deal."

Anne had already spoken with Pleasant, who had cabled Charles, and the plans were made. Cecelia would go with Anne to New Orleans for a month's time to rebuild her strength after the miscarriage. There was shopping there, and the balm of new sights and sounds to help her heal. She would rest, regain her strength, and return home, the woman they all knew and loved. The family had worked it out with the sure finality of a cotton exchange. But Cecelia was too weak to argue, too desperate for a bit of freedom to care whether things went according to their plans or what she would do . . . if they did not.

Chapter Twenty-two

❧

William stood at his office window, hands linked behind his back. As commissary in the army, he looked down onto the gravel courtyard, surveying his troops. New Orleans was not his favorite post, but after a year, these men had become family. Yes, almost more family than Ellen. Hating the South and being away from her parents, she had opted to return to Ohio, live apart from her husband, and wait, as she said, for William to get the military life entirely out of his system.

She had not become the kind of wife he had hoped for. Nor was she the sweet, understanding girl with whom he had grown up. But there was, William believed, a just penance in accepting that. He had brought this loveless, largely platonic life upon himself the day he had walked away from that Augusta church.

He went back to his desk and to the letter he had been trying, for most of the morning, to write to Ellen. That, he did with great regularity as a concession to his feelings. Her words to him before leaving New Orleans the last time still played in his mind.

"I hate this army and what it has done to us! And Lord, how I despise the South! It's insufferably hot here, steamy, and full of invalid pretensions!"

William had thought of reminding her that he liked the South very much, that the people here had always been good to him, and that there was a kind of comfort here he could find nowhere else in the world. But she knew all of that already. And still she spoke as she did.

"I'm not yet ready to give up on the army," he had blandly replied as she packed to leave.

"I believe you mean you are not yet prepared to commit fully to your wife and children."

It was a low blow, and he reeled from her venom. "You are the one insisting on returning to your father!" he had charged.

"If *you* were more of a man to us, I suspect I would not have to go back again!"

He squeezed his eyes and shook his head to chase away that bitter image. For better or worse, Ellen was his wife. They had two young children, and that was that. His assistant, Sergeant Saunders, came through the door just then, and the thoughts vanished. "You will never guess what I've got, sir!" the tall, tow-headed soldier playfully teased as he held a hand behind his back.

Philip Saunders was a slim young perfectionist with a high nasal drone, but William liked him, which helped at a moment like this. "You're right. I won't."

"Spoiled sport."

"You know I'm a far too serious sort to be a fan of games."

"Oh, all right, then." He pulled his hand forward, revealing two tickets. "What do you say to two third-row-center seats to *Measure for Measure*, starring only the most talked about actor in all the country, one Mr. Edwin Booth?"

Despite Saunders's annoying penchant for boasting, William had to admit, he was better than anyone he had ever known at working the system—any system, to get precisely what he wanted for his superior, or for himself. William was impressed. Everyone he knew had been trying to get tickets to the latest play by the acclaimed actor. "Well, then. I'm thrilled for you," William deadpanned, and went to sit at his desk.

"Be thrilled for us both, since I want *you* to accompany me!"

"Me? I should think I would be the very last person on earth you would wish to take."

"You would, would you?" he said wryly, pausing for a moment with a finger poised theatrically at his cheek. "All right. The truth of the matter is that I've followed the Booth family for years, and sadly it seems, here in this vast cultureless wasteland, *you* are the only person I know cultivated enough to appreciate seeing one of them perform Shakespeare."

William scratched his head and leaned back, considering. "When is it?"

"Tomorrow evening. Curtain is at eight. Now, you aren't going to tell me that you're busy. I know for a fact that your wife hasn't been here for weeks, and you're far too stuffy to retain any sort of *public* mistress who would possess your time."

"True." He shook his head. "Mrs. Sherman *is* well gone. . . ."

"Then it would do you good to get out a bit. Come on, what do you say? Join me for an evening you're certain never to forget?"

"All right," William finally conceded with a weak smile. "It *is* just one evening. What harm could it really do to join you at the theater?"

He had dressed with impatience and haste, his cap askew, his uniform collar not quite so crisp as it should have been. William had never cared a great deal for his appearance. But he cared less so at this stage in his life, when oil to tame the hair and a neat shave seemed pointless. He paused to glance into the long, gilt mirror in the theater lobby. Dragging off his cap, he tousled his copper waves with a sweep of the hand back from his forehead and chuckled at his rugged face and the newly grown stubble of a copper beard. *I'm certainly not the promising sight I was at West Point, so many years ago, that's for sure. Young, idealistic . . . inspired by love, and so many youthful things. . . .*

William glanced down at his physique, still slim and taut as a boy, standing now actually thinking himself just slightly dashing in his full dress uniform, dark trousers, and single-breasted, dark blue frock coat with gleaming brass buttons and epaulettes. Mature now, and successful, his eyes still glowed with a longing for something, some experience in life beyond the ordinary—something he had not yet found.

He still could not vanquish old dreams. The images that plagued his sleep always involved violence and war—and strangely, they mixed as though they belonged with memories of Cecelia.

He cursed them not only because his mind foretold war, but also because the memory of a summer long ago never fully left him, even now, as a husband to someone else, and father of two small children. He thought sadly of those children, a daughter and a son back in Ohio with their mother. He had not seen them for months. They were young children learning to care more for their Grandfather Ewing, than for their own father. He was being punished for the unpardonable sin of trying to make it in the world on his own accomplishments.

William thought of Ellen and felt only the cold, heavy rush of disappointment. They were still companions, confidants, and the power of history bound them. He wrote to her regularly. She wrote to him. And there was comfort in that. But they had settled, far too quickly, into the emotionally vacant rhythm of marital complacency.

Philip Saunders tapped his shoulder, and William pivoted away from the gilt mirror, bringing himself back to the evening. He felt engulfed by the crush of theater patrons and the din of excited chatter, as the velvet and gilt lobby steadily filled to capacity for Mr. Booth's first Louisiana performance.

"We'd better take our seats. We've only a moment or two before the curtain goes up."

William nodded, but as they were swept in with the crowd toward the door, he was stunned into immobile silence. It was not possible. Not here in New Orleans, as it had happened in Augusta. No God could be so cruel.

He closed his eyes, then opened them again to chase away what could only be vestiges of last night's unsettling dream. Still, from behind, and at a distance, the slim shape . . . the elegant turn of her neck . . . the color of her hair . . . and God help him, even the way she moved.

But of course it was impossible. Cecelia was long married now, happy somewhere near Augusta, and certainly the mother of a number of children.

Children that would have been mine, but for a fault I alone bear.

A barrel-chested, silver-haired woman in a large hat stepped in front of him as they moved into the theater, and the moment vanished. *Foolish heart!* he chided himself as he sank into the seat. Only after the house lamps were dimmed did he realize that the image that had so reminded him of Cecelia was sitting before him, in the front row, her form clothed now in shadows.

As the actors came on stage, and wild applause erupted for Booth, William's heart crashed wildly. He did not see the stage or the actors, nor did he hear their lines. He saw only the woman. And he thought only of Cecelia. William was transfixed by the gentle rise and fall of her shoulders with the rhythm of her breathing. A moment later, she turned her head slightly and, in the dimly lit theater, he saw that it *was* her. Cecelia was sitting with another woman, not with her husband. Why, he wondered in that dark and shadowy place, did that minor fact matter at all? It changed nothing. She was married.

So was he. There were children. Commitment. The bridge that had once so tightly linked them had gone forever.

He sat motionless, watching her. He was greedily drinking in every moment, every breath, knowing how quickly it would all end.

In that darkened theater, as Booth played Vicentio, Duke of Vienna, a dozen scenarios raced through William's mind. Things he might say. Ways he could stop her from leaving, get her alone to speak to her. As Booth boldly gestured and his actor's voice filled the dark anonymity of the theater, Good Lord help him, William realized that even now he would leave Ellen in a heartbeat—abandon his disappointing marriage for another chance with Cecelia. . . . Would she do the same after all these years? What had her life been since their fleeting words and that single dance they had shared in Charleston? Was she happy now? Content? Was she any more in love with the person she had married than was he? Would it be better to know for certain, or to wonder?

After what felt like a lifetime of baritone lines and applause, he leaned over and quietly murmured to Philip that he was ill and needed to leave the theater. When his assistant leaned forward to rise and leave with him, William pressed a silent hand on his forearm, bidding him to remain.

I shall ever love and protect you, he heard his mind say in the darkness. Yes, a naïve youth had said that to her once, and he would be a man of honor for her now. William would not destroy her marriage with his dreams. He meant to live on those dreams for the rest of his life.

Cecelia stood in the lobby watching him dash alone into the night as if he were running from something. She was not certain he had seen her, but she would have known William anywhere. It was those deep, commanding eyes, the color of which she had never seen anywhere else in her life. The gaze of those eyes had found her so many times before, in life and in her dreams. Now, they had found her across the room before the performance began, and she had fought hard against her instinct to go to him. Cecelia stood alone, body trembling, heart racing over what to do next.

"Was that him?"

Anne put a hand on her shoulder, and Cecelia turned around in the empty lobby. "Yes."

"Then what in heaven's name are you standin' *here* fo'?"

She inhaled sharply. "He's married."

"So are you! So am I! Fo' all that seems to mean."

Her expression was full of desperation. "What about Charles?"

"Yo' husband who struts about Savannah with his mistress so openly these days? *That* Charles?"

Cecelia paused, closed her eyes, and felt the familiar jolt of indignation she always did when she considered Charles's affair.

"I just don't know if I can," she softly said.

"The better question, my dear heart, is"—Anne looked at her—"can you afford to live the rest of yo' life not havin' tried?"

William had taken a hack parked in a line of other rented carriages along the curb outside the theater. Cecelia described it to the driver who, for a large cash inducement, followed it quickly into the night. The coach lamps before them lit the way down a narrow tree-lined street. He then stopped before what looked like a small saloon, with golden light spilling out in an arc from the large bay windows and a regularly opening front door. As William emerged and was paying for the ride, Cecelia's driver approached the carriage. She waited in the cold, empty hack. Her heart was racing; the blood was rushing through her mind so that she could barely think. She watched the two men speaking in the glow of the carriage lamps before her. William's face was bathed in a shimmering golden glow. He looked, she thought, like perfection.

Tell him only that an old friend seeks a private word, she had nervously directed her own driver, who stood now with William and the other driver at the open carriage before her in a circle of golden lamplight. A new fear struck Cecelia. She felt a chill rise up from the pit of her stomach. What if William resented her? Resented the presumption? After all, it was she who had turned away from him that night in Charleston. It was she who so wrongly had sought to blame circumstance solely on him.

Cecelia wrung her hands as the men continued speaking back and forth, and she thought very nervously about bolting from the hack and running off into the night before William saw her. If he should despise her now—or worse, feel indifferent to her, she was entirely certain she would not survive the knowing it. But somehow, fate had placed them together yet again for a reason. Of all the places in the world the two of them might be just now, this could not possibly have been an accident.

Cecelia shifted and fidgeted on the cold leather seat, certain she would come completely out of her skin as William began to walk with the driver toward her. *Please*, she began silently to pray. *Don't let him hate me too awfully much fo' how things have turned out between us now.*

The next moments changed everything completely. A sad kind of recognition lit his eyes as William climbed into the hack beside her and closed the door. A heartbeat later, she was buried deeply in his arms, her head against his chest, and she melted naturally against him as he embraced her.

"I had no idea you'd seen me," he murmured into her dark, chamomile-scented hair. "I tried so hard to leave the theater, to let you have your life—I was about to drink myself into bourbon oblivion in that saloon over there to make up for it."

There was no pretense here. No explanation. Only love and history, and what had been done to keep them apart. He pulled her harder still into the curve of his chest so that she could feel the heat of his body against her own.

"I'm sorry fo' the things I said in Charleston, fo' how I blamed you."

He touched her face as if she were a precious jewel. "You did nothing to be sorry for, but believe in me."

"I didn't believe enough."

There was desperation in their murmured words and contrition on this dark, forgiving street where they were known by no one, and where rules did not apply. Suddenly in the blackness of the night, William kissed her as if not a single day had passed since the promises they had made so long ago, and Cecelia kissed him back. The driver was tapping down onto the top of the carriage. He wanted to move on to a new fare, and they must decide.

"Is your husband with you here?"

She touched his short beard with a gentle finger. "He's in Savannah. And yo' wife?"

"Gone home to Ohio." They kissed again, more deeply and passionately, this time. "But the barracks are—We can't go there."

Her breath shuddered in his ear. "I have a room alone at the Saint Charles Hotel."

Without another word between them, William stepped out into the night and spoke with the driver. Cecelia watched him with a curious calm. She should be scared, but there was no fear. They were owed this, no matter what the morning would bring.

I love you, she thought fleetingly. *And I always will. Come what may.*

Her room on the second floor of the hotel was dark and cool. Anonymous. William pushed the door closed. They heard the latch click as they stood together wreathed in shadows. Gauzy curtains blew around an open window near the bed.

"Would you kiss me again?" she asked him in a whisper.

William cupped her face gently in his hands. She felt him trembling, almost as much as she. "I still love you," he said, his voice breaking.

"And I will always love *you*."

The years slipped back further still as William drew her down onto the bed, the springs giving gently beneath their weight. He was kissing her passionately, at her mouth, throat, hair, the moonlight through the window making a silhouette of their joined bodies. *This is a sin,* she thought wildly, feeling him touch her breasts beneath the lace bodice of her dress. But she could not convince herself that it was wrong. *He was mine first . . . and I was his.*

Then he saw the cross he had given her. William fingered the gold chain that lay against her ivory skin, but he could find no words. She had kept it. It had meant something dear to her. She saw now in his eyes that he knew that.

As he peeled her dress away, then touched her bare skin in long, sensual caresses and sweet, slow kisses, Cecelia felt herself shiver. She then watched him undress. The night air through the open window was cool, and his mouth on her skin was so unbelievably seductive and warm. Finally, he was inside her, moving gently. It was the thing she had dreamed of for so many years as Charles had pawed and prodded her. What it would have been like with William . . . *always William* . . . His tenderness aroused her swiftly to a place nearly forgotten, such a long time ago. She wished they could stay like this forever. But that was a fool's dream: happily ever after.

Each powerful thrust inside Cecelia took her farther from those thoughts, those regrets, and toward the hot bursts of pure pleasure he was creating within her. She was lost to anything else, no longer caring about dreams, or forever—only this.

Afterwards, wrapped in his powerful embrace, their legs still interlocked by each other's, Cecelia finally felt her heart begin to slow and the room take shape again. The pale rose-colored sunrise very slowly showed though the curtains beside them.

"I should go," he murmured. "It's nearly morning."

"Please stay. No one knows us here. Can we not give ourselves that one, small gift?"

Later, they made love again as the sun turned from rose to shimmering gold and came up fully, spreading its warmth through the window over their glistening, sated bodies. Then, exhausted and content, they ordered a breakfast of eggs, toast, coffee, and grapes, which they fed to one another on top of the bed, kissing between bites and giggling like errant children.

"Go out with me," William bade her, fingering the cross at her neck as Cecelia sipped her strong black coffee.

She chuckled at that and reached out to touch the line of his jaw. "Where?"

"Anywhere! I don't care! Just walk with me, *be* with me, as if we were any other couple."

She felt a sudden, sharp stab of truth hit her, and she rolled onto her back, away from him. William lunged for her and lay beside her, stroking her hair. "But we aren't that, are we?" he tenderly asked, knowing by instinct what she felt.

Cecelia's eyes glittered as she looked into his. "No, you're right. The devil with what is, or isn't. Pretense may be all that is left us in the world. There are some lovely shops along a lane just around the corner. Let's walk awhile together past them."

She left a note at the desk for Anne, then let William pull her arm through his as they strolled out of the hotel and into the broad, cool autumn daylight as any other married couple might. William wore his uniform, and Cecelia had chosen a beige dress with black trim, and a matching wide-brimmed hat. She felt happier than she had been in her life. They passed a garden full of pink roses, their heady fragrance engulfing them as Cecelia tried drinking in every sensation. She must forget none of this; it would have to last a lifetime.

They passed an old bookshop, a milliner's, and then a crisp, little white-trimmed shop with a bow window and crystal and silver displayed on forest green velvet. An oblong, silver music box emblazoned with a royal crest caught Cecelia's eye as they paused at the window, linking their arms more tightly. "Isn't that lovely." She smiled, gazing up at him.

"It certainly is unique. I've never seen one like it before."

"Nor I. It's exquisite . . . It makes me think of London." She felt playful all of a sudden, and almost serene. "Did you know I met the queen?"

"I'm sure you thoroughly charmed her." William smiled, too. "You're not so different from that box. Elegant, complex . . . something well worth keeping. If one could only hold on to you."

Cecelia chuckled softly. "I do believe you've a bias, Captain Sherman."

"Guilty as charged, ma'am."

After they had walked awhile longer, a sudden cloudburst forced them to dash into a quaint corner restaurant with Irish point lace curtains over the windows and a roaring stone fireplace at the back of the room. Not hungry, still they ordered lunch and a bottle of wine from a cozy table they had taken near the fire, just as the rain beat down like pebbles against the panes of window glass. They sat beside one another and held hands but ate little, as if both of them could feel the dream slowly coming to an end. When the rain let up and they left the restaurant, they returned to her hotel room.

Alone with her again, William leaned on the closed door and raked both hands through his hair. The small mantel clock chimed three o'clock as he tried to rein in a mounting sense of desperation. Seeing it, Cecelia came to him, and they held one another.

"God help me!" he murmured hoarsely into her hair. "I will live every day of my life in the shadow of us! And it haunts me already, Cecelia! What we could have had—what should have been *ours*!"

"It was never all yo' fault," she softly crooned. "You need to know that my maid threw away my letters to you! Letters beggin' you to meet me befo' I married Charles. It's not all of it yo' fault, as I foolishly made you believe in Charleston! Whatever happened, we both played our parts in where we are today!"

"Damn them all to hell! God, I damn every last one of them!"

She reached up to touch his face. "We *meant* to be together. That at least is somethin'."

"I'll leave Ellen! I'll go to Ohio the moment I can and explain things to her!" His eyes glittered with dark, tormented purpose. "Of course I will provide for my children, and I hope you will want me to be a part of their lives. But we need to be together, as we should have been all along! It's no accident we both ended up here in New Orleans like this—now. This is our chance!" They clung to one another against the door in a frantic way as if to change everything, when they knew it would change nothing. "I won't lose you again!" William desperately warned her as he touched her face, kissed her mouth, and then pulled her powerfully against him. "We will find a way! We *must* find a way!"

A sudden knock on the door silenced them both. "Cecelia? Are you all right? Are you there, darling?"

"It's my stepmother," she whispered against his neck, her heart beating as quickly as William's. "She knows everythin', but she'll still be concerned fo' me. I've got to speak with her, explain what's happened."

"And I've got to report in," he reluctantly confessed on a sigh. "I was expected at a meeting an hour ago." His eyes fell on hers, those deep and wonderful eyes, just before he kissed her again. "You *will* be here when I get back?"

"I love you, William Tecumseh Sherman, with every part of my heart," Cecelia said in reply.

He was so entirely happy at what had happened for them at last, that he was halfway back to his office before he realized she had never really answered his question.

Chapter Twenty-three

❧

Anne convinced her that she had no choice but to return home.

William and Cecelia had been given a small jewel of time, Anne had told her. But there were too many other lives at stake now, too many people to hurt—the children most especially, if they meant to make it more than that. In the end, she convinced Cecelia to leave New Orleans before William could have time to return to the hotel and change her mind. Certain that she had gone, Anne then left for Augusta an hour later.

Cecelia's return to her life at Shelman Heights was bittersweet. There was no guilt over what she had done, or sense of shame. She and William had deserved their one precious night. But Anne was right. Because of Pleasant Stovall's manipulations to keep her from William, Ellen and her children did not deserve to forever bear the brunt by losing him.

"Take yo' loss, and turn the pain into a shape," Anne had urged her as they said their last good-byes in the misty New Orleans autumn morning. "Then pour that pain into somethin' of value in yo' life. Through the years ahead of you, believe me, it will make the pain somethin' easier to bear. It is the single regret of my life that I didn't do that myself."

She had no idea of what "value" she could be to anyone. Yet, in spite of the long journey home, Cecelia was at peace. Her peace ended when a letter arrived, handed to her by a grim-faced Charles. Pleasant Stovall had written to tell them that Anne—dear Anne, the friend, the only mother she could remember having—had contracted typhoid fever on the way home. The situation was grave. Cecelia and Charles went to Augusta at once.

Josiah met them out on the red brick carriageway beneath the low-hanging line of magnolia trees that closed off the Stovall mansion from the street. His deep mahogany face was dull with sorrow as he helped Cecelia from the last step and onto the property of her family home.

"How is she, Joe?" Cecelia urgently asked, fear spiking her voice and expression.

"Doc Benson and yo' sisters is wit' her, Miss Cecelia," he said somberly. "But it don't look good. No ma'am, it sho'ly don't."

She brushed past him, her heavy bell-shaped skirts rustling as she moved up the stairs. She was tearing off her gloves and bonnet as Charles silently followed her into a house that already looked dressed for a funeral. The shades were drawn low over all of the windows, and there were garlands tied with black ribbon adorning two of the tables. The only scent was, not from the flowers Anne had always loved so much, but rather the scent now came from camphor and bourbon. In Anne's bedroom sat Cecelia's two weeping elder sisters.

"Where the devil is Father?" Cecelia asked in a rushed tone of panic which her sisters did not meet. Instead, one of them stood and somberly came forward to embrace Cecelia.

"He can't remain here. It's too painful, he says, knowin' what's gon' to happen any time now."

Cecelia pushed past Marie, the eldest of Pleasant's many children, to the doctor who stood at the basin near the window washing his liver-spotted hands. "Can you not do somethin' fo' her?"

"I'm afraid not. It's the fever. She's in God's hands now."

Tears she had been determined not to surrender welled in her eyes as she lunged for Anne's bedside. She was so thin already, and so ghostly pale in such a short span of time, Cecelia thought, remembering her laughter as they had strolled the cobbled streets of New Orleans mere weeks ago.

"Father should be here! She *needs* him to be here!"

"You ought to tell her, Marie," her other sister, Caroline, urged.

"Hush now!" Marie shot back. She was such a big, imposing woman, accustomed to being regarded, that for a moment the room fell silent.

"Tell me what?" Cecelia asked with a panicked glance at each of them. "Tell me, then, for God's sake!"

"He's with *her* already. Poor Anne isn't even dead, and Father is wooin' her replacement!"

Like a swift blow to her stomach, the shock made Cecelia want to vomit. She felt the bile rise in her throat. Gripping her chest, she sank into the empty chair across from Caroline. "You cannot be serious!"

"It has been gon' on fo' months now, I'm afraid." She shook her head woefully, the coal dark ringlets brushing softly at her cheeks. "Her name is Cleo Hill, and when Marie and I confronted Father, all he would say was that he can't bear to be alone in his old age."

Cecelia had gone deathly pale. Her words sputtered out. "Is he gon' to *marry* this Cleo woman?"

Caroline looked as if she had bitten something sour. "He says, as soon as it's 'appropriate.' Good Lord Almighty, if there is such a thing!"

The mere thought that her own father could entertain such a plan, much less fully and unapologetically intend to carry it out, was inconceivable—even after what he had done to Cretia. She leaned forward and brushed the back of her hand gently across Anne's cheek. Her skin was fiery hot, and her breathing was labored. Cecelia ached at the thought that a woman for whom she cared so deeply should die like this.

And it made her consider her own marriage—Charles, and his flagrant interest in other women. How quickly might *she* be replaced? Charles controlled everything. There was no future. No purpose. Only servitude, acquiescence, and more pregnancies.

She needed something of her own. Something to make a difference. Shelman Heights, like the children, her beautiful blessed children, was of Charles. Her heart ached now, and had for a good many months, for something all her own—something of value, although she had no idea at all what that was likely to be.

"She's askin' fo' you!" Caroline called out desperately, drawing Cecelia from her thoughts.

She glanced back at the bed to see that Anne's eyes were slightly opened and her hand was up, motioning to her. Cecelia's heart began to beat swiftly as she swept back to the bedside and perched onto the edge. She took up Anne's blazing hand disregarding the danger of contagion. "I'm here," she murmured, feeling the pressure of tears again. Cecelia leaned nearer, squeezing her stepmother's hand. "May I get you somethin'? Water? Anything? Lord, there must be *somethin'* I can do fo' you!"

The reply was a slight shake of the head. There was nothing anyone could do for her now.

"Oh, how I despise myself that I didn't give you a real chance sooner to be as important to me as you are at this moment—and I swear to you, I will regret that fo' the rest of my life!" she murmured. "Please, fo'give me."

Anne's reply was a very faint smile just before she closed her eyes.

"Make a difference," Anne had said, not long ago. Cecelia remembered it now, a silent whisper across the days as she held Anne's hand. *Turn your pain into a shape . . . and then pour it into something of value in this life. . . .*

As she came down the stairs, in the shadowy light of the foyer, she saw Georgie standing at the bottom, his face ashen with concern. But he said nothing, only looked up at her expectantly. That was his mother upstairs dying, and of course Georgie, no longer a child, knew about their father's dalliances. He knew how his mother had been betrayed. Her heart broke for his disillusion the way she once long ago had suffered her own.

"She's restin'," Cecelia offered, reaching out to him as she lingered on the bottom step. "This came for you," he said, holding out a package. Cecelia took it and looked back at her brother, her mind filled with images of Anne—moments they had shared, the way she looked now.

Absently, she drew off the packaging and opened the box. There was no note. No card. But once she saw what lay inside, she understood. Her heart began thundering in her ears. It was the silver music box with the royal crest. Cecelia's lungs constricted, and for a moment, she could not breathe. Simple. Understated, so like William. The box alone expressed his feelings to her. "*You're not so different from this box . . . elegant . . . complex, well worth keeping, if one could only hold on to you.*" The box would be precious to her forever, for the oasis of time it represented.

"Thank you," she mouthed to her brother, even as the tears slid down her cheeks.

Georgie Stovall thought the tears were all for his mother. And, more than anything, Cecelia wanted him to believe that. "Make a difference," Anne had bidden her. And it was William who had first given her the notion of how. Perhaps now, it was time to do just that.

❧

Cecelia stayed in Augusta until the next morning when Anne died. Then, unable to attend the funeral with her father there feigning sorrow, she left for her home on the Etowah River, her heart pierced by many things now. By her past . . . by the world in which she had lived . . . by the future she saw for herself if she did not drastically change the direction of the road which lay ahead.

Chapter Twenty-four

A war for the U.S. with Mexico had come and gone. Kept from action there, too, through administrative duty, William fought the devil of unrest. Plagued also by his sense of honor without love for Ellen, he attacked his personal weaknesses head on. In Sept 1853, William did as Ellen long had bidden him. He resigned from the army that had sent him toward temptation in the South. His brother, John Sherman, trained as a lawyer, now held a seat in Congress, and old Thomas Ewing maintained his powerful alliances in Washington. Those connections netted William an offer to manage the bank Lucas & Turner, in San Francisco.

It was as far away from the South, and from Cecelia, as he could take himself.

Pleased at having won the battle at last, Ellen and the children left the safe harbor of her father's home in Lancaster, Ohio, and joined him out West. Both of them had hopes of making a fresh start of things.

But William's life seemed wrapped up in a kind of fate that knit people he had known more closely to him. It had begun with seeing Bragg, then Cecelia, and now again, one Sunday afternoon, someone else. As he and Ellen left Catholic Mass at Saint Stephen's Church on a bright spring day in 1856, they walked toward their carriage at the end of a long line of waiting carriages that lined the curb outside.

"You see there, Cump, it doesn't really wound you irreparably to sit through an occasional Mass with me," Ellen teased, strolling beside him in a new blue velvet bonnet with a silk ribbon and modest blue-and-red gingham dress. She was a larger woman now than she had been when they married, and her hair had changed, showing a few shafts of silver already. But, once again, she looked up at him with the adoring gaze that she had in their youth. The one that once had won him. It was that look to which he tried desperately now to cling.

"Let's not speak too soon. A delayed reaction is possible," he bantered, patting her arm, which was wound with his.

The children had gone ahead with Mrs. McGuffey, their governess, giving William and Ellen a few rare moments alone on the shady and cool tree-lined street. It had been a pleasant sermon, William thought. Not overly long or preachy, and he actually hadn't minded it much. But he would guard that closely, for to reveal it to Ellen would be to open himself up to a whole new onslaught of pleading to convert. William had nothing particular against the Catholic Church. He simply was not a Catholic. Out of deference to his widowed mother, who had died just last year, he felt compelled to cling to his own Protestant heritage.

It is more than that, and you well know it, a small voice inside him silently chided as they walked. And he did know. To Catholics, adultery was an unpardonable sin. And he already bore the heavy weighted guilt for that which had gripped his mind and heart and held him squarely for over eighteen years. He would not—could not—pay more dearly than he already had for that.

A man, drunk, lay sleeping in an alcove of an office building beside the church, his legs outstretched on the sidewalk. William did not realize it until Ellen stumbled over his scuffed black boots and then caught herself on a wall. As William glanced down at the man, his own face went ashen.

"*Sam?* Good Lord, Sam!"

Ellen tugged at her husband's arm. "Come away from there, Cump! A man like that may be dangerous!"

"He's drunk!"

"Precisely!"

William bent down, seeing that, of all people, it definitely was someone he knew. It was his West Point classmate, Ulysses Grant. In spite of his shabby black beard, his features and coloring were unmistakable.

"Help me get him up, Ellen, get him to our carriage! He needs a strong pot of coffee, and then a bath and perhaps—"

"I will do no such thing!" she gasped at him.

William shot his wife a look of reproach so bold that her tone softened beneath it. "I just don't think we should be mixed up with a man like this, that's all."

She wouldn't tell William that anyone from the West Point days was a tie back to the mysterious girl—Cecelia—and her own unsettled fear that the powerful past could still upset their fragile future.

"Oh, for Lord's sake, Ellen! Sam was a friend at the academy! I'm obliged to help him, if I can. It's a point of honor!"

"Your first obligation, Cump Sherman, is to me! And *I* don't wish to see you involve yourself with a drunk!"

"Where is that Catholic charity of yours now? If this is an example of what that church breeds, then I'm damn glad I never converted!"

"You can be the most obstinate man!"

"As *you* can be a great disappointment!"

Her face blanched at his words, and her hands fell to her sides. Other people walked on around them toward their own waiting carriages as the oak trees tossed leaves down around them. "That was very low of you, Cump."

"Your selfish behavior was lower still."

"Oh! I *knew* San Francisco would be bad for us! This air certainly is not doing a thing for your reasoning!"

His face was crimson with anger. "I hear you've been writing as much to your father, complete with your homesick rambling again, hoping, I'm sure, that he will insist you return to him!"

"Father is only trying to help me bring you to your senses, and get *all* of us home to Ohio where we belong!"

San Francisco should have been a good choice for them. But so far from Ohio and her family, Ellen was desperately homesick. She blamed William for it and for the financial crash of 1854, from which California was only now beginning to emerge. In the interim, real estate had declined, which doomed his bank to a profitless future and crippled William with debt.

Now, William was appalled at her incessant selfishness. In the face of that, he cared nothing for the presence of the people around him who had stopped to listen to their argument and to glare at the drunken man at their feet. "I, *not* the great Thomas Ewing, am your husband, as much as you might wish it otherwise!" Then he stooped and lifted Grant's hand.

"And just what the devil do you think you're doing?"

"Helping a friend!" he called angrily over his shoulder.

"What shall I tell the children?"

"Why not read them a Bible verse until I return! The one about the Good Samaritan seems to come most quickly to mind!" he said before he turned away, then left her to find her own way back home.

It took a pot of very strong coffee and a meal of pot roast and mashed potatoes before Grant seemed even vaguely aware of where he was or who was helping him. Only when his bloodshot eyes filled with tears and he surrendered his face to his hands did William lean across the table very gently to cover his hand with his own, and to speak.

"Do you want to talk about it, Sam?"

Grant finally looked up, a wreck of a man and, before he spoke, grimaced. "It's been a long time since anyone has called me that. Sure does take me back."

William's voice was very low, and warmed by true concern in a restaurant filled with busy conversation, the rattling of dishes, and the clink of glasses. "What happened, Sam? You were always so full of fire. I half expected you to be a general by now!"

Grant laughed. It was the deep and rheumy sound, William thought, of a much older man. "I could sure use a drink."

Without reproach, William ordered him a shot of whiskey and watched as he drank, and Grant's eyes slowly widened then steadily cleared. A moment after that, he was ready to talk.

"I didn't mean to let it get so far out of hand. Or to get so far from the goals I'd set for myself." He exhaled a heavy and very weary breath and fingered the whiskey shot glass, seeming suddenly in no particular hurry to finish it. "I'm posted over in Monterey and actually did make it to first lieutenant last year."

"Did you?" William smiled. "Well, that's grand."

"I suppose they thought I'd distinguished myself in the Mexican War. But all of that is a world away from my life back in Ohio."

"That it is."

"Ohio, that is, *and* the woman I love." He looked up at William, his eyes wide and very sad. "In the beginning, the whiskey helped me not to dwell on missing her so much. Now, it only makes me miss her more. Tell me Cump, you ever miss anyone like that? . . . A longing that is physically painful?"

"I can only imagine," he said, drawing in a careful breath.

He ordered Grant another whiskey, and one for himself. As they drank and spoke of many things, Grant was shocked to discover that William had never seen action in Mexico, and that he had later withdrawn from a military career altogether.

Grant managed a few small bites of apple pie a waiter had laid before him onto the bare, oak table. "What happened to you? Exemplary cadet like you, working in a bank?"

William sighed heavily. "Life, I suppose. And my own wife's wishes."

"Children?"

William nodded. "Four."

"Oh, that's right. Van Vliet told me once about your wife. One of the cadets' sisters. Southern girl, wasn't she? From Georgia, if memory serves. A real love story with the two of you. Like Romeo and Juliet, her brother wanted to keep you apart at first."

He flinched. "No. I married a girl from home. We grew up together, so I suppose it was fated." William knew that Grant could see another truth in his eyes, and it made him suddenly anxious to leave. "Speaking of my wife, I really should be getting on home. So let's get you up to that room I took for you, and get you cleaned up. You'll feel like a new man after you've had a hot bath."

An hour later, outside on the street, the two men shook hands as Grant waited for a hired carriage to take him to the train depot. "You've been a good sport today, Sherman."

"You would have done the same for me."

"Do you expect we'll ever meet again?"

"Not likely. With the bank closing here, I've taken a new job as a school superintendent back in Louisiana. I was stationed there once, but now I'll see it as a civilian. And you will become something grand in the army."

"You're not going home to Ohio, to your wife's family?"

"The time is not right for that yet. But I certainly do miss it there."

Grant shook his head. "I always looked up to you at West Point, Sherman. You were preparing to be some kind of soldier. If you'll forgive me, it seems a terrible waste, with you so perfect for a military career."

"My family wants those days over," William sighed, "and so they are."

Grant smiled and clapped William on the shoulder as a gust of cool wind rose up suddenly off the San Francisco Bay. "I keep hearing rumors that we're headed for a War Between the States if the South keeps up this wild talk of secession. If there is a war, our side'll surely want all able West Point men like yourself back in uniform."

"I doubt it will ever come to that. A war like that would devastate the entire country."

Grant shook his head. His eyes were clear now, William thought, and so blue that they reflected the sky. "Then I pray to God, you're right, Sherman. If that's the only way our paths might cross, I do pray that we never do see one another again."

Chapter Twenty-five

OCTOBER 1860

Cecelia sat on the wide veranda of graceful Shelman Heights eight years after New Orleans, as the autumn fog of late evening lay like a heavy blanket in the trees, down by the water's edge. Her gaze was focused very far away. Out here in the still silence with her book, she read greedily in the moments when she was alone. Around the veranda, the trees and shrubbery holding the last of the dogwood blossoms were thick, hiding her from the world beyond. Charles, thankfully, was in Savannah on business or she would never have dared to bring the book out from beneath her bed. She had read that Queen Victoria wept reading *Uncle Tom's Cabin*, so troubled was Her Majesty by the sheer inhumanity of slavery.

"You take very good care of yourself, Miss Shelman, that in the coming days for your country, you don't find your heart divided more than it already appears to be. . . ."

Cecelia had never forgotten the young queen's sage words to her from that surprise meeting years earlier. They had played on in her thoughts through the years, and troubled her as she slowly, and yet passionately, had come to terms with her own feelings on the incendiary subject of slavery.

For Cecelia, Harriet Beecher Stowe's book had opened up an entire world, and brought her a thirst for discovering everything she could about the Underground Railroad and the abolitionist movement.

She knew Cretia had remained deeply, and dangerously, involved in helping fugitive slaves as the political unrest had risen to a fever pitch. If Abraham Lincoln was elected to the presidency next month, as it appeared very likely now he would be, Southern leaders felt they had no choice but to protect their way of life and leave the Union. According to the newspapers, many of the states were planning to do so already, Georgia among them. When Cretia came outside onto the veranda with her, it was well after dark. The back door creaked, then clattered to a close behind her.

"The children?" Cecelia asked, rocking a steady rhythm in her white cane rocker and reaching up to take Cretia's hand affectionately.

It had taken her several years to entirely forgive Cretia for what she had done to keep her from William. For nearly a year after she discovered Marcellus's letter scheme, Cecelia had found it difficult even to speak to her. But over time, and after another difficult pregnancy and birth, during which Cretia never left her side, Cecelia remembered all the reasons for their devotion to one another. All the reasons she would keep the identity of Cretia's mother a secret. Hurting Cretia with the truth now could not bring back the past. Nor could it change her future.

"Margaret is sayin' her prayers, while the children are lettin' Mammy Ruth chase them round the nursery in their nightclothes."

Cecelia smiled. "They do love to tease that poor woman, but she sho' is good to them."

"That's a fact." She glanced at Cecelia's book, which sat prominently, and intentionally, on Cecelia's lap.

"Miss Cecelia, now what are you doin' bringin' a book like that into Master Charles's house? He'll skin you alive—or mo' likely *me*—fo' givin' you the idea!"

"He'll do no such thing because he'll never know I have it."

"You can't keep secrets from Master Charles!"

"*You* certainly have. Look at all you've accomplished!"

"*I'm* not his wife!"

"For as often as he's here these days, I don't think I'm in much danger."

Cretia did not dare to argue that point. The gossip in town was that Mr. Shelman continued his affair with the wealthy young widow in Savannah, the city in which he spent an extraordinarily large part of his time.

"Truth is . . ." Cecelia looked at her. "I want to help you."

"Help me do what?"

"With the Railroad. I want to help as many of yo' people go North as I can."

Cretia studied her, her dark brow furrowing suspiciously. "It's not a job fo' you."

"Why not? Because I'm white? I've heard there are dozens of white folks involved in—"

"Because you're you!"

"Don't you patronize me, Cretia!"

"Don't *you* ask me if you can't take the truth!"

"If you have some problem with my help, you tell me straight out!"

"You're a Southern woman! Wife of a mighty powerful landowner, who just also happens to own slaves! You want folks whose whole lives are wrapped up in this one last hope to trust you?"

"I would *never* betray you!"

"I know that, but they don't!"

"Can you not tell them?"

"It's a risk I couldn't take!"

"Well, it's damn nice to know you have a heart 'bout someone other than *me*!" The air thickened in the silence. "I'm sorry. I didn't mean that."

It had hurt so much, losing William, knowing Cretia, of all people, had been a party to her greatest pain. But she had meant what she had said, and she had lived by it for a long time. There was no point in airing all of that now. No amount of her venom would ever change history.

"There's nothin', I promise," Cecelia said as Cretia studied her warily. "Please," Cecelia bade her. "Let me help you. I want my life to mean somethin'! Yours—doin' as you do—savin' lives, seein' people to freedom, is far better than mine will ever be if I don't do this!"

"Well, if you get caught, if they hang *you* there'd be plenty of folks who'd care. I'm no account. Just another dead darky, and one less to fret over runnin' away."

"Don't talk like that! You know what you are to me! Friend, companion, and the one woman in this whole crazy world who can understand my need to make a difference!"

"This ain't a joke, Cecelia," she said. "And there's no room with these people fo' good Samaritans who're gon' to fold under pressure of interrogation!"

"I won't fold."

"Can you handle the unexpected?"

"Of course. My life should tell you that!"

"Surprises you hadn't counted on?"

"Absolutely!"

"Like knowin' yo' house here has been a station fo' two years fo' the Underground already?" Cretia took Cecelia's upper arms, gripping them tightly. Her eyes were wide and dark and full of shimmering purpose. "This ain't a game. It ain't a diversion fo' the afternoon because you're bored with life. These people have hopes and dreams, just like you—and they've got them wrapped up in one small chance, one shot fo' a lifetime that might pass fo' somethin' close to normal."

"I am committed," Cecelia declared in a deep, steady tone Cretia had never heard before. "Please. Let me help you."

"I want yo' house to stay as a station."

"Done."

She looked as if she were still studying her lifelong friend and owner, the decision not yet made. "And I'll want you to help with an escape, directly."

"All right."

"Tonight."

They both heard Cecelia swallow. "That's quite sudden."

"My people have waited a lifetime."

"All right, then. Tonight it is. Just tell me what to do."

Mammy Ruth put the children to bed. Charles was still in Savannah. His being there so often, Cretia confessed, had been a blessing, as it made the station more available. And after Christmas last year, he had bought another male slave to tend the grounds. But when Charles was away, Pait, tall and quiet, a man with a strong slim body and a good heart, helped her with the tasks of the station. Just after sunset, as the crickets came out in force and filled the air with their night music, there was a soft knock at the front door. Cecelia, who had been absently working a needlepoint flower in the small parlor nearby, felt her heart jump. This was it, she thought. The beginning. There would be no turning back after tonight. She moved to the door and met Cretia in the foyer.

"You sure 'bout this?" Cretia asked her.

"Absolutely sure."

A very tall black man slumped against a column, head lowered to his chin, outside on the front veranda. Cretia dashed toward him and only as he came out of the shadows and into the light did Cecelia realize that he was badly wounded.

"Dear God!" Cecelia gasped.

"He's been whipped! Quick! We need to get him to a bed! Call Pait to help me get him up to my room!"

"Of course!"

"Then fetch some water, towels, camphor, and bandages! I'll need yo' help with this one! He's as bad off as I've seen!"

Cretia directed her with more confidence than Cecelia had ever heard, and she was grateful for it—she had not expected this heart-thumping fear to intimidate her. All her life Cecelia had played by the rules, and this first very sudden foray against them was terrifying.

She stood in the doorway too stunned by what she saw to think or to move. The large man slumped motionless, stripped to the waist. His bare feet were muddy and blistered, and the brown pants he wore were ragged and frayed at the ankles. But it was sight of the deep, raw, and bloody gashes slashed across his back, like great red cords, that stunned Cecelia into immobility. All her life, first her father and then Charles had reasoned that slavery was a good institution, that it gave blacks a secure place to be, gave them a home . . . food, a purpose. And because she had never seen this sort of brutality, injustice, and inhumanity herself, Cecelia had chosen to believe her family. It was easier and safer than believing that what the abolitionists said might actually be true. She cursed her own naïveté, wondering how many she might have helped before now if she had only opened her eyes wide enough.

Pait silently tossed the wounded man over his shoulder and carried him upstairs to Cretia's garret room. As he stood in the doorway with Cecelia, Cretia examined his wounds.

"Quick! Fetch me some whiskey fo' his pain!"

Cecelia flew back down the stairs, her skirts rustling in the pale gray silence of early evening, relieved, even for a few moments, to be away from the sight. How could anyone have done something so horrid?

After she returned to the small room, Cecelia watched helplessly, handing bandages and medicine to Cretia and Pait as they worked together—a seamless, natural team, until the stranger was clean and comfortable. She had been moved to tears as Cretia sang softly to the wounded man while she worked over him and he finally fell asleep:

> *Oh, freedom over me!*
> *And before I'd be a slave*
> *I'll be buried in my grave*
> *And go home to my Lord, and be free.*

Downstairs, Cretia put a hand on Cecelia's shoulder as Cecelia quickly dried her eyes, trying her best to show the strength she had convinced Cretia she possessed.

"I sing it to all of 'em," she said. "They say it gives 'em hope. Keeps them strong."

As she glanced at Pait, who stood, a tall and silent shadow behind Cretia, Cecelia was certain she had seen a look of awe in his eyes. And she had never really looked at him before now, never noticed Pait as anything apart from the other slaves, to whom she was fair and kind, but previously unaware. Now, in the glow of Cretia's triumph, he seemed a formidable partner.

Cecelia shook her head and, for a moment, closed her eyes. "I'm sorry. I should be stronger."

"It's a powerful sight the first time you see barefaced injustice."

Pait was shaking his head in silent agreement. Cecelia saw that his eyes were a rich milky brown and that his black face had lovely depth and texture. She wondered what horrid stories of mistreatment were locked away in his mind behind that gaze.

"Is it always so bad?" Cecelia asked haltingly.

"Sometimes worse. Was a man, 'bout a year ago, died in yo' own cellar down there, from bein' beat. All he'd done was call his owner *mister* 'stead of *massa*."

Cecelia recoiled, arms wrapping around her waist as she felt a rush of loathing. "What can I do for the man up there now?"

Cretia gripped her shoulder and squeezed it. Her gaze did not waver. It was as strong, and determined as was she. "You doin' it. Without you to let him heal up there and sleep, instead of bein' in that damp cellar, he'd likely never make it to freedom one day. Each leg of the Railroad is crucial. Ain't any leg mo' or less so."

Cecelia managed a small, grim smile. Here was a glimmer of salvation. "I *do* believe Charles'd kill me right here on the spot, if he knew."

"But the good Lawd'll love you on into fo'ever. I expect knowin' that is gon' make up for the risk."

And for Cecelia, it did.

"Thank ye, ma'am," the man mouthed, little sound coming out past the pained, shallow breath as he struggled to speak.

Cecelia squeezed his hand tightly. Bending over this injured man reminded her of Anne. "Turn your pain into a shape, and then pour into something of value in this life." It was what she was doing here, now, with this man, and with the others she intended to help. She never would have known selflessness if she had found a future in Ohio with William Tecumseh Sherman after that first West Point summer. And, for Cecelia, that realization was healing.

"It'll be all right. You're in the best hands there are," Cecelia whispered, and patted the blue-black skin of his hand as she glanced up at Cretia with shreds of the same grim smile from last night.

"Name's Horace, ma'am," he murmured suddenly, then coughed deeply. ". . . Horace."

Cecelia glanced again at Cretia, who told her, "He believes you have a good heart, doin' this. He thinks if he dies today, that someone in this ol' world knew him is what matters."

Cecelia took up his hand again, so dark against her pale skin, and squeezed it. "Thank you, Horace," she said, her voice breaking. "But you aren't gon' die. Not in my house, you're not! You've got to know freedom and a bit of happiness first, you hear me?"

The man nodded weakly, then closed his eyes to rest. It was a moment, and he was a man, who had changed her life, and Cecelia knew she would never forget it, or him.

"Pait's a good man."

Cecelia made the declaration as she and Cretia were alone out in the warming kitchen the next morning, making hot chicory to drink, as coffee rations had long ago run out. Mammy Ruth was across the room, hunched over, pressing the pulp of a melon through a sheet of gauze for the sugar, another commodity they no longer could buy.

"I expect he is," Cretia replied.

"Are you fond of him, may I ask?"

Cretia glanced up, wiping her hands on the white apron tied at her waist. In the silence, the tone of Cecelia's question fell upon her. Her hands stopped then, and her expression was full of self-defense. "Not how *you* mean it."

"And may I ask why not?"

"I ain't never gon' have those sort of feelin's fo' a man."

Cecelia knew she meant after what Pleasant Stovall had stolen from her. That would always be one of the darkest clouds over their enduring friendship—that and what had happened with William Tecumseh Sherman.

Cecelia took Cretia's hand and squeezed it. "We can't, either one of us, live on in the past."

"There's just no future fo' me with a man."

"I think Pait may have a different feelin' 'bout that."

"He's a help with the work. That's all."

Cecelia shrugged her shoulders and poured the chicory liquid into a china pot, knowing she had pushed enough for the moment. And this did not feel over to her. Not nearly so.

Over the tense opening weeks of April 1861, the first shot of war having been fired in South Carolina on Fort Sumter, a collection of Southern states took their stand, seceding from the Union. They included Alabama, Florida, Mississippi, Louisiana, and, as Cecelia had long feared, Georgia. As the first seceding states adopted a constitution and elected Jefferson Davis as their president, Cecelia went secretly and bravely against the grain. As days passed and the newly elected President Lincoln made his inaugural address, she and Shelman Heights played host to more than forty-three desperate slaves seeking their freedom. Some, like the man who called himself Horace, were kept upstairs until they were strong enough to travel on to the next station. Others, when Charles returned home, lived for days, or even weeks, in the relative safety of the cellar, until the next station opened up.

For Cecelia, participating in the cause became an obsession, as it had been all along for Cretia. It was, she told Cretia, as if all the moments of her life had led her to this one, strongly defining place where God had given her the chance to do something of value. God, Anne—and William Tecumseh Sherman.

As she rode in her carriage across long dirt roads, along vast cotton fields, hiding duos of runaway slaves disguised as her servants, Cecelia thought of Anne's plea, her prayer for meaning. It entirely sustained her now as they all risked everything to get to the next station on the Underground Railroad. She was no longer a naïve Southern daughter. She had become a noble woman. Slavery was wrong. The South was wrong. This way, she could make a difference as Anne had bidden her. Her life as a Southern wife in a loveless marriage could mean something—if she remained brave enough to shoulder these risks.

After one ride to the Mississippi border, she returned home to find a letter had come from Augusta, sent from Pleasant Stovall's new wife, Cleo. The perfumed missive was filled with news of the birth of her second child. But along the bottom she had written one other thing, as an afterthought: Cecelia's father wanted her to know that Marcellus, Bolling, and Tom had all signed up with the Confederate Army to fight for the Southern cause. They had left a day earlier. Along with them, so determined to be a man in their father's hardened eyes, had gone Georgie Stovall, the brother of Cecelia's heart and her link back to Anne, whose memory faded from her a little more each day. *God, keep him safe,* Cecelia prayed. *Just, please, bring home Anne's boy—and mine—alive.*

Chapter Twenty-six

❧

William read the latest plea-filled letter from his brother, now a United States senator, as he sat behind his grand carved desk, the superintendent of the Louisiana Seminary of Learning. He felt some sense of relief. John wrote that powerful old Thomas Ewing had set up a meeting for Cump with President Lincoln. As May of 1861 came, the president was seeking to put all West Point graduates into federal uniform. This was a second chance at a life for which he had trained. A way to find greatness in the middle of the mediocrity in which he floundered. The flame of unmet ambition within him flared.

He pushed a stack of papers around absently on the top of his desk as if he were searching for something. But he would find nothing here in this dimly lit office with its heavy desk and cases full of dusty books, in this school full of tensions. In spite of his own distance from the conflict, the school quickly became a microcosm for the rest of the country, poised to erupt at any moment.

William glanced out the window again, at a grand and full old magnolia tree, such a lovely symbol of the South he loved. Its leaves bristled in the breeze. Ellen would be furious. Especially when she discovered that her own father had a hand in his posting. Damn! Why did that infernal woman always insist on putting herself on the opposite side of whatever he desired? In a wave of frustration, William shoved the papers off the desk and onto the floor with a sweep of his hand.

"Goodness, Cump!" Ellen entered, bearing his midday meal, as always, along with her own particular brand of smiling reproach. "This *is* quite a little mess you've made for yourself! If you were one of the children, I would send you to bed without your supper!"

When he turned around slowly, she was smiling. He rose and went to take the hamper from her. "But I'm not, am I?" He kissed her cheek absently, hating it when she spoke to him as she did one of their children. "It was kind of you to bring this, my dear. Thank you."

"As your wife, I consider it my duty. And my pleasure, of course."

"Of course."

As he sat back down behind his desk, Ellen settled into the chair opposite his. The only article remaining on the desk now was the official-looking letter from John. Her fingers flew to her lips.

"Come now. It cannot be a total surprise to you that they would want me back in uniform."

Ellen lunged forward across the desk, her fingers clutching the polished wood. "You cannot think of going! You've a new life here! And we have been given a new chance!"

She was frowning at him, her smooth, round face strangely puckered with disapproval. "I'll not move around again as a military wife, Cump. I warn you, I'll go home to Ohio again before I'll subject our children to an unnatural existence like that!"

An existence many military wives lived, for the men they loved. "I would follow you anywhere that made you happy." The echo of Cecelia's words from so long ago settled on top of the silence. William chaffed at the woman before him. "Isn't that what you want anyway? To go home to your father again?"

"That's not at all true!" Ellen replied, a bit too quickly as she moved away from the desk, straightening against the accusation. Her lips were tightly pursed.

"Isn't it?" He settled his eyes on her. "You knew what I was before we married, and yet you went through with it anyway. And you've done little else since then but set about changing me!"

"I've known a good *many* things about you, William Sherman—and I went through with it anyway!"

"What the devil is *that* supposed to mean?"

She stood and spun around, her heavy skirts rustling and her small opal earrings glinting in the filtered sunlight. "Take it as you wish!"

William sprang from his seat and went after her around the desk, grasping Ellen's upper arm in a vise grip, his eyes on fire. "No! You meant something by your remark, some reference to my past—"

"I knew perfectly well that there were other women in your life! You wrote me yourself from your post at Piccolata about your affection for Mary Johnson and then Mary Lamb after that!

Useless attempts to heal an unbearable hurt . . .

"And I have every reason to believe there were others before Picolata!"

"What reason?"

She tried to free herself from his grip. "You're hurting me!"

"You've made an accusation, Ellen. I simply want you to see it through!"

"Very well, then. I cannot bear the thought of knowing you were with another woman! Any woman! Loving her, holding her . . . whispering the things to her you have to me! The mere thought of it makes me violently ill!"

Struck, William stepped back. But his shocked gaze never left her sight. "I cannot change my past, Ellen, nor how I became as I am. Yes, there were other women before we married. I never hid that from you!"

"Did you confess every one with this great honesty of yours between us?"

William spun on his heel, slamming the palm of his hand onto his forehead. He was exhausted and furious, a dangerous combination. "Oh, blasted! That is simply over the line!"

"Well, did you?"

"I married *you*, Ellen, not any other! We have a life! Children! Another on the way! Why can't that be enough?"

"Because it's not enough for *you*! Don't you see? You wear the truth of your heart, of your desires, in those incredible eyes of yours! I'm not blind, Cump! I see the ambition burning there, the disquiet! The need for something never fully realized! You're not just going back to the military because Mr. Lincoln asked you to! You're going because *you* want it! You could deny that to me all day long, and the truth would still betray you! Your *eyes* would betray you! You were right about one thing! If you're going to war, I *do* want to go home! I want to be there with my family—have this baby there, surrounded by them! Because at least with them, there is the peace of knowing fully where I stand!"

William softened, putting a gentle hand across Ellen's shoulder, then drawing her into a careful embrace. "I don't want you to go."

"And *I* never wanted you to love another woman! But there you have it, just the same."

She was not tearful, but motionless and board-straight—entirely closed off to him. It was as if she had read his mind about Cecelia. But William was simply too tired of fighting Ellen to consider anything beyond the sheer impossibility of that.

After he had fallen asleep, Ellen rose from their bed and went, barefoot and silent, to the old trunk Cump kept up in the attic. It was his military trunk, full of old uniforms, his saddle, sash, sword, and letters. It also harbored the single pencil sketch of a young woman who had haunted her for too many years. These were pieces of the past he had laid away, yet saved all these years because they mattered to him.

As she carefully unrolled the old paper sketch, Ellen felt a shiver snake through her.

Cecelia—of course it was her, damn her phantom image! And if not for that mad moment in time when Ellen had tossed her letter to the flames, the mysterious Cecelia, she knew, would now be Mrs. William Tecumseh Sherman. In the beginning, she had felt victory in her success, then guilt, and now simply resignation to things no amount of manipulation could change.

William was a wild and restless bird she had caged. She had been clever, persistent, and she had won. But seeing the expression in his eyes earlier today, as he had spoken of the new war, had stirred the restlessness all up again. It had brought thoughts of Cecelia and almost, *almost* a confession of having found this sketch. What had driven Ellen was the hope of making him confess that Cecelia, whoever she was, now meant nothing. But Thomas Ewing always said one should never ask a question if one could not bear to hear the answer.

She glanced down again and traced her finger over the youthful, feminine face with features so completely different from her own. In fact, this woman, this stranger, was the complete antithesis of herself. Dark, slim, and Southern, with her ebony ringlets, William had sketched her with such a tiny waist, in a dress with a wide bell skirt full of flowers and lace. This was no one's poor relation or country tart. And there was a spirited quality in her expression. It was one not unlike William's, that leapt right off the page at her. Kindred spirits? Soul mates . . . and her own greatest enemy.

He had never once, in all their years, asked to sketch her.

After another moment, Ellen carefully rolled up the sketch again and hid it away back in the trunk. She was right to go home now. If their marriage was to survive, she could not follow him around the country—as his memories did. Ellen would have to *make* Cump come to her. God willing, she could make him choose her over war—as she had made him choose her over a mysterious Southern belle.

Ellen had gone back to Ohio, and a daughter was born to them, whom she had chosen to name Ellie. Feeling the deepening estrangement between them, Ellen wrote to William of her decision about the name—as if it were an afterthought. Still riled by her husband's ambitions and his mysterious past, she had not requested his opinion in the matter.

In spite of his reluctance to test himself after so many years, and in the face of his wife's disapproval, William heard President Lincoln's call. At last, he went to the trunk himself and drew out the sword, sash, and saddle he had laid away, agreeing to return to the army, in the rank of colonel of the Thirteenth Regular Infantry.

On his way North, William stopped in New Orleans to see his old West Point foe, Braxton Bragg, who long had urged him to come for a visit. What he found, he had not expected. Bragg met him for lunch in the restaurant of the Saint Louis Hotel, tall and dashing in the crisp, gray dress uniform and white gloves of a Confederate officer. After they had embraced heartily, Bragg chuckled and slapped William across the back. "Those steely eyes of yours always did betray you, my old friend. I see I have rendered you speechless."

"Quite." William smiled as they sat down across from one another at a small linen-draped table. It was only then that William noticed the large gathering of gray uniforms around them, and an uneasiness descended on him. This South that he had loved was very swiftly becoming enemy territory, and *he* was the enemy.

They ordered drinks, and Bragg, far more distinguished-looking now with his height and imposing bearing, waited for it all to sink in.

"I've accepted a commission from President Jefferson Davis to command a new state army. He was glad to get all the West Point men he could steal from Lincoln, with the war so fully blown now."

William was cautious. "I'm sure he was."

Bragg leaned across the table, lowering his voice sincerely. "You're at a crossroads, old friend, and you've always loved the South—understood us as if you were one of our own. Hell, you once planned to spend the rest of yo' life among us!"

"Tell that to the boys at the Louisiana school I just left, to whom I am forever Billy Yank."

"To my Johnny Reb!" Bragg scoffed, slapping the edge of the table for effect. "Those are boys, and these are times that call fo' men! We need you, Cump! You'd be an officer of the highest standin'. I could see to it. We could fight side by side to protect our way of life down here!"

"*Your* way of life, Braxton."

"It would have been yours, too, you know, if you had married Marcellus Stovall's sister, as you once were so intent upon doin'."

William stiffened and glanced around the room. "But I didn't," he answered crisply, looking back at Bragg.

Braxton Bragg downed his bourbon as a male servant in a starched white jacket lay a china plate brimming with pot roast before each of them. "You know I wouldn't offend you fo' the world, and I'm sorry if I did. It's just that I see such greatness in this fo' us."

"Perhaps on opposite sides."

Bragg's thick, dark brows arched. "So you would actually fight with Lincoln against us?"

"Not against *you*, Braxton. *For* maintaining the Union."

"The same Union that wants to tell us how to live our lives down here—that we have no states' rights to make our livin' as we choose?"

"Yes, *that* Union. The one that wants to remain a *United* States of America."

"Do you ever wonder how yo' life would have been different now if you *had* married that Stovall girl—what was her name?"

"Cecelia," he flatly replied. "Her name was Cecelia."

"Ah, yes. That was it." He leaned back in his chair, his darkly bearded chin between his thumb and forefinger. He was silent for a moment. "Talk of her makes me remember that dance, all those years ago, how foolish we both were. Do you recall that captain—who was to be honored our first year at commencement? The one who helped you navigate to win yo' dance with Cecelia from me?"

William had not thought of him in years, or the kindness he had shown on that one fateful night. "Lee, wasn't it? From Virginia." He suddenly remembered him warmly.

"Robert E. Lee, the very one who has been put in charge of the entire Confederate Army."

William's surprise showed on his face as he set his fork back onto his plate. "Is that a fact? He seemed such a loyal fellow, a real military career man."

"And so he is. Devotedly so. Turned down Lincoln cold for the same post on the other side. Apparently his devotion to his Southern roots outweighed his other concerns. I heard he told the president he could never fight against his Virginia friends and neighbors."

William respected honor, and found that he respected Robert E. Lee.

They finished their meal, speaking of less volatile things—of family, of children—and when they finished and Bragg walked him out into the street, William felt that great bittersweet pull between loyalty to the past and devotion to principles he believed in.

In the Louisiana midday sun, they embraced, and William saw the shine of tears in an old friend's eyes. "Good luck," William said, meaning it.

Bragg eyed him for an intensely silent moment. "Please, Cump. Stay here in the South. Fight with us. Fight with *me*. I'm the commander now of this new army, and I have the authority from Governor Moore himself to name you a brigadier general, if you'll agree!"

William arched his brows. His lower lip dropped. "That is impressive."

"What do you say? Stay. Fight with us. You're loved here. We need you."

"I can't." Seeing the expectation on Bragg's handsome face, William went on. "Damn it, I'm a Yankee, Braxton! I will forever be a Yankee. And as much as I feel the deep, hot burn of the call to return to the military—as much as I ache for that—more than you could ever know . . . I can't do it on your side of things. I don't support slavery or even the idea of states' rights. Not the way the Southern states mean to use it."

Bragg drew a breath, then exhaled deeply. He studied his old friend for a moment before he spoke. His words, when they came, were a sad warning. "We'll likely fight against each other in the comin' months."

"I pray God that doesn't happen."

"*We* will win, you know," Bragg said.

"I'd like nothing better for *you*, my old friend." He drew Bragg then into a tight and desperate embrace on the crowded, carriage-lined street of New Orleans. "But not for the United States. For the sake of the country, the North is about to break you."

He thought now how swiftly life changed. From marking examinations in a Southern boys' school as an anonymous authority to defining battlefield combat on the front lines. There was no turning back now from the conquests and adventure that had both eluded and beckoned William Tecumseh Sherman for decades.

Chapter Twenty-seven

On July 31st, 1861, William charged his mighty bay across the broad, grassy plane of a strange place in Virginia, called Manassas by some, Bull Run by others. He rode hard at the head of a ragtag collection of Union troops. The Second Wisconsin Militia put under his command, their bayonets raised and muskets pointed, were nothing more than a collection of farmers who wore a confusing and dangerous uniform of gray flannel. With them, marched the Scottish Highlanders, wearing their ancestral kilts. They marched with yet another distinct collection of men, the Irish troop. Along with the Scottish Highlanders, the other novices brandished bayonets, tempting fate, feeling ready for the conflict ahead.

But all of them were green as the grass, William saw. These boys playing soldier tore at his heart, so unprepared and untrained they were for what he knew must lie ahead.

Suddenly, musket balls were whirring past William, blue-white smoke filled the blazing July sky, and men were falling in the volley of yellow dust, crimson blood, and throaty cries of agony. After a career of inaction, William Sherman was instantly in the thick of it, trying to rein in the pandemonium that had swelled up around him in confused men and terrified boys.

Confederate cavalrymen had charged them with a sudden ferocity that threw them all off guard. Things progressed in a strange, twisted reality. Men flew from their saddles amid the powerful volley. A rebel officer, in his gray coat and red sash, slashed at him with a saber. William dodged the blow. His heart was throbbing, hammering into his burning, dry throat. Beside him, one of his own men, a Wisconsin boy, took the similarity of his own uniform to the Confederates to confuse the rebel. In an instant, the boy plunged his bayonet into the side of his Confederate opponent. The curiously familiar dark-haired boy tumbled from his mount into the tall grass and smoke beside William. In an odd moment as the enemy lay in the grass looking up, his eyes met William's. They were dark. So dark. And yet familiar. But there was no time to consider it, and he moved on, hollering orders and dodging bullets.

The battle raged, and there was heavy combat for hours, each side attacking and then retreating in a hail of rifle musket fire and cannons. William's men were falling around him now, mangled bodies, blood streaming from limbs, nostrils, and open wounds. Very swiftly, his fervor for victory became a clear need for retreat. The Confederate Army was winning. No matter how many West Point maneuvers he and the other officers employed, carnage grew around him. Cries of terror. Screams of agony. Dust. Blood. Fury. This bit of hell, he knew now, was what he had missed in the Mexican War.

Boom! A bullet grazed his own shoulder. William felt the warm sting of pain. Then the blood. Around him was confusion, fear, and the risk of desertion by his entire regiment. Through the blue haze of a battlefield steadily littered with bodies, William knew that to save what men he could, he would need to make one last stand. As his horse was struck, William gave the commanding cry for one last powerful volley behind which he ordered the bulk of his men to retreat. These green, frightened boys would live to fight another day, but only if he knew when to quit.

Later, as night began falling around them, silence engulfed their wounded and still reeling masses making their way into the safety of the woods, William came upon a group of his Irish soldiers gathered around what appeared to the corpse of a young Confederate soldier, kicking it and jeering. But, as he drew near, walking his own wounded horse through the men, William saw that the soldier was a fair-skinned, dark-haired young soldier. And though badly wounded, he was still alive.

William felt his heart quicken with a strange recognition as he drew nearer the crumpled pile lying in a scarlet pool, only to realize then that it was that first rebel soldier who had received the bayonet blow beside him in the battle's opening tumult.

"Stop!" William called out, and the gruff sound of his voice echoed through the woods.

The Wisconsin soldier, covered in battle blood, turned to him in surprise. "It's just a Reb, sir. The boys here were just fixing to finish him off, put him out of his misery."

"Touch him again, and I will personally shoot you myself!"

William removed his gloves and handed them to a young sergeant who shadowed him. He knelt beside the boy who had been wounded in the abdomen. Blood spilled from the opening in his gray coat, completely covering the two hands that tried to stem the flow. How was it that he had wandered this far? He must have come from determined stock. And then the thought hit him as hard as any musket fire, as William gently brushed a swag of dark hair from the boy's pasty, perspiration-drenched face. That same strange thing jerked within him. The hair. The shape of his face.

"Sergeant, my canteen!"

William knelt in the dirt, held the boy's head, and gave him a swallow of water. His eyes were glazed, dark half moons of agony as William brushed the flies from his wound. "What's your name, son?"

It took a moment. "Stovall, suh. George P. Stovall."

William's heart wrenched with horror—and he knew. "You from Georgia, son?"

"Yassuh. Augusta, suh." He coughed. The water came back up in a mixture of blood. "I wonder . . . Could you get a note to my family, suh? . . . I don't believe I'm gon' be able to do it myself. . . . Please, suh. Tell them that I was a brave soldier. Even in the hands of the enemy? . . . My father would like to know that. . . . I think, at last, he'd be proud of me."

Tears blurred William's eyes, then fell into ribbons cutting through the layer of dust on his craggy cheeks. He leaned very close to the boy, who was so near to death. "Your sister would be proud to know it, too."

The gaze was a vacant stare, the words whispered. "You know my sister?"

"A very long time ago." He stroked George's hair back from his face, offering what comfort he could for Cecelia's sake to the boy; but for circumstance, he might have known him well. "I'll see that your family gets the message, son. You have my word."

≈

Following the Union's bloody defeat at Manassas Junction, in the battle of Bull Run, William's troops waited for orders with no food, blankets, or tents in a cold downpour of rain that had descended on the plains of Virginia. The cold seared the men's bodies and their resolve to fight on after so gruesome a loss. To William it had been a devastation.

Two weeks later, President Lincoln and the Secretary of State personally rode into camp in an open carriage to review the troops, offer support, and to make William Sherman a brigadier general for his bravery. But the promotion mattered little. The death of George Stovall had thrown him into a deep spiral of depression, exemplifying horrifically the torn state of his life for the past two decades. He had lost Cecelia again and again, and then held her dying brother in his arms. No matter how much whiskey he drank to blot that out, the misery was more than he could bear. He was fighting his Southern friends like Bragg—and in a way, he was doing battle with Cecelia herself.

The mistake he had made in Augusta, all those years ago, believing hearsay rather than going to the church to fight for her, haunted him even here, and he believed, for the rest of his life.

For longer than he could remember, William had wanted to test himself in battle. Now all he wanted to do was be free of the stench of death and the tormenting reminders of it. When President Lincoln sent him to Washington, and then home to Lancaster for a few days of reflection, William went without resistance. He was changed, uncertain if he would ever return to battle, Union cause or not. At the moment, the price seemed far too high.

To her surprise, and at great risk to themselves, Josiah and Setty Mae personally brought the letter to Shelman Heights. Cecelia knew, the moment she saw them standing together at her front door, that the news they bore was bad. She leaned for a moment against the doorjamb at the wide front entrance and tried to catch her breath. Cretia lingered in the foyer like a shadow behind her.

"What's wrong? she asked Cretia's father.

"Can we come in?" Setty Mae asked. "It be a long ride from Augusta dis time o' year."

"Forgive me, of course. Please come in." Josiah removed his straw hat and stepped onto the rich Aubusson carpet.

"It was dangerous for you to come alone," she said, heartily embracing each of them.

"Massa Stovall, he git us da pass sayin' it be all right, Miss Cecelia," Setty Mae said, and the tears that filled her eyes were Cecelia's undoing. "And we wanted to do it fo' you."

"It's Georgie, isn't it?"

"Yassum, it is."

Her hands flew to her mouth, as if she could somehow contain the horror that rushed up, pushing forward, taking her over. "Dis letter, it come yesterday." Setty Mae offered it to her with a trembling hand, but Cecelia spun away and sank brokenly onto the bare part of the wood floor.

"No . . . God . . . ," she murmured from behind her hand. "I can't lose him, too!"

As she wept, Cretia moved forward, exchanging a stricken glance with Old Joe and Setty Mae. After a moment, Cretia took the letter. She read a few lines to herself, and glanced up, her expression desolate. When Setty Mae nodded support, Cretia read it aloud, as Cecelia had taught her to do long ago.

Dear Mr. Stovall,

I am writing to inform you that your son, George Stovall, has been killed at the Battle of Manassas on this, the 28th day of 1862. While I was not personally with your son at his death, due to my own injuries sustained that day, I was assured by my staff that the Union officer who discovered him, and at peril to himself, later bore his body personally to our encampment. He said that your son died honorably.

Please know, sir, that, while your son is no longer of this earth, he had the comfort in those last moments of life, having known human touch and caring by a particularly honorable Northern officer, who identified himself to my sergeant only as William, and then left before I could extend my thanks.

Wartime makes strange enemies, Mr. Stovall, and even sometimes friends of these men, and I trust that it brings you some comfort knowing that there was one Yankee, for whatever mysterious reason, who felt it important to show honor to your boy. . . .

On the floor, arms around her knees, as though she were trying to fold in on herself, Cecelia rocked back and forth. "It can't be true. Not Georgie. It's not true. It's not! Damn this awful war!"

They tried to help her up, but she was shaking her head and rocking. The others exchanged a worried glance, their faces strained.

"Should we call up a doctor?" Setty Mae asked.

"Ain't nothin' he got that's gon' help her with dis."

Cretia reached out to touch Cecelia's face. She wanted to ask if there were something she could do—but Cecelia was trembling so wildly, the sobs coming from her now a deep, wracked sound—that she knew the answer already. There was nothing anyone could do. As with William Sherman and Anne, this was a loss Miss Cecelia would feel for the rest of her life.

It was William. There had been only one small clue, and yet she knew—the voice of her soul had confirmed with absolute conviction that it had been him. And she believed in the voice that had come to her, because she knew the man William had always been destined to be. It made it a little easier believing it was her great love's face into which her brother last had looked. There would have been kindness there, a more gentle death.

Cecelia lay in her bed, quieted now by an earlier dose of laudanum. Relentless thoughts of family, connections, loves, and losses scampered around in her mind. She was certain, more than ever, of what must happen. Old Joe and Setty Mae were here. Cretia was here. That could not have been by accident. The truth was the one good thing that she could bring out of Georgie's horrific death. Life must go on. She must do this for all three of them.

Late that night, nearly midnight, Cecelia crept down the stairs, holding a single white candle in a brass holder. Somehow she had known who would be there, awake still in the dark calm of the late hour. And she was. Setty Mae was sitting in the drawing room on a tufted stool near the fireplace, gazing into the flames but seeing something far beyond them.

"May I join you?"

Setty Mae turned with a start. "Fo'give me, Miss Cecelia. I ought not be down here. You needs some tin'?" She struggled up off the stool, her big body tense in the shadows and darkness. "What can I get you? Milk? Water? A bit of da massa's bourbon, hep you sleep?"

"Setty Mae, please. My house is yo' house. You must know how dear you are to me. How dear *all three of you* are to me. You're welcome in *any* room."

She sat quietly on the small damask-covered settee beside the stool, where the fire cast a deep, golden glow over both of them. "You gon' be all right, chil'?"

Setty Mae had meant about Georgie, and even thinking of him again now, of the horrid death he must have suffered, so far from those he loved, made the tears come again. But Cecelia wiped them away and stiffened her back. Perhaps she could no longer help her brother, and that pain would linger for a very long while, but there were three other people she *could* help in this life. Cecelia reached out her small hand and surrendered it to Setty Mae's heavy warm one. Her touch was good and reassuring.

"It's gon' take some time," she said honestly. "I wish, mo' than anythin', that I could have helped him. It's too late for that now. But it's not too late for you, Josiah, and Cretia."

Setty Mae gave her a startled look, and she felt the hand that held hers go very limp. As Setty Mae shrank from her, her eyes suddenly were as cold and dark as black onyx. "Chil', you knows I love you like you was my own." Her voice quavered. "But you ain't got no right talkin' 'bout dat."

Cecelia leaned forward, undeterred. "Don't you suppose Cretia has wondered at all why you and Josiah came out here together? What yo' true connection is to one another?"

"Da good book say my secrets be laid bare to da Lawd. Das enough fo' me."

"Don't you *owe* her the truth befo' it's too late, just as it's too late for my brother?"

Setty Mae scratched a spot on her meaty forearm, considering that uncomfortably for a moment. "I ain't thought 'bout much else fo' most these las' years, Miss Cecelia. What it be like havin' my on'y chil'—my girl, know da truth. . . . Lawd, we was so scared. . . . But what we all did to keep us all together back then, now likely be the one ting make her hate me fo'ever." Her black eyes shimmered with obsidian tears. "Her hate would sho'ly be my own kind of death."

The creak of a floorboard behind them gave, and they both turned to see Cretia. She was standing in the shadows, in the arch of the parlor door entrance, her entire body trembling as she braced herself against the wall.

"Tell me it ain't true." Her voice broke, hoarse with shock as Setty Mae rose slowly on her stocky legs. Cecelia put a hand to the tired old woman's back in support.

"It's why you *really* came here. Why the good Lawd brought you all together now. Here," Cecelia whispered. "I beg you, Setty Mae, look at my life, and don't throw away this one chance now with a lie."

Cretia moved a step slowly into the light. "It ain't true, by God! My mama was sold over twenty years ago, by Master Pleasant! Papa tol' me so himself!"

The fire cracked and then flared. "Ester was da one sold." Setty Mae's voice quavered. She was trembling.

"*She* was my mama!"

"No, Lucretia. Yo' name and yo' blood came from *my* line . . . not hers."

The three, a family of women now, stood in a circle, moonlight playing across Cretia's wild face. "How could you have told that kind of lie!"

"We all have our reasons," Cecelia gently interjected. "We do what we must, sometimes, to get by. Don't punish yo' mother for what we all, at times, have done."

She was sorry the moment the words had left her mouth. Cecelia had meant never to bring it up again. But it hung there between them now, and Cretia's eyes bore the pain of so sharp and sudden a blow.

"Look. I'm sorry," Cecelia went on in her gentle tone. "But yo' mother meant well fo' you. Sho'ly you can see that. There was danger to you all in my father discoverin' the truth."

"I was dere for ye, Lucretia," Setty Mae said in a soft, wounded tone.

"Not as my mother!"

"I never *once* pushed you 'way from me—only 'way from da danger of knowin' what Josiah and I done!" She moved forward, brushing a hand across Cretia's cheek, wiping away a tear in the movement. "I was dare in da only way a slave woman can hold on to her babies. By doin' whatever it takes. We did it fo' you, Lucretia, girl. Fo' all three of us . . ."

The soft words and tender touch of a remembered childhood that had all come from Setty Mae, slowly drained away the shock of the moment. Feeling that shift, because she knew her child, Setty Mae brought Cretia against her breast, folding her into the same loving arms she always had offered, and they both felt a fragile new life beginning. It was a good thing, a shining moment in sadness and tragedy that seemed never ending.

Chapter Twenty-eight

It was a horrible, violent, and bloody war. And in spite of heavy casualties at places like Bull Run, Shiloh, Antietam, and Gettsyburg, the Confederate Army, under Gen. Robert E. Lee, refused categorically to surrender. Whatever William believed he had missed in the war with Mexico, he had gained in spades at costly and horrific battlefields where the bright blood of young boys spread onto wide grassy plains and changed the American landscape forever. A year after the horrendous battle of Bull Run, William Tecumseh Sherman was a brigadier general, returned to his post and now serving under one of the most unlikely men from his past—Ulysses S. Grant.

The next years of the war were full of clashes, and there were both losses and victories. The fortunes of the Confederacy now were clearly in decline, and yet still they would not surrender. In battle, and in strategy tents in rain and in blistering heat—all up and down Mississippi, Tennessee, and Kentucky, William's friendship with Grant had solidified. Grant privately recalled their past, their San Francisco meeting when he was at his lowest, and was spurred on now by the common goal for which they fought. In the South, after Bull Run, William Tecumseh Sherman had become famous.

After the Battle of Shiloh, a year later, he was infamous.

And once the decision had been irrevocably made for William to return to the military, Ellen had, for all of her manipulations to the contrary, supported him. He needed her letters and her support to survive the horrors of war. The cries of the wounds and dying was the worst. It was a sound that would live within him for the rest of his life. Daily, he saw raw, open, gaping—fatal— wounds that had not killed men immediately, but would later. He held their hands, prayed with them, and cried with them, as well.

Confederate or Union, he saw with great horror as they lay dying that they were all just boys with families, wives, mothers. Stories. Loves. Lives not to be lived. And seeing their deaths, on both sides, had changed him yet again. One in particular remained in his heart and mind—George Stovall.

For her part, a world away in the still safe haven of Georgia, Cecelia read greedily anything she could find about the battles, keeping up with William's ascension in the Union military she was supposed to despise, and praying privately for God to keep him safe from harm.

Her own involvement with Cretia in the Underground Railway had become her redemption. It was many things to her: a substitute for a loveless marriage, a way to forget the past, and the work by which she one day hoped to define herself to her children.

To Charles, she was a trophy, long ago won, and long ago tired of. He returned to Shelman Heights only when the image of a happy marriage mattered. Cecelia rejoiced that it was a preciously infrequent occurrence. Tonight, unfortunately, was to be one of those rare exceptions. Charles was entertaining several businessmen and their wives from Atlanta. For appearance' sake, his own wife, not his Savannah mistress, was required to be by his side.

But much had changed for the South. The Union blockades, and their strangulation of cotton and rice exports, had sent most cotton barons like Charles well on their way to ruin. The "white gold" with which he had won her now was useless. Stores were empty of merchandise and food. New fabric was impossible to obtain, and much of the old clothing and upholstery were needed for bandages. Draperies and dress fabrics were gone from fine homes and modest homes alike. Not only wounded soldiers, for whom there were no more hospital beds, but refugees crowded the streets, making most places in Georgia now unsafe, as they scavenged for what they could.

There was so little to buy, even if Charles had possessed the money. But like most other wealthy Southern men who had long taken creature comforts for granted, Charles Shelman was learning to live without, and to sell what representations of his former life he could. Costly art, china, and family jewelry. That was the main intent of this evening's dinner. But what scarce bits of food one could buy were nearly as precious as jewels.

In light of that, the meal they intended was the precious use of stockpiled goods and liquor that were running dangerously low in the padlocked cellar of Shelman Heights. With any hope it would help the more well-off men to open their wallets. Cretia stood looking with her at the very best they could do for this evening of vulgar pretense with the limited resources under which they now suffered. Cecelia's evening dress, passably fashionable at a distance, was a combination of three old dresses, the parts of which had not yet frayed or thinned. But in the thick of wartime, there were no longer crinolines or hoops to conjure the distinctive and feminine bell skirts. Those, like most other usable fabric, had gone to the front lines for bandages.

"I'm afraid that's 'bout the best we gon' do," Cretia frowned, studying her own handiwork in the long, gold-framed mirror.

"It doesn't matter. This is all just a way to get Charles back to his tart in Savannah so we can get on with *our* work." Cecelia sighed, spinning away from her own image and tucking the tiny gold cross she still wore beneath the collar of her dress. She wore it for luck. And every day the South saw more of this horrible war, she felt the need for luck just a little more.

The evening, after that, was a tiresome affair. A group of well-bred Southerners and their wives, doing their best to pretend that times and their fortunes had not been changed by the decimating power of the Union forces. Still, to keep Charles from her bed tonight, and to be rid of him tomorrow, she entertained them in her home with a smile. They danced in her parlor, and she laughed at their foolish tales of how close they were to all-out victory over the man they called, "that drunken Yankee leader, Grant, and his henchman, Sherman."

"May I have the pleasure?" A morose balding little man bowed to her and extended his hand for a dance as the quartet she had hired began to play. One glance at Charles, and his expression told her acceptance was essential.

Cecelia was only casually acquainted with their neighbor Porter Saxton, but she knew he was a wealthy investor, who also kept a large home in Atlanta. Saxton had long maintained an extensive art collection, and the desire to add to it. Many of the paintings in Charles's collection were bought in London that summer when they met, and they were now of great value. Charles was intent that his passing interest in art now see him through the financial devastation the war was already bringing.

"Certainly, Mr. Saxton. I would be delighted."

Bored instantly by his syrupy smile and the glint from his small, gold-framed spectacles over an upturned pug nose, Cecelia swallowed a yawn—bored, that was, until he spoke. "You've garnered quite a reputation fo' yo'-self, Mrs. Shelman," he said as harmlessly as if he were complimenting her hairstyle.

"I beg yo' pardon, suh?"

"Yo' work, Mrs. Shelman. Yo' very important work."

"Pardon me, Mr. Saxton, but I'm afraid you've mistaken me for someone else."

"Oh, no ma'am," he softly drawled, smiling all the while. "There is no mistake. Which is precisely why I've gone to such lengths to be here this evenin', *and* to have this dance with you."

"My husband believes you are interested in the sale of some of his artwork fo' yo' own home."

"He does, doesn't he?" They twirled, then bowed to one another. The patriotic song, "The Sunny South," played by the quartet, hid the intensity of their conversation. "Yo' work with the Railroad has been very impressive. The number of slaves you have helped lead to freedom is worthy of admiration."

Her face paled, and she tried to let go of his hand, but he only held hers more tightly as they twirled. "How could you know 'bout that?"

"It serves only to tell me where yo' sympathies lie."

"And yours, Mr. Saxton, are not with our Southern brothers?"

"Only the ones opposed to the abomination of slavery, Mrs. Shelman."

"Well, I certainly don't see how I can help you."

"With yo' own husband newly commissioned as a general in the Confederate Army? And you, therefore, in the proverbial catbird seat, a position I trust he still knows nothin' about," he chuckled. "Now that *is* humorous."

"A Confederate general? Charles?"

"You truly didn't know? Lovely, resourceful woman like yo'self, now that does come as a surprise."

"My husband and I lead separate lives, Mr. Saxton. This evenin' was his idea."

"Oh, dear." His cheerful smile fell as they danced. "Now that *does* complicate things."

"What things would those be, Mr. Saxton?"

"My hope that you would agree to carry information you glean from yo' husband through to the North to help them bring our misled Southern brothers to their knees, once and fo' all."

Cecelia laughed out loud just as the music ended. She appeared to the rest of the room as if she were reacting to some harmless anecdote he had just told. "You cannot be serious!"

"I am—quite. We assumed you would be the quintessentially perfect operative."

"Operative? At betrayin' the South?" She lowered her eyes and stiffened her spine. "Helpin' slaves is one thing, Mr. Saxton. What you propose is quite another."

"Do you not already *do* as I propose, nearly every day?"

"I help slaves help themselves, sir. That is quite a different thing from betrayin' my land."

As they neared Charles together, Saxton began to smile and then chuckle blithely as he leaned toward her, as if she had just returned their lighthearted banter. "I had no wish to offend, I assure you, dear lady. Fightin' the war from inside would certainly hasten its end, and potentially save many of those Southern lives that you seem to hold so dear."

"My head is spinnin'!"

"These are young boys who are dyin', Mrs. Stovall. Young Southern children. You could help end that. You can *help* yo' homeland."

"I can't think!"

They stopped a few feet from Charles, and Saxton nodded to her with a smile, as if thanking her for the dance. "I shall leave my callin' card with yo' *servant* girl. Then I shall wait for word from you. I trust I will not be disappointed in yo' reply."

There was no way to see the proposal as anything but dangerous for her. Rose Greenhow, the infamous Confederate spy, sat at this very moment in a Yankee prison cell for having been caught at the very same thing, albeit for the other side. And there were the children to consider, plus Cretia's welfare, and her work with the Railroad. Cecelia was good to none of them as a convicted and imprisoned spy.

A spy!

She shuddered at the extraordinary thought. But these were extraordinary times made of risks and chances taken, lives lost, for the most noble causes.

She felt the sting of Anne's death now most bitterly. Father was married again, and Cleo had given him a third family. It felt to Cecelia like the unraveling of the years of healing Anne had struggled for so long to bring to their family. There was no home there in Augusta for her anymore. No reason for her to return.

There were few things, besides her children and her work, that meant anything to her at all.

Charles strode into their bedroom as she sat up in bed, propped by a spray of pillows. The distant sound of Yankee shelling tore at the otherwise serene calm of late evening. As Charles undressed near her in the lamplit shadows, Cecelia thought how little she had come to feel for this man. Even as the father of her children, he still was a stranger. And she hoped nothing so much now as that he would leave tomorrow for Savannah without giving her yet another child he would neglect before returning to his mistress.

"So, then," he said unexpectedly, sliding beneath the bedcovers beside her but keeping a mercifully welcome distance between them. "Have you somethin' to tell me?"

Cecelia put down her book, a small volume of poetry, and looked at his face, full and blotched red from drinking. "I don't believe I do."

"For someone with nothin' to say, you were awfully chatty this evenin' with Porter Saxton."

Her heartbeat quickened. She steeled herself—the war and her work had made her very good at that. "I hadn't noticed anythin' unusual."

"Was he forward with you?"

She met his gaze squarely. In the lamplight, her black eyes glittered. "Would it matter if he were?"

"You are still my wife, Cecelia."

"Legally, perhaps."

"Ever the quick one, aren't you? Sharp spirit and an even sharper tongue."

"I'm surprised you still notice."

His brows merged, and for a moment, he looked to her as if he might strike her for that sharpness he once had professed to adore. "What did Saxton want?"

"Oh, for heaven's sake, Charles. Pleasantries only. He was yo' guest, a potential buyer fo' yo' art, as you said, so I was pleasant to him."

"Some say he is involved with that evil Underground Railroad helpin' the darkies, and that now he is a spy against his own people fo' the Union."

Cecelia let out a small chuckle. "Then why in heaven's name are *you* doin' business with someone like that?"

"Difficult times call for an occasional compromise of one's values." He leaned over and then, in an uncharacteristic show of affection, he took her hand. "I've been waitin' for the right moment to tell you this, my dear, but I suspect I shall run out of those moments very quickly. The point is, I am proud to have accepted a commission in the Confederate Army. I'm gon' fight fo' our home, our ideals, and fo' all that we hold dear, and I'm gon' beat the Unionists at their horrid game all by myself, if I must!" Charles looked at her expectantly. "Have you nothin' to say on the matter?"

Cecelia drew back her hand from him and began to smooth out the bed linen over her legs. It was a movement designed to avoid his touch. "I assume that if it were important to you, what I thought, you well would have consulted me befo' you had taken so bold a step."

Charles sank back into the pillows, away from her, letting free an audible sigh. They were silent with each other again, the great chasm that had formed through the years only widening now. "I leave for Savannah in the mornin'."

She looked away from him and across the room into the darkness. "I assumed as much."

"If Saxton comes to you again, if he proposes you help him in any way, I will expect you to wire me of it at once."

"Why in the world would Mr. Saxton want anythin' from me?"

"Look, Cecelia. You may not be the brightest woman, or the wisest wife the good Lawd ever gave a man, but you are the one I chose, and therefo' the one I must look after, in good times and in bad."

"Yo' confidence in me is truly awe inspirin'."

"My dear, these are dangerous times, and our enemy, in their desperation, will look fo' the weakest links in the chain to break that chain entirely. Everyone knows yo' darky is treated just like a free woman, prancin' round town in those fancy dresses and shoes you used to buy her befo' the war, so it is only natural that some may conclude you oppose our Southern ways."

Cecelia bit her tongue, choking on the hostility she felt for this man. "You really don't know me at all, do you, Charles?"

"Go to sleep, Cecelia," he said blandly, turning away from her onto his side and drawing up the bedcovers. The squeak of the bed springs with his heavy movement was the only sound as Cecelia extinguished her bedside lamp and lay, for a time, in the darkness.

"Charles . . . ," she finally said. "Was I ever anythin' mo' to you than a conquest of my father's cotton business?"

"Was *I* ever anythin' mo' to *you* than a way to forget yo' vile Yankee lover?" When she did not answer, he tartly added, "I suppose we both shall just have to go on wonderin', won't we?"

Cecelia was not certain if it was more for herself—to spite Charles—or to avenge Georgie's senseless death, that she sent Pait to the grand and sprawling Saxton house the next morning, on the outskirts of Rome. She was angry with the South for starting a war that had slaughtered so many, and if she could help it be over a little more quickly, as Mr. Saxton had said, then so much the better.

Her answer to him was clear and brief. She would help the cause in any way that she could, so long as it did not threaten or involve either her children or her female servant, Cretia. There had been too many losses in her life to also suffer the deaths of any of them without going completely and irretrievably mad.

The first job came swiftly. Two days later, a Negro servant from the Saxton house came bearing a note of thanks for the delightful evening his master had spent at Shelman Heights. The real message was delivered verbally. She was to take a carriage ride east out of town to Walnut Hill. There, beneath the corner of the large, white rock she would find a coded message. From a pouch in her hair, she was to take the note she had been given, stow it beneath the rock, and then take the message she found there, concealing it in her hair in the same manner.

In those first, early assignments, she was merely a courier of the secret dispatches, told nothing of the contents of the messages she bore, most of them in code. What she was told was where to deposit them and what to do if she were captured. She should swallow the note quickly and then use any ingenuity she found necessary to escape.

Over the weeks that followed, Cecelia learned quickly how to spot Confederate or Federal patrols, and how to avoid them. Neither side would understand or take kindly to her spying. But she kept away from the main roads and always had an airtight story at the ready. This was a purpose. This work had filled her full of life again. The more challenging work, she was told, would come when Charles had something important to confide in her that could be used against the South.

∽ఁ∾

Pait was silent as he followed her outside, back behind the stables, to the white clapboard outbuilding that once had held dozens of roosters and hens, when they'd had them before the war. Now Cretia carefully plucked the few precious eggs left by the last three hens, placing them in the basket on her arm as gently as if they were gold. Today there were only half a dozen eggs, and Cretia knew they would all go to the servants. The Shelman children had eaten eggs the last time there had been any, Cecelia would say, and then she would give them to Mammy Ruth with strict orders to prepare them the way she most enjoyed.

As Pait closed the door behind them, Cretia spun around. "What the devil you doin' in here?"

"Lawd, but you is a fine woman, Lucretia," he said in a deep baritone voice tinged with awe.

Cretia swatted the air. "Don't you be startin' up again now. Just because of that one time b'tween us out here, don't mean every time I come out this way, I'm gon' be wantin' you."

He smiled broadly at her and crossed his arms over the wide expanse of his chest. "Don't it, now?"

"No," she said stubbornly. "It don't."

He moved slowly toward her, across a floor laid thickly with straw, his long sinewy limbs glistening with sweat from the summer sun. "You is my woman, Lucretia."

"I don't belong to no man, Pait!"

"You knows dat ain't so, and *I* knows it." His arms went around her waist, locking her into his tender embrace and pressing a kiss gently onto her neck. "Someday we gon' make a family."

"We're slaves, you fool man! We *can't* have what white folks have!"

"Dat ain't what Miss Cecelia say. She say we as right together as rain," he declared, trailing a line with his finger down the length of her bare arm. "And when dis war is over, I *am* gon' marry you, proper."

"Slaves can't marry! That ain't gon' change! Pait, you are as crazy as a loon!"

"Don't you jes' see if I don't."

Cretia rolled her eyes.

He smiled, bright and wide, and convincing. "Believe me, gal, it gon' happen. Sooner or later, I'm gon' *make* it happen . . . jes' like I done wit you 'n' me. . . ."

As gently as if she were delicate glass, he lay her down into the mound of straw near the back wall and lowered himself over her. After she had softened, letting him kiss her, Pait chuckled against her neck. "So you do care 'bout me, after all?"

"I care just fine," she said softly as her eyes rolled to a close and she wrapped her arms around his neck.

Chapter Twenty-nine

NOVEMBER 1863

Inside his camp tent, sealed off from reality and the rest of the world, promoted to head of the Army of the Tennessee now, William drank alone. He also tried to forget that it was Braxton Bragg, of all people, entrenched and waiting in the mountains before him. But there was never enough whiskey to silence the haunting sound of a little boy's laughter—*his* own son, or the vision, mere days later, of the old priest hovering over the small, lifeless body. Everywhere he saw Willy's face. His little smile was as deeply imprinted there as the hope a father had held for his son's future. He could not eat for how sick it made him. Only whiskey and cigars brought him any moments of peace at all.

God, he had not wanted them to come!

After all, this was wartime, and the air was full of danger.

But Ellen had written him frantic letters that she was desperate to be with him. Considering what had happened to him after Bull Run, the depression into which George Stovall's death there had plunged him, William found himself softening to the notion. It had been so long since he had known a woman's touch, and he missed it. He even missed Ellen and the familiar affection they sometimes found. After the Vicksburg campaign, and too much fighting that found him weary from battling old Braxton Bragg, and Ellen promised to bring the children, William had relented. Seeing them—Willy especially, so like himself, with the same flaming copper hair and interest in war—had been a brief balm on the wounds he had felt for so long.

They had spent precious summer days, and Willy, so fascinated by military life, quickly became the pet of his father's troops, easily learning the manual of arms and receiving an honorary sergeant-at-arms rank from his father's men. He gloried in his son's expression as the men presented Willy with a sergeant's uniform to wear with them.

"Did you see it, Papa? It has real brass buttons! Look!"

"I see, son." William had smiled with the greatest pride as Willy stood at attention before him.

For the first time in a very long time, William was at peace. He had, he believed, outrun his past, and the consequences of it. But those days ended as quickly as they had come.

At a place called Chickamauga, Bragg turned sharply on the Union troops and soundly defeated them. The victory by his old West Point friend was a resounding blow, and William could feel that, once again, the tide was about to turn against him. When he was ordered to return to work with his troops, repairing a destroyed section of railroad, he took his family with him on the steamer *Atlantic* as far as Memphis. It was there that he was informed by the doctor that Willy had contracted typhoid fever.

William cringed again now, remembering it, and took another deep swallow of whiskey.

"What hurts, son?" William had helplessly asked, sitting as he had for hours by his bedside.

Willy's child voice had been thin, barely audible. "Only knowing that I'm going to die, and not be with you and Mama anymore."

He ran a hand across his weary, bearded face now and squeezed his eyes, the moments before his son's death made real again—agonizing in his mind. "You're *not* going to die, Willy!" he sternly rebuked this child, his favorite, because he could not bear to say anything else. "And I will thank you not to say that again!"

He wasn't certain what it was, but something suddenly made him aware of the presence of the black-robed, Catholic priest behind him, a stout old man he had approved of for Ellen's sake. But having him there with Willy only served to deepen his own guilt. *This is my fault. Because I have sinned . . . It's because of Cecelia . . . My son—Willy is to be the price for New Orleans . . . for loving her* . . . The old priest was shaking his head, silently telling him not to give a little boy—his precious boy—hope for the impossible. William wanted to kill the old priest himself for that look alone.

Out in the sitting room of the suite they had taken at the Dartford Hotel, he could hear Ellen and his daughters softly weeping. The haunting sound only intensified his guilt. The same God who had given him Cecelia and then taken her away could not be so cruel now as to punish him further by taking his dearest son. But that was precisely what He was about to do.

This God of Ellen's, this spiteful Catholic God was his enemy.

In those next moments, holding Willy's small, burning hand, when anyone would make desperate promises to stem the tide of the inevitable, William could speak not a single plea. It would not be answered. It was pointless. He was despised by God who had waited to mete out a punishment when it would bring the most devastation. This corrosive God who destroyed everything William had ever truly loved.

Silent tears fell into the softness of William's bearded cheeks as his mind conjured the image of Willy at the moment when he closed his eyes. "It's all right, son," he had achingly murmured, leaning closely, touching the soft child cheek with the back his hand. "If God wishes to call you to Him, He will carry you up to heaven in a beautiful white chariot, and Mama and I will meet you there again soon. . . . Wait for me, will you? . . . Wait for me."

Willy made a small motion, and William could feel the thick, dark shroud of death falling slowly around them. He closed his own eyes as the priest behind him began to murmur gentle prayers for the dead. "Stop it, you fool!" William lashed out. "He isn't gone yet!"

"My son." The priest's meaty hand was on William's shoulder. "He has left us."

"No!"

"General, please—"

"Stop! I won't hear it!"

"General Sherman, your boy is with the Lord now. We must all make peace with that."

"Never! I will *never* do that!"

The priest had moved toward the bed and leaned in, making the sign of the cross over Willy's slim, lifeless body. After helplessly watching the small, precious life disappear, William had shuffled into the sitting room, feeling entirely apart from himself. He saw it all again in his mind. The pain had shaken him to his core. Ellen had glanced up from the white handkerchief poised at her chin. Her eyes were bloodshot and full of tears. He wanted to comfort her, but that was impossible. Seeing the expression on his face, she began to sob loudly into the handkerchief, and their daughters encircled her, sobbing in their own keening wails of grief. He could offer nothing, give them nothing, for he was empty of every sensation but the pure, swelling grief that had overtaken every fiber of him.

He must get away, be away from all of them, as it was a grief no one could share. Willy, so much like him. So much a part of his heart. Gone . . . and only a child. So many dreams not realized. A life so prematurely snatched away. William had felt estranged from God after losing Cecelia, but the death of Willy was a wound that would never heal. A hate that would live within him, from now on, where love once had been.

Beyond grief, and unable to banish the image of Willy's bright face from his mind, William had moved through his nightmare, throwing himself back into the goal of winning the war, and doing it solely for the boy who believed him to be a great military hero.

For Willy, he thought. *For my son, I will go on, and be the man you believed me to be, even when I refused to believe it myself*.

Alone in his tent that night, as Ellen, the children, and Willy's casket sailed home, William wrote a note of thanks to the Thirteenth Regiment who had been so kind to his son.

The child that bore my name, and in whose future I reposed more confidence than I did in my own plan of life, now floats a mere corpse, seeking a grave in a different land, with a weeping mother, brother, and sisters clustered about him. For myself I seek no sympathy. . . . But Willy was or thought he was, a sergeant of the Thirteenth . . . he had the enthusiasm, the pure love of triumph, honor and love of country which should animate all soldiers. God only knows why he should die this young . . .

Behind him lay Bull Run, Shiloh, Antietam, and Vicksburg. Ahead, Sherman and Ulysses S. Grant prepared to move into Tennessee, and ever more closely toward Georgia—and, they hoped, a full Union victory at last.

"I don't care *who* he will not see! I'm going in!"

The deep voice outside the tent flap just then was gruff and familiar. William set the empty whiskey glass on the table beside his cot just as a young sergeant held back the flap. The memories skittered mercifully back to the corners of his mind. "Excuse me, General, but——"

"Out of my way, boy! This is the business of one general to another!"

"Make that *three*, if you please!"

Suddenly, before William, stood two distinguished and uniformed men he had not seen in nearly a decade but whose imprint on his life made it seem like yesterday. "Van?" William looked up incredulously. "Is that really you? And Ord?"

"In the flesh, you old dog!" Edward Ord chuckled as the three men embraced tightly and with the affection of years and memories.

His expression was now a smile. "But how? I mean, we're in the middle of a bloody war, for Pete's sake!"

There was a small pause, a hesitation, and William knew. "Ellen wrote to you, didn't she?"

Stewart's hand was on his arm. "She's worried about you, Cump. She loves you. Hell, we all do!"

"Lincoln thought a couple of days of bivouac for Ord and I were called for. So here we are."

"Hell, we should send a scout up to that mountain, ask Bragg to join us, and make it a party!" laughed Stewart Van Vliet.

William poured himself another whiskey as the cool tone settled between them. "Oh, that's right. Our old friend who wants to kill the lot of us now."

With William's back to them, Ord and Van Vliet exchanged a worried glance. "You drinking alone there," Stewart cautiously called out. "Or can anyone join in?"

William spun around with the bottle in one hand and a glass in the other. In the daylight, with the tent flap still open, they could see how haggard and scruffy he looked. Grief had aged him even more than the war.

"Sergeant!" William bellowed. "Bring a couple more glasses and another bottle. Can't you see I'm entertaining in here!"

Ord and Van Vliet both sank onto William's cot, William into a camp chair beside them. "It was good of Ellen to put this together," Edward cautiously said as the sergeant came into the tent and poured drinks for the other two generals before him. "Let's take a small detail and go on into Knoxville for a couple of days. There's a hotel there where a man can have a bath, and pretty enough Southern girls, desperate enough for money to be available for a tumble or two, to make any man forget his troubles for a while."

William's face fell forward into his hands. "That won't change a thing," he finally said.

"Neither will staying drunk," Stewart countered.

William looked at him with a glassy, dark-eyed stare. "But it helps get me through the damn day, and that's really all that I can hope for."

"You deserve one hell of a lot more."

"What I *deserve* is to rot in hell, and that is what the good Lord apparently has in mind for me." He slumped back in the chair and emptied the glass of its amber liquid.

Again Ord and Van Vliet exchanged a glance. "It might help if you talked about it."

"I've lost the only two people in the world who I can honestly say I ever truly and completely loved." The chuckle that followed was a bitter, hollow thing. "In light of that, gentlemen, talking feels about as vulgar as the sort of bivouac *you* are proposing."

"At least go into town with us then," Edward gently pressed. "No women. No pressure. Just a few days away from here, away from war."

"I do believe this war, and my drive to win it, is the only thing keeping me sane, if you want to know the truth."

Edward leaned forward and put a hand on William's knee. "Please, Cump. We promised Ellen."

"My wife's a good woman," he relented on a weak sigh.

"The best."

"Oh, all right. I guess Bragg will still be up there waiting for my best shot a couple of days from now."

"That's the spirit!" Van Vliet smiled. "Just a couple of days, then back to him!"

He had spoken the words but he had never really meant them so fully as he did now. Ellen *was* a good woman—a woman who, in her own complicated way, loved him deeply. And, at last, as the three generals, old roommates and lifetime friends, rode together toward town he no longer blamed her for the unpardonable sin of *not* being Cecelia.

Chapter Thirty

❦

Even as Union troops moved through Mississippi early in the spring of 1864, the devastation wreaked by war reverberated into Georgia as a warning of things to come. Mississippi homes, from stately and elegant to humble, were pillaged for food and livestock, then looted for gold or things that could be sold. What was left was often burned to the ground as President Lincoln insisted upon making a statement. What remained once the troops left were the charred skeletons of once graceful Southern mansions, homes, and businesses. Food became even more scarce than before. Meals mainly now consisted of what people could grow, along with a rare egg from the few precious hens they so closely guarded.

What met William, now given command of the entire western army by Grant, were fierce and blinding days of bloody, all-out battle. Hurting and yet determined to break through toward Atlanta, William was renewed to beat Johnston, and get the hell out of Georgia. Atlanta, known as the "Gate City" of the South, was full of arsenals, foundries, and William knew that its capture was essential to end this war. But to get to Atlanta, first he must pass through Cartersville and Rome.

He spurred his horse on with a jab of his knees. The sudden thunder of approaching horses startled him. His head snapped from left to right. His skin tingled with the by now familiar premonition of impending attack. There were Confederate trenches he had been too tired and too preoccupied to see. A sudden movement in the trees, and the hair on the back of his neck told him that it was an ambush.

William gave the cry, hollering for the mass of weary Union soldiers on foot and horseback behind him. Waves of gray-coated soldiers rushed down at him like a water from a fountain. They poured toward him from the rocks, crevices, and brush, and William felt his heart throb, his blood pump in that way it always did before he killed a man.

Brandishing long, glinting sabers over their heads, Confederate troops charged at his Union forces. William ordered a charge nonetheless, refusing to give in to the fear and the disorientation of being surrounded. His horse bucked, and he shot his revolver at two Confederate soldiers charging him. One fell to the ground beside him. In a smoky haze of confusion, other men fell, arms flying out in defenseless surrender, gun barrels boomed, and the clang of sword blades sliced the smoke-filled air. The familiar smell of blood and death moved through it, tainting each breath he took, further still. The smoke from artillery fire left a blue haze, clouding the shapes of men who lay mangled and moaning along a path like fallen dominoes. Some Confederates. Some his own Union men and boys.

The man who had been felled beneath him suddenly whipped a gray, long-barreled pistol from his shirt, pointed it directly at William, and drew back the hammer preparing to shoot. He had been fast, but William was faster. He thrust a boot heel into his palm and the pistol careered into the mud. Only then did he realize that they knew one another. A day of reckoning had come for William, at last.

The Lord giveth, and the Lord taketh away. . . .

"Get up, you son of a bitch!" William growled from the back of a horse that whinnied and reared up.

Marcellus Stovall gazed up at him, older but clearly the same man he had been twenty years before, now with sweat dripping from his temples. He gripped his thigh, from which blood oozed beyond a gaping bullet wound. The Lord had taken Cecelia, but he had given him back Marcellus, allowing him, at long last, this sudden retribution.

"You can see that I can't! It's my leg!"

"Pity it wasn't clean through your miserable heart—if you even have one, that is—for how you destroyed mine!"

Around them more men fell, shots rang out, and hollers of savage brutality and agony pierced the smoke-gray morning sky.

"Still that, is it?" Marcellus lifted a brow, his chest heaving from the exertion and from the pain of a gunshot wound. "My sister has been married fo' years now, and so, I hear, have you!"

William leapt from his horse, mud spattering up on his boots and trousers, as he grabbed Marcellus by his shirt collar. "I ought to kill you, you miserable bastard, for what you have cost Cecelia and me!"

"Do it, if you can!" Marcellus bellowed his taunt amid gunfire and retreating Confederate troops. "But you don't have the guts, do you, you yellow dog Yankee! Just like you didn't have the guts to come after her all those years ago, and fight, no matter *what* obstacles I tossed befo' you!"

William ground his boot heel into Marcellus's chest, his dark hair, now tinged with shafts of silver, as he jerked back into the mud. It felt hideously good. Freeing. The desire to torture and to kill this man beneath his boot heel overwhelmed William on a wave of frustration and hate.

And then, quite suddenly, it stopped—flowing out of him like cool water.

His eyes were still blazing with contempt, but need for violence had vanished. There was nothing it would change. Nothing it would help. She was gone. He must live with that now and be worthy of the belief Cecelia had always, *always* had in him. "You're just not worth it—" he finally said. "Not for what it would do to Cecelia to know *I* was the one who killed you," he brayed bitterly as he vaulted back up into his saddle.

"Where you gon'? Sherman, you can't just leave me here! Come on, man! You can see I need help! Help me!"

"I expect one of your Reb friends, who've retreated, will return after we're gone. That will have to do, I'm afraid." William turned his horse around and gave the call to his men to advance onward. Then he turned back to Marcellus Stovall one final time. "Knowing you might well lose your leg, and remember me for the rest of your life because of it—looks like that'll just have to be revenge enough!"

It had been raining steadily for days. It was a thick, gray, blinding rain that had saturated the ground all around Rome and Cartersville, rutting roads and killing the last of the precious stores of livestock. Cecelia found herself hoping it would be enough to keep the Union troops from breaking through and crossing the Tennessee border, as rumors assured they were about to. As much as she wanted this appalling war to be at an end, she knew only too well that it would have to get worse before it got better. Would William be involved?

She had read, like everyone else, that he was now Lincoln's great commander. For as long as they had been apart, William Tecumseh Sherman had never been very far from her mind or her heart. She prayed for him, and she feared for him every day, God help her—and far more than she ever did for Charles.

As night fell along the great and glistening Etowah River, a wild thunderstorm broke across the Southern sky, and the parlor lit a sudden, bright silver. Margaret, Lelia, and little Charles sailed down the staircase in their nightclothes.

"Mama! Mama! Is it the Yankees? They're shootin' at us, aren't they? Are we gon' die?" Lelia cried, and Cecelia ran to her, scooping them all up in her tight embrace.

"It's all right, my darlin's." She smiled calmly at them, smoothing back Charles's unruly dark hair from his sweet, cherub's face. "It's only a bit of thunder. Angels playin' ball up in heaven! We're all quite safe here. I promise."

They were calmed by that as they clung tightly to Cecelia, and even as a powerful banging sounded on the knocker at the front door. Cretia came into the parlor and Josiah, yes, kind Old Joe, went to answer the door. A month before, Cecelia had asked her father's new wife for the use of Josiah and Setty Mae at Shelman Heights. With the children still so young and Charles away at war now, she needed more help that she could trust, she explained. Cleo Hill, her father's third wife, was only too glad to be rid of two old Negroes who were an uncomfortable link to Pleasant's past.

Cecelia glanced up. Standing beside Josiah, rain-soaked and out of breath, was Porter Saxton, a drenched hat in his hand. Cecelia shot to her feet. "Cretia, take the children into the kitchen fo' a piece of sugar cane. I'll come and see them in a few minutes."

Without objection, Cretia and the children filed into the corridor, with Josiah closing the carved parlor door behind himself. "Good Lawd!" she said, nearing Saxton. "You look a sight! Come sit by the fire and warm yo'self! Shall I pour you a drink?"

"Bourbon," he flatly answered, holding his hands out to the gold and warming flames that licked the fireplace hearth.

"What on earth are you doin' here? You told me you would never come on yo' own?"

"I know. But this is different."

She knew that, several days ago, Union troops had moved across the Tennessee border into Georgia, and the position of Cartersville and Rome made them very near danger. "You've got to get yo' family out of here! It isn't safe! My operatives tell me that Union troops will sweep down from that hill behind town by sundown, the day after tomorrow. Johnston, that Confederate devil, knows it, and is prepared to ambush them. This entire area will be overrun with fightin', lootin', and soldiers!"

Cecelia was cautious. She handed him the nearly full glass and waited for him to drink it. "I do appreciate yo' concern, Porter. But I can't imagine you've elected yo'self town crier fo' all of the residents 'round here."

He looked at her in the firelight. His spectacles were bent, his face bruised and battered. "No. I need you to do a job fo' me."

"You mean let my children and slaves go to safety while I point myself directly into the lion's den?"

"Precisely."

"You're out of yo' mind!"

"No, Cecelia, I'm desperate! My neighbors are on to me, and I've been reported. God knows, I'd do it myself, with the risk, but I can't get a pass to go anywhere but visitin' a few friends' houses, like yo's, just here in town!"

She spun away from him, wrapping her arms around her waist. "You ask too much of me. I have children! My husband is at war! If somethin' happens to me, they'll be orphaned, and what then?"

"They will live the rest of their lives knowin' that their mother was a brave and honorable hero."

She turned back to him, her expression fearful. "I can't do it!"

"Cecelia, I'm desperate, and you've never let me down! I have no one else I can trust, and a woman on a country ride foragin' *fo'* food *fo'* her children is the perfect ruse to save the lives of hundreds of men. Take one of yo' Negro women with you fo' cover, and I can provide a Union pass. If the Yankees are warned, and they win this one, vanquishin' Johnston, they could well bring an end to this whole, wretched nightmare! *Please.* I beg you, just listen!" He pulled a coded message from a pocket inside his jacket and held it out to her. "In two days, a Union general, Joseph Hooker, will join General Sherman, bringing advance troops across Two Run Creek. They will be vulnerable there to a great massacre by Johnston, and that will lay the commander's entire army bare. You've *got* to get a message to General Hooker, who is on the main road from Allatoona, that a huge brigade of Confederate soldiers are waitin' to ambush the troops in the rugged forest land 'round New Hope Church. If Hooker hears the message is from me—specifically from me, he will believe you."

Cecelia felt a chill. "Can I not take the message right to General Sherman, if the opportunity arises?"

"He's a hotheaded renegade, that one—far too wild and reckless to have the sort of power Grant has given him." He rethought his indictment for a moment. "Cecelia, look. Hooker has learned through experience to trust me, as a Southern man who he well might fear. I haven't had the same luxury of experience with General Sherman. These are men's lives at stake, and Sherman's lack of knowledge of me could well lead, not only to a massacre of all of them, but to an escalation of the battle down here!"

She shouldn't have continued, but the words came across her lips anyway. "Is General Sherman really so reckless?"

"Don't you read the papers? They say he had some mysterious Southern weakness—likely a woman if you ask me—that has driven him to the edge of lunacy befo', and, general or not, no one is ever quite certain what he will do next!"

Like everyone else, she had read the stories of William's emotional difficulties once the war had begun. She had read, along with everyone else, that he had, for a time, even been relieved of his command, and questions had followed about his sanity. But no one knew the William she did. Saxton could not know that surely William would believe *her* warning of danger . . . Wouldn't he? . . . But what if the papers were correct? She, after all, had lived her entire life in the South, and he was a powerful general opposing that. If Porter Saxton were right . . . *God, if he is right,* could her enduring love for William Tecumseh Sherman, the man, cloud her thinking about Sherman, the troubled general . . . and thus endanger the lives of countless Union soldiers?

Saxton brought her from the turmoil of her thoughts by facing her directly to him and holding her forearms tightly. "Cecelia, please. No matter what happens, give me yo' word, you'll give the message only to General Hooker. Yo' *word* as a Southern woman, Cecelia."

Part 4

❧

I know that I had no hand in making this war,
and I know I will make more sacrifices
than any of you to secure peace.

—WILLIAM TECUMSEH SHERMAN

Chapter Thirty-one

By May 1864, Georgia was swallowed up now, too, into the tumult and chaos. Its residents lived in the same daily fear as did other beseiged Southerners. Throughout the cities and towns, as it had been all across the South, cotton supplies were being burned to keep them out of enemy hands. What they did not destroy—anything they did not destroy, was either stolen or looted by Union troops. Great houses that were not burned to the ground were, in many cases, taken over as Union headquarters.

Cecelia had not seen Charles for almost eight months. Amid the chaos, he wrote to Cecelia that his unit had faced wild fighting across the border in Tennessee. The letter had taken a month to arrive. Only God knew how things stood now. His men had suffered a horrific number of casualties, and he had been wounded, although not seriously. What he had seen had, he said, changed him unalterably. As the war progressed and they lost everything they had, except for Shelman Heights, Cecelia found her husband's letters increasingly full of references to reflection and an uncharacteristic kind of humility.

In their time apart, he had come to realize what was important in life, and he had been, he said, a fool. When he returned home—God willing, and if she would have him, he would, he declared forcefully, renounce his ways and return to her as a proper husband. But as she read his letters, with the far-off sound of cannon fire and ammunition coming in on a breeze through her open windows, Cecelia was not certain she—or they—could ever go back. Too much had happened.

His years of infidelity. Her infidelity in New Orleans with William. Deaths. The war.

They would first need to see one another, and only then could she decide if there was anything there at all upon which they could try to rebuild not only their fortunes, but their marriage, as well. Late the next morning, after Porter Saxton's unexpected visit, Cecelia folded a letter from Charles just as Cretia stumbled into the firelit parlor from outside. Her face so was ashen, her lips parted in such a way that Cecelia felt a welling of panic even before Cretia spoke.

Cecelia stood, the forgotten letter whispering to the floor. "What is it?"

"It's not good."

"I can see *that*!"

"It's Mr. Saxton!"

She gasped. "Oh, God, no."

"They hung him, bold as life! And, the good Lawd save us all, it was a message to *you*!"

"*Me?*" She squeezed Cretia's forearms tightly, her own face alive now with panic. "What are you talkin' about?"

"They just cut him down from that ol' oak tree at the end of yo' carriageway! They think you're involved with him! You've got to see it as a warnin' to you!" It was decided then and there. Cecelia had been determined to stay at Shelman Heights, to protect the only thing she had and Charles had left in this world from the horrible looting and pillaging that would certainly befall it if it were abandoned. But Porter Saxton's ominous warning now rang in her ears. Her children were not safe here, nor were her slaves. They would need to leave this house where her babies all had been born, and they could only pray that, when the war was over at last, there would be a home—someplace left to return to.

God, what would they do to this place? she wondered, turning slowly around to look at the mirrors and the wallpaper, the paintings, carpets, and furniture, all of which she had personally chosen. She felt the violation even before it occurred. But occur it would. These were the dark days of the war, and General Grant and President Lincoln had grown tired of Southern resolve. *They must bring us all to our knees to make us surrender,* she thought sadly. *And that is precisely what they have done.*

There was no choice. This horrible war needed to end, and she owed it to the memory of a brave Southern spy to finish the work he had begun.

"Cretia!" she said, bursting into the warming kitchen, where a group of Shelman slaves were huddled together, talking in low tones. "I want you, Josiah, Setty Mae, and Pait to pack what you can. Tell them to take the children, and all the rest of you, out into the woods. The Yankees will be here by sundown and the house won't be safe any longer!"

"You is comin' with us, ain't you?" Pait asked.

"I will meet you there. But first there is somethin' I've got to do."

"No! I can't let you!" Cretia objected, her eyes like black saucers, filled with fear. "Those men who killed Mr. Saxton gon' get you next!"

Cecelia smiled without feeling it. She needed to reassure all of them. "They have to catch me first. And the one thing Porter Saxton taught me was how to take the greatest care. It's only a pity he didn't practice it properly himself."

"Please don't," Cretia argued. "We gon' lose the house *and you!*"

"I will find you. I promise. But I owe this to Porter and to the whole country to do what I can to bring this war to an end befo' every last Southern boy is dead and buried!" *And I have to protect William, if I can.* . . . "Please don't fight me on this, old friend. Help me. Take the others, go into the woods, and I will find you."

"I am stayin' here, Miss Cecelia."

Josiah stood near the door. "Setty Mae and Cretia gon' protect yo' young. And dey gots Pait. But *I* gon' stay and see to yo' prop'ty, fo' all you done fo' us."

Cecelia's smile was a bittersweet grimace. She appreciated the brave stand he was willing to take in her behalf. "I can't ask you to do that."

"You ain't asked. I gots to do it, same ways you gots to do what you do. We owe you, Setty Mae and me. I *is* stayin'."

Cretia had helped her dress, disguising the coded message inside her tightly twisted hairstyle beneath a riding hat. She held the road pass Porter Saxton had obtained for her tightly in her hand. She couldn't allow herself to think about his death—or that the same fate could befall her if she were caught. It was too horrible. Nor could she bring herself to take Cretia with her, in spite of how it might protect her if she were caught by troops from either side. She must go bravely, and swiftly, then meet them all in the safety of the forest beside the river and wait until it was safe to go home. That was the best she could do with the war now, at last, on her very own doorstep.

She held each of her children tightly and then kissed them, forcing herself, through steely determination, not to cry. It would not be fair to them to see weakness in her when she demanded bravery from each of them. The sound of artillery shelling in the distance cut through their farewells.

"Take care of my babies," she whispered to Cretia, pressing a slip of folded paper into her hands. "And if somethin' happens to me, I've written it out that no one else but *you* is to raise them. You understand me?"

"But ain't nothin' *gon'* happen to you," she said softly, tears shimmering in her coal-black eyes, and it was not a command but rather a pure and simple declaration. "I know the good Lawd—He gon' see to that."

Chapter Thirty-two

❧

William paced outside the door flap of his military tent in the muggy air of a late spring afternoon and watched the sky, with night fast approaching, darkening for rain. His high boots were mud caked, his coppery beard and hair were wild and unkempt. He had tried for an hour to write a letter home to Ellen. But, here in Georgia, so full of the ghosts and memories—and consumed by his orders to destroy a place he had once found sacred because of the woman he had loved here—the words to his wife would not come.

He'd been informed several days ago that his old friend and now rival, Braxton Bragg, a key Confederate general, had been relieved of duty as the Rebel side grew more desperate to find the path to victory. Poor Bragg, with whom he had broken bread, gotten drunk—and against whom he had done battle at Tunnel Hill. It was strange regrets this war made, and that filled William at the thought, knowing how much pride Bragg possessed. But bitter memories and regrets, for William, had long since become a way of life.

Nighttime was easier, when nothing was demanded of him. When there was no sound of killing, or death. At least not here in this camp. Yes, night, when his soldiers had retired from the hot, hopeless days, and he could give way to his thoughts of how to win this wretched war, how to bring the Confederates to their knees so that he could go home.

Yesterday had been the battle of Snake Creek Gap with hundreds of his men now dead. In the days before that, they had battled at Adairsville, and then at Two Run Creek. And a blur of so many battles and deaths since he had put his uniform back on. He'd had enough of war. Of death. His own son's included. That, most especially, was a loss from which he would never recover.

As the evening wind grew stronger now, William stopped his pacing and held out his hands to the fire, his unruly copper hair made gold in its light. Here on the field of battle, he slept little, smoked too many cigars, and drank far too much whiskey now that the conflict had entered its fourth bloody and violent year. He moved through the South at the will of Lincoln and Grant, who urged him to bring the people to their knees through violence and pillage. President Lincoln had been very clear that a prideful people would surrender only when they were entirely broken. Horrible as it was, Grant assured him, ruthlessness was essential.

"Excuse me, General Sherman, sir?"

William spun around, a streak of lamplight from a light on a camp table beside his chair lay across his cheek. His nerves were raw from lack of sleep, and from Grant's insistence that he and his men hold their position here, at Allatoona Pass for two days of rest. He would have preferred squeezing off the head of that Confederate scoundrel, General Joseph E. Johnston, while he had the chance, and so finally be done with him.

"What is it? Can't you leave me to a bit of evening's peace?" he growled at the new young and annoyingly innocent-looking aide whose name he could never seem to remember.

"It's Conrad, sir. He's just returned from reconnaissance over near Rome, and damned if he didn't bring himself back a Southern spy!"

"Well, it sure as hell wouldn't be the first time, Sergeant! I'm sure Conrad is well versed in how to handle it."

"But General," the boy pressed. "Conrad sent me to you, specifically. The spy they captured . . . is a woman, sir."

William heaved a great sigh. Would this wretched war leave him no peace at all? So Georgia, too, was awash with the dangerous likes of Belle Boyd and that scurrilous traitor, Rose Greenhow, here to torment him now.

"Oh, all right, then. Have Captain Conrad bring the conniving Southern flower in, and we will decide together what the devil to do with her once we know just how dangerous she is."

He pressed back the flap and walked into his tent to wait there. Sergeant Weston could bar the door, and the lady more easily that way, and force her to confess what he could in short enough order for him to get at least a bit of sleep later tonight before it all started again tomorrow.

While he waited, William walked to his desk and poured a stiff whiskey from a cut crystal decanter his men had seized last month at a plantation in Tennessee. The heavy Turkish carpet beneath his feet had come from the same raid.

"Southerners are a proud lot you've got to break entirely to make them surrender." He thought of Lincoln's strong directive and closed his eyes. Yes, this war had hardened him. He cared about so little any longer. Suffering . . . death . . . the destruction of lives and . . . *Cecelia?*

As he looked up and opened his eyes, it was her face that met his in the tent's shadowy golden light. Unmistakable. A dream for so long. And yet now was it to be a reality, here of all places? No matter the years, he would always recognize that face that he so had loved, that he had heartbrokenly sketched and then quietly treasured for two decades.

"This is the woman, General. We seized her out near Tyler Junction. Before we could search her, I'm afraid she swallowed something, so we couldn't see if there was any danger to us. We bound and gagged her before she could yell for help, then brought her straight to you."

"Untie her!"

"But General Sherman!"

"Now!"

Complying, the young officer untied the rope and then the scarf at her mouth. Perspiring, her hair matted and loose from its once stylish knot, she grimaced but held her head defiantly high.

"That will be all, Sergeant," William managed to sputter, his eyes locked upon her and his mouth gone as dry as desert sand.

"But General Sherman! A woman alone like this in your tent! And it's nearly dark outside!"

William arched a brow and linked his hands behind his back, showing no sign at all of the furious pounding of his heart. "Well, Sergeant Prescott, as it is beginning to rain, would you have me interrogate the lady outside? Show our civilized ways to the South like that?"

"Well, no, sir. But I just thought—"

"You may wait outside. You may *both* wait outside. I will handle this on my own. I shall call when *and if* I need you."

Once they were alone, William pulled a sweat-stained canvas-back camp chair out for her, and motioned for Cecelia to sit. He sat facing her on the edge of his cot. After a long while to collect himself as best as he could, William found his voice. And still the words broke as he spoke them. "It's good to see you, Cecelia."

"A surprise, I should imagine."

"Quite," he added tenderly. "I suspect it's too much to hope that you found yourself here in my camp . . . intentionally?"

"Actually, this way we have of running into one another appears to be one of life's great ironies." They both heard the far-off boom of artillery shelling. "It is wonderful to see you, William," Cecelia said in a low voice, her eyes settling powerful on his. "Strangely, now that I'm here lookin' into yo' eyes, it feels as if no time has passed at all."

A smile played at the corners of his mouth, but he fought to keep his composure. "As if we could be those same two naïve people who met all those summers ago at West Point."

"I'm certainly not naïve any longer," she said in a voice he found surprisingly weary and jaded for how little she appeared, outwardly, to have changed. Her face was still smooth, her cheeks pale, and her dark eyes capable, all on their own, of captivating him completely. She was still a delicately bred Southern woman. Only her coarse cotton dress and rough brogan shoes showed how much her life in these past years must have changed.

"So you're a spy now."

"And *you* are a great general." She met his gaze head-on, not shrinking from the disapproving tone upon which it had come. "A general bent on levelin' Georgia."

He stood in the echo of that and looked away from her, toward his desk, the candle lamps, anything but at those deep, black eyes of hers that had ruled his heart, even in her absence from his life.

"What I am *bent* on is helping to end the abomination of slavery and winning this damnable war! There was a time when our goals in life were not so far apart."

"That was a long time ago, William. I'm not the same girl you knew back then."

He spun around, meeting her eyes once again, feeling their power to wound him fully. His voice was low and pain-drenched. "The heart doesn't change, Cecelia. Not that much. I know mine never has."

"I told you a long time ago that you were destined fo' greatness. I'm glad to know I wasn't wrong."

"Even though we find ourselves on opposite sides?"

"You would be surprised," she softly said.

He moved a step nearer, then stopped. "God, but you're as beautiful as the day I met you."

The rain beat heavier now against the canvas above them, creating a kind of cocoon around them. What they had both felt so deeply for one another filled the small tent now. The air between them very swiftly grew dangerous and uncomfortable. The rain and the tension stopped time. Stopped *them*. Cecelia shot to her feet. Her body was rigid; her fists were clenched at her sides. "Perhaps it would be best if you just threw me in the brig or shot me as a traitor, and had done with yo' duty!"

"As any prisoner, you must be fully interrogated first," he said, biting back a sudden smile. She realized then how absurd her outburst with him had been.

Cecelia sat back into the chair, forcing herself not to think of how many men's lives there were at stake as William reached for the half-full decanter of whiskey and two glasses.

"Seeing as how you've left your Southern world of gentility behind to operate as a spy, I assume you can handle a glass of this."

"Actually, I've never tried it. But present circumstances seem to warrant an exception."

He chuckled at her as she finally picked up the glass and swallowed. Her quickness and wit, her spirit and sheer determination—all the things he had fallen in love with so deeply—were there before him once again, blazing so brightly, as if they had never gone from his life.

The years and the circumstances slowly washed away, with the sound of the rain. The other people who had long been a barrier were gone between them, too. Here, with the war raging all around them, death and loss and unspeakable tragedy, time had taken them back somehow to a lost time of gentle innocence and peace.

"Good God! I do believe this is gon' to make me drunk!" Cecelia coughed, grasping her throat, then began to laugh. "I feel as if I'm on fire!"

William drank his entire glass in one desperate swallow, as Cecelia sipped hers in the more genteel manner he had expected of a proper Southern wife, not a Confederate spy. But she did not stop, he observed with admiration after her third swallow in succession, the love rushing back at him uncontrollably.

No matter how close he felt or what they spoke of in those minutes that became an hour, then two, inside his tent beneath the battering rain, he did not tell her about the cruel death of her brother George. He could not confess that he had been the one with him when he died. He did not mention how he had sworn Savannah and all of Georgia—her homeland—as a gift for an American president she must believe was as evil as Satan himself.

Instead, they drank and spoke of other things—of Ellen, of William's children and his changing life. Cecelia told him that she and Charles were managing their marriage now, a day at a time, but that after years of betrayal the road ahead of them was a long and difficult one. Cecelia did not reveal her years of bitter isolation and hopelessness. That could do neither of them any good now. Finally, they spoke about William's young son, and what the boy's death had meant. As he had known they would, tears he had not been able to shed with his wife came now with Cecelia.

"There are some sources of pain," he told her haltingly, "from which a man never recovers. Losing a child is one of them."

"I'm certain you did all that you could."

"There is always more one can do in *every* circumstance where there is failure, Cecelia."

"I don't agree with that," she said gently. "Sometimes things just have a way of gettin' beyond our control."

"I could have insisted he stay with his mother in Ohio. And I will live with that knowledge for the rest of my life—as I have had to live with other things." They were both silent again before William said, "And what of your own life since we last saw one another? Have you children of your own?"

"I have been blessed with four."

"I'm so glad for you," William said with a heartbreaking sincerity he could not keep from his voice. Tears stood in his eyes, then fell on his tired, weathered face.

"I dreamed fo' a very long time, William, that I would have them with you."

"It's too late for us now, isn't it?"

"Impossibly late," she murmured in reply as the spring rain beat a torrent against the canvas tent around them. "Still so tough, aren't you, to all the rest of the world."

"You'll have to remain here with me for a little while longer, it seems. At least until the rain lets up. So that I can tell them your interrogation is finished."

Her eyes were wide and shining up at him. "It has been my dream since New Orleans to be with you again, William. To look into those wild, beautiful eyes of yours—to spend time alone with you."

"Should I fear what you came here to this camp intent on doing?" he asked.

"I hope you believe I could never do anythin' that would cause harm to you."

"I do believe that."

"You're gon' destroy it all, aren't you? Right through to Atlanta, like they're sayin'."

"There's no other way, Cecelia, to bring the opposition down."

He remembered then that, she, too, was a part of that opposition to the Union, and all he had ever wanted was to protect her. Still, life had made of him, not her husband, but a soldier. And now, God help them both, he swore allegiance to that.

They spoke of many things over the next hours, but they purposely avoided talk of war. They were inconsequential things, and tentatively spoken, at first. But quickly, their old rhythm with one another returned, and they were at ease in the way only old lovers can be. She still could never ask him to leave Ellen, nor would she. But this place, this tiny canvas-covered island, as New Orleans once had been, was theirs.

Knowing what it could not be, their lips met anyway, gently at first, and he touched the curve of her neck. "Nothing about us has changed. Nor shall it," he murmured huskily.

"Give the message only to General Hooker. . . . Your word, Cecelia!"

She wanted to tell him—ached to tell him, but Porter Saxton's dying plea still stopped her. Cecelia pressed her lips to his in response, silencing the pleas she could never answer. "I have always loved you," she said instead. "I will *always* love you."

It was a perfect, isolated moment, separate in time and space, as William's body enveloped hers. He pressed her back onto the stark military cot, not caring about the soldiers standing in the mud and the rain just beyond the tent flap, or any other threat that could part them again. Cecelia wrapped her arms around William's neck and let him unfasten the buttons of her dress. As he did so, she kissed him, her mouth open, hungry, and willing. She wanted to care about Ellen, about Charles, about the risk to their children if this went on. But God help her, she didn't care any more this time than the last. No one was taking tonight from her—from them—just one more night to last a lifetime.

As his kiss deepened and grew more desperate, his strong hands moving down the length of her body, Cecelia felt the joy of youthful passion she had long forgotten, and she needed to drink up every moment with him. Yes, this man. A part of him would always belong to her.

Oh, he smells delicious, she thought, *with that familiar scent of musk.* He straddled her body with his own long, taut bulk, removing her dress and underclothes. How had she lived all these years without this? Without a man, the one man, who truly and completely worshiped her? The feel of him, his body, the fragrance of his skin, and the warmth of his breath engulfed her completely.

William's mouth was on her throat, his fingers gentle on her breasts. He arched over her and suddenly she was drowning, lost entirely to sensation and wild desire. When it was over, and they lay wound in one another's tight embrace, a cool sheen of perspiration on their smooth, bare bodies, William kissed the top of her head, and his touch made her feel like shattered glass. Fragile fragments of love, devotion—and duty.

Before dawn, still lying beside William, Cecelia woke to the distant sound of the bugle and the sweet trilling of birds among the branches of the tall pine trees that surrounded his encampment. In the grainy, gray early light, her eyes were bordered with tears. Shivering helplessly, she looked over at his peaceful, sleeping expression as he lay with her beneath the rough gray-green military blanket. A hot rush of anguish pelted her suddenly, as reality met daylight, and the tears pushed forward, clouding her vision.

With a sense of fate that would ever devastate her heart, Cecelia hesitated, then faltered, but she knew there was no longer any question. What they had promised one another last night was a fool's promise. Yet she also knew that if he woke and touched her now, just one more time, she would give up everything to stay with him—for he was and always would be the one true love of her life.

And that life led her, led them, to this moment and place, this achingly bittersweet connection. She regretted nothing. She loved him. But to protect William—and everyone else who would be hurt—she must call upon all the strength life and this horrid war had brought her—and she must force herself to walk away.

Bereft at the idea, Cecelia grudgingly rose and dressed, never taking her eyes from his tanned, worn, and grizzled face. She needed every last moment, every image of him her mind could capture, even as the torment settled upon her. How different might both their lives have been, she wondered, slipping on her shoes and then tying the ribbon at her throat. If they had defied the odds and married, was it possible that today he would be commanding Confederate troops to victory, instead of battling them to the loss they surely faced?

He was a grand, magnificent, and misunderstood man who wanted only to see this war, and its injustices, end. And she hoped that history would look upon him more favorably one day than the anger with which he was looked upon now. Especially here in the South that he once so had loved. She drew in a sharp breath.

Dear God, I cannot bear it!

Finally, as activity began around the tent and she knew William soon would wake, Cecelia pressed a last kiss to her fingertips and then to his lips. Two long tears had dried on her cheeks but the swell of pain was beyond tears. They were not defeated in this, she realized defiantly with an unexpectedly victorious last glance back. They must both make commitments to their other lives, and leaving was the only way she felt capable of making a stand—for both of them. But she was not entirely setting him free. Not so his heart. Feeling a cool rush of morning air, she clung to the tent flap, lingering for a final moment. William may have married Ellen, and she, Charles—the North may well be forever divided from the South—but something greater about each of them would ever belong to the other.

No one could stop them loving one another.

Fate be damned! It may well force our lives apart yet again, my love, but no one, nor anything, can ever change what we are, nor what we will be for all eternity. I know that, she defiantly declared, *as sure as the sun will come up again tomorrow, and again after that! I will remain the love of William Sherman's life—the woman he would seek to ever love . . . and protect . . . And I will pray every day left of my life that there will be another chance, and then another, to see you . . . to be with you like this, again.*

Chapter Thirty-three

Some part of him had known she would be gone when he woke. He knew the kind of woman Cecelia was. And nothing in either of their circumstances had changed since New Orleans. Across the room, a small lace handkerchief lay in a ring of morning sunlight through the window flap. William stood on unsteady legs and went to claim it. He clutched tightly to the slip of fabric, and it felt like holding a part of her—perhaps because he wanted so badly for that to be true. Last night had been a gift, but she was a spy for the Confederates that he had let go, and this was war.

He knew he would never see her again.

As he clasped the fabric to his heart, and for a moment closed his eyes, his sergeant came in. "General, that woman, the one who just left—"

"Not now, damn you!" He could not bear it just now, defending himself for letting a Confederate spy slip through his grasp. He had given away nothing, nor had she asked him to.

"But sir, she wasn't . . . What I mean to say, General, is that she left something for you. For all of us really. She urged me not to wake you, but she insisted I read it, which I did before I let her go on to General Hooker's camp, with two soldiers as an escort."

William opened his eyes and looked at the small slip of paper in the sergeant's fist. "It was information, sir. From one of our Union spies on the inside. The woman from last night, she isn't a *Confederate* spy, General Sherman! It turns out she brought information from that top secret operative, Porter Saxton, and through very dangerous territory! She was on a mission to deliver it directly to General Hooker, your advance-column, sir, and no other, which is why she didn't confess it to you directly."

William ran a hand across his face. "Well, I'll be damned." His instinct to let her go out of love had turned out to be correct.

"You can say that again, sir. Turns out, that crazy Southern gal risked her life, not at all like Belle Boyd, but *for* the Union!"

William rode away from his dismantled camp toward a hail of shellfire and musketry bullets, cursing the sky and the cruel god who inhabited it and all the forces at work for taking from him the only two souls he ever truly loved. He ached physically, as if a part of his body had been ripped away, both for Willy and for Cecelia. The wound made by being with Cecelia and losing her yet again was one from which he knew there would be no recovery. Ellen was his life, and Cecelia had gone because she knew that. She had left the handkerchief to make certain he knew they were finally—yes, finally—at their end. And yet it was Cecelia Stovall who would go on forever possessing his heart. She told him she had changed, and now he understood how much.

Cecelia had emerged as something so much richer and more complex than she had been even when she was young. He mused now how she had always told him he would one day find his own greatness—and yet she was the one who had found magnificence.

As William rode through the spongy, muddy earth the rain had left, he urged his horse on, digging his boot heels in the animal's huge flanks until he was riding at a furious gallop, a cold wind blistering his face, tossing his hair. *"You are brave and wonderful, and I will love you forever,"* he could hear himself say.

It was a voice he would hear for the rest of his life.

After the battle of Allatoona, when they were saved from a wrong turn that would have cost thousands more Union lives, William rode across a grassy plain along the Etowah River with a battery of his men who were searching houses in the area for any food they could find to feed their starving and battle-weary troops. He still had not made his own peace with the destruction

Lincoln and Grant urged him to set upon these fine, stately old homes. But war was hell. Yes, one day, when he had time for reflection, and he wrote this all down for posterity, he would tell the truth precisely like that.

As Confederate troops licked their wounds and tried desperately to fight on, Atlanta lay ahead to be conquered, and William Tecumseh Sherman had been chosen as the one to conquer it. Then he would march his troops to Savannah and the sea. And hopefully then, it would be over. But this day, a detachment of Union soldiers he led had come upon another stately Southern mansion standing high on a bluff overlooking the river. Another to pillage, he thought sadly, and then burn to the ground, as Lincoln commanded.

Grim-faced and weary, with the roar of cannon fire in the distance and smoke on the horizon, William leaned on the pommel of his saddle. He drew a hand across his brow as he waited outside in the courtyard of a white-columned mansion. But for the grand view of the Etowah River that lay beyond, he thought, and for all of the graciousness and gentility in its appearance, it was just another massive house surely built on the backs of too many nameless, faceless slaves.

A moment later, he was distracted by an elderly black slave on the front steps as his soldiers searched the house for food and valuables. "Oh, Lawd . . . Lawd. I sho'ly is glad Miss Cecelia ain't here to see it wit her own eyes," he repeated to himself. "I sho'ly is."

"Good God," he murmured, washing a hand across his grizzled, bearded face. William looked up at the man, narrowing his gaze. He knew the man from long ago. "Miss Cecelia, sir? Tell me, *not* Miss Cecelia Stovall."

"Yassuh, da same. But now she be Mrs. Shelman, suh."

It had been two months since she came to his camp and then left him one final time. The pain and the memory of that night lingered within him still, so that his heart began to beat very fast. He closed his eyes for a moment and fought the lump he felt in his throat as the memories of so many bittersweet moments rolled across his mind. *Just one last time . . . to see her once more . . .* "Is your mistress here now?" He managed to say, "I should have a word with her if she is."

"Oh, no suh! Cap'n Shelman is off to wah. Bless da Lawd at las', Miss Cecelia, she be refugeed up in da mountains wit the chil'ren, suh. I is da only one lef' here."

"What is your name, sir?" William asked him in a kind tone.

"Josiah, suh. But folks round here be callin' me Ol' Joe."

"Well, Josiah." William smiled. "Say to your mistress for me that she might have remained in her home in safety, that she and her property would have been protected."

He nodded gratefully. "Yassuh."

"You've known Miss Cecelia for a long time."

"Since she was a baby, suh."

"You have such cruel eyes, sir. And I pity your enemy. Ah, how you would crush him! . . ." William looked at the old man and felt a smile play at the corners of his mouth in a time when he'd had so very little to smile about. He felt warmed by looking at a face he was certain Cecelia had known and loved for a very long time.

"Josiah?"

"Yassuh?"

"I wish you to give her a note from me when she returns."

William leaned back in his saddle, feeling the ages-old tug at his heart that thoughts of Cecelia always brought. How star-crossed they had been for so long. And how magnificent, through adversity, such a simple Southern girl had become. The warm summer breeze tossed his hair as he took a folio of calling cards from his saddle bag. "Captain," he instructed the soldier on horseback beside him. "See to pen and ink for me. I've a need to write a personal note for the lady of this house."

"Yes, sir, General."

William swung his leg over the saddle and stood in high, dusty boots on the lovely brick-covered pathway leading up to her house. There were roses and iris, just as his mother had grown in their garden when he was a boy. How bittersweet and how splendid, a fleeting connection between the two women of his heart. This was a lovely home, and he hoped with all his heart that she had found some bit of happiness here.

As William began to scrawl a note, balanced on a traveling desk held by his captain, dusty, worn Union soldiers began to file out of the house, laughing and joking, their arms laden with gleaming silver, porcelain, and bound carpets.

"Put everything back where it was!" he loudly declared, a hand poised in the air. The men froze in their tracks. They looked at William, and then at the subordinate beside him. The rest of the grounds were swarming with the blue-coated Union troops. In the echo of General Sherman's command, they stopped, as well.

"But, General, sir," argued one of the men whose arms were most full.

"This is just like all the other Reb houses we've gone into! The men can surely benefit from all this!"

"Not under my command, they won't! I *said* put everything back!"

William had become something of a legend with the men, not only for his impressive battlefield skill, but also for his even temper and caring. One soldier turned around and headed up the steps, then another, and another. He glanced back at the words he had written, making certain they were as he wished to write.

My Dearest Cecelia,

You said once that you would pity the man who would ever become my enemy. Do you recall my reply? Although many years have passed, my answer is the same now as then. I would ever love and protect you.—That I have done. Forgive all else. I am only a soldier.

William T. Sherman.

William folded the letter then and sealed it. Before he handed it to his captain, he touched a finger to his lips and pressed it along the line of the ivory paper—a silent, last good-bye. The war was nearly over, he knew. So did the devastated people of the South. He would be returning to Ohio soon, to Ellen—a war hero in the North and a great enemy of the South. As Cecelia knew that last night in his camp, he knew that he would never see his love again. One day, perhaps, he would grow accustomed to that. But right now it hurt like hell. The wind was blowing harder, a rich Southern inferno. *How appropriate*. He smiled. A sign. Like so many other things about being here.

He looked back up into the sunlight at the weary old black man standing so tentatively, his hat in his hands, on the brick carriageway, surrounded by Union soldiers yet undaunted. "You need not fear me, sir," William said in response, removing his own hat respectfully. "Go back into the house and make it ready for the return of your mistress, as the end of this awful conflict is not far now at hand."

"Yassuh. I do it."

"And Josiah—"

"Suh?"

"I'm quite glad to have met you again."

He tipped his head. "Has we met befo', suh?"

"A long time ago, Josiah, when we were both much younger men."

Josiah remained a moment longer, looking up into the silvery hot sunlight as if he might find an answer to some unspoken thing lingering there. More of the soldiers were passing him, silently returning the stolen goods. Finally, he looked directly back at William. "Miss Cecelia, suh, she cared fo' a Yankee once, long time ago. If dat gentleman was anyting like you, General, suh, I can say I sho'ly does understand why he be in her heart to dis day."

"Thank you, Josiah," he managed to say. "Coming from you that actually means quite a lot."

Josiah turned away and went up the three wide front veranda steps, then pivoted back around one final time. As they looked at one another, the silence came with a knowledge. "I watch over her fo' yuh, suh."

"I'm afraid I'll have to count on you about that."

"It'd be a privilege to do it, suh."

As William rode away, determined tears shimmering in his tired eyes, he left a contingent of soldiers at Shelman Heights. They had been given specific orders from the commander of the Union Army himself to guard the property with their lives until the end of war.